W9-ALV-319

A NATION

—OF—

STRANGERS

Also by Ellis Cose

THE PRESS

A NATION

—OF—

STRANGERS

Prejudice, Politics, and the
Populating of America

Ellis Cose

William Morrow and Company, Inc.
New York

It is the policy of William Morrow and Company, Inc., and its imprints and affiliates, recognizing the importance of preserving what has been written, to print the books we publish on acid-free paper, and we exert our best efforts to that end.

Library of Congress Cataloging-in-Publication Data

Cose, Ellis.
    A nation of strangers : prejudice, politics, and the populating of
America / Ellis Cose.
        p. cm.
    Includes bibliographical references.
    ISBN 0-688-09337-X
    1. United States—Ethnic relations.   2. United States—Race
relations.   3. United States—Emigration and immigration—History.
I. Title.
E184.A1C654   1992
305.8'00973—dc20   91-22734
                                                                    CIP

Printed in the United States of America

First Edition

1 2 3 4 5 6 7 8 9 10

BOOK DESIGN BY ROBIN MALKIN

For Lee

CONTENTS

INTRODUCTION

In Search of the Perfect American

Less than a decade after ratification of the U.S. Constitution, Congress debated a twenty-dollar naturalization tax proposed to help retire Revolutionary War debts. Almost immediately the discussion went far afield of revenue needs and focused on the value of American citizenship—and of the dispatch with which it should be awarded.

Jeffersonians argued that naturalization should be made as effortless and inexpensive as possible, for America had been founded in part as an asylum for refugees in search of sanctuary. To charge so much money, they believed, would be a hypocritical repudiation of the young republic's political heritage and would place citizenship beyond the grasp of many of those most worthy. What, they demanded to know, was the essential difference between denying suffrage to those without property and refusing citizenship to those without twenty dollars? If a lawyer could be licensed for ten dollars, remarked John Swanwick, a citizen certainly should be certified for less.

Federalists advocated a more restrictive course. Citizenship, they argued, was too precious to confer lightly, and should perhaps be reserved for those born in America and for those who had paid (fighting the British) with their blood. At the very least, they reasoned, it was worth twenty dollars. Representative Robert Goodloe Harper dismissed the notion of America as asylum to the world's dispossessed. That concept, he explained, had originated during "a moment of enthusiasm" in the blush of the American Revolution.

Eventually the politicians compromised, effectively agreeing with North Carolinian Joseph McDowell's assertion that in fighting for liberty, "We did not mean to confine it to ourselves, nor to sell it to others." The proper assessment, they decided, was five dollars—enough to give the treasury a boost but not so much as to give the impression that citizenship was for sale, or to place it beyond the reach of any deserving person determined to have it.

Two centuries later, the House again reverberated with arguments over the value of U.S. citizenship as legislators debated a proposal to award visas (and permanent resident status) to well-to-do foreigners willing to create American jobs. Congressman John Bryant of Texas condemned the measure, calling it "the sale of American citizenship to anyone with one million dollars." Colleague Tom Campbell agreed: "However beneficial the investment may be . . . America would, for the first time in its history, be granting a statutory preference for citizenship based on wealth."

Substantially more than the value of twenty dollars has changed in the years separating the two debates. Still, for all the progress America has made in growing from a nation of 4 million to one of over 200 million, many of the citizenship issues that bedeviled politicians then continue to do so today. How many newcomers can the country comfortably absorb? What should be required of those seeking admission? Will the native-born suffer if foreigners come in? In answering such questions—in deciding what qualities and assets a prospective American should possess—the nation is also forced to define what an American is. And that definition has expanded greatly over the years.

The first U.S. naturalization law (passed during the second

session of the first Congress in March 1790) reserved naturalization for those "aliens being free white persons." Eventually judges and politicians were faced with the dilemma of determining who was "white" and who was "free." But at the time the meaning was clear enough. As the U.S. Supreme Court concluded several decades after the law's passage, "No one supposed then that any Indian would ask for, or was capable of enjoying, the privileges of an American citizen, and the word white was not used with any particular reference to them. Neither was it used with any reference to the African race imported into or born in this country; because Congress had no power to naturalize them, and therefore there was no necessity for using particular words to exclude them. It would seem to have been used merely because it followed out the line of division which the Constitution has drawn between the citizen race, who formed and held the Government, and the African race, which they held in subjection and slavery, and governed at their own pleasure."

The English, or those of English descent, made up three fifths of the white population in 1790. The largest non-English-speaking minority—Germans—made up less than 10 percent. Colonial political leaders assumed not only that Americans would continue to be white, but that most would continue to be Protestants of British origin. By the mid-1800s, however, that assumption was vanishing beneath a wave of Irish-Catholic and German immigration. Following the Civil War, blacks were granted naturalization and citizenship rights. Later in the century, a new flood of immigrants arrived—many of them Jews or Catholics from Eastern and Southern Europe. In the 1940s, Chinese, East Indians, and other Asians were made eligible for naturalization. By the middle 1980s, the English flow had become little more than a trickle. Great Britain ranked twelfth as a place of origin for newcomers—behind Mexico, the Philippines, Korea, Cuba, India, Mainland China, the Dominican Republic, Vietnam, Jamaica, Haiti, and Iran.

The changes in law and in immigrant ethnicity were driven by a complicated array of forces. The decision to protect and enfranchise blacks in the wake of the Civil War made denial

of citizenship to native-born Asian-Americans unconstitutional. Growing U.S. involvement in global affairs made
ethnically discriminatory immigration laws increasingly embarrassing, and simultaneously stimulated interest in coming
to America. Also, from the beginning, America had made herself a haven to those seeking safety and opportunity. Though
that responsibility often has been shirked, the nation has never
stopped taking it seriously. Two centuries ago, Representative
Albert Gallatin quoted the Declaration of Independence to his
fellow legislators to remind them that one reason for breaking
with England was the king's impeding immigration to the New
World. Similarly Ronald Reagan, in his farewell presidential
address, extolled America as "still a beacon, still a magnet . . .
for all the Pilgrims from all the lost places who are hurtling
through the darkness toward home."

In trying to live up to that calling, America has repeatedly
faced tension between the desire to welcome and the impulse
to exclude; and again and again she has asked herself whether
a nation professing to believe in human equality could create
harmony among peoples fundamentally dissimilar—in color,
culture, means, and expectations.

Often the answer has been no. Certain groups have represented such peril, or appeared in such unexpected numbers,
that the nation, swept up in hysteria, has rushed to stop (or
restrict) the influx. Catholics, Jews, Hindus, and Bolsheviks have,
at one time or another, all been classified as grave threats to
everything America represents, as have Irish, Italians, Germans, Romanians, Chinese, and countless others. Over the
years, the red flag of foreign menace has proven to be such a
potent distraction that politicians and others have regularly
employed it to mask an array of questionable policies and de-
vious purposes. As a consequence, immigration policy has often
been held hostage not only to prevailing prejudices and passing panic but to narrow, partisan political intrigues.

Yet again and again, America has been forced to acknowledge that xenophobia is fundamentally incompatible with the
Constitution and the Declaration of Independence—documents that have worn infinitely better than the prejudices of

the men who created them. Such acknowledgments have been made easier by the passage of time, which invariably has revealed the foreign threat to have been exaggerated. They have also been made easier by the process by which yesterday's menace becomes tomorrow's political interest group. For as the formerly shunned groups amass political power, they unfailingly work to exorcise the demons of their past.

Again, America has entered a period of rapid ethnic change. Hispanics, Asians, blacks, and "minorities" make up one fourth of the nation's population, and the proportion is growing. In an April 1990 cover story devoted to the "browning of America," *Time* magazine summed up the shift with: "Someday soon, surely much sooner than most people . . . realize, white Americans will become a minority group." Later that year, Congress passed the most sweeping immigration-reform package in decades, one that sanctioned immigration levels not seen since the turn of the century.

In the past, such transitions have signaled outbreaks of regional panic, and citizens have worried whether America can absorb so many who are so different from those who "made America great." Always, those fears have been ultimately judged not only groundless but a diversion from the larger task of allowing America to become even greater.

Aquí Estamos. Aquí Nos Quedamos. ¡Y No Nos Vamos!
Anonymous.
Handbill posted in Washington, D.C.

1

Roots of Intolerance

From the beginning of the period of colonial settlement, America attracted devotees of a huge array of faiths— Presbyterians, Congregationalists, Baptists, Methodists, Quakers, Roman Catholics, and Jews—all in search of religious freedom. Nonetheless, at the time of the American Revolution, an estimated 98 percent of Americans were Protestant. That was no accident. For many of those Protestants so feared pollutious from competing sects that they refused to sanction religious freedom for others, and America had become not so much a haven for the world's theologically oppressed as a refuge for dissenting Protestants.

During the early seventeenth century, Massachusetts Puritans prohibited anyone from settling without permission and limited the vote and all political power to fellow believers. Connecticut, which did not limit suffrage to any specific sect, denied it to Quakers and atheists. Over the ensuing decades, Virginia, South Carolina, and several other colonies prohibited non-Protestants from full membership in their communities. Even Maryland, founded as a refuge for persecuted

Catholics, early on discovered liberalism had limits—and in 1654 repealed the Toleration Act passed five years earlier to safeguard the Catholic minority. Three and a half decades later, Maryland restricted entry of Irish-Catholic servants, as did South Carolina and Virginia.

Each colony, of course, made its own rules (subject to the restrictions of its charter and the power of its governor) and not all were so distrustful of competing faiths. After Roger Williams and his Anabaptist followers were expelled from Massachusetts, they founded a colony at Providence dedicated to accepting others. And when the Quakers, considered heretics in New England, were whipped, mutilated, and ordered to leave, they found compassion and shelter in Rhode Island. Similarly Pennsylvania, founded by Quaker William Penn, was a committed sanctuary from religious persecution. Yet even the most liberal colonies harbored a deep suspicion of Catholicism, a religion with all the trappings of a rival political sovereignty. So despite the colonists' heightened sensitivity to issues of religious freedom, by the arrival of the eighteenth century, only in Rhode Island did Catholics enjoy full religious and political rights.

Such attitudes set the stage for major problems of Catholic assimilation. And non-Protestants were not the only groups to which settlers were antagonistic. In the early 1600s, when England began substituting exile to the colonies for certain crimes previously punishable by death, colonial leaders responded with resentment, and many eventually responded with statutes and resolutions designed to keep undesirables out. In 1670, Virginia enacted a law barring ship captains from unlading "jail birds" and others guilty of capital crimes who "deserved to die in England." Maryland enacted a similar law, as did Delaware (which barred not only felons but paupers). Parliament, however, ignored the measures; and just as America would long continue to harbor suspicion of Catholics, she would remain convinced, decades after independence was won, that Europe was still using the New World as a dumping ground for her most irremediable losers.

In the mid-eighteenth century, as Germans poured into

Pennsylvania, many non-German settlers insisted the new-comers were of inferior quality. Significant German migration had begun in the late 1600s by Pietists lured to the New World by William Penn's promise of freedom for their nonconform-ing Protestant beliefs. Over the next several decades, the German flow gradually increased, propelled by the combination of puffery from America and difficult economic and political conditions at home. By the 1740s, German immigrants (many of them indentured servants) were arriving in Pennsylvania at the rate of thousands per year and represented an array of religious (though primarily Protestant) sects.

The Pennsylvania Colonial Assembly noted in 1755 that earlier German immigrants had consisted of families "of sub-stance" and "industrious sober people," but of late they had become "a great mixture of the refuse of their people." Ben-jamin Franklin vehemently concurred, calling the German ar-rivals as "ignorant a set of people as the Indians." "Those who come hither," he wrote, "are generally the most stupid of their own nation." Franklin found them unaccustomed to liberty and inept in utilizing it. Concerned about their effect on the En-glish language and American culture, he urged that the Ger-mans be more broadly dispersed. The disdain felt for the Germans was unlike that previously incited by Irish "papists" in that it singled out an ethnic group rather than a religion and indicated the stirring of a belief that foreignness alone could represent a threat.

As early as 1782, Thomas Jefferson questioned the wisdom of actively promoting immigration. At the time, he reckoned America's population at approximately 3 million, and calcu-lated that the number was doubling every twenty-seven years and three months. In something less than a century, noted Jefferson, America's natural growth would give the settled areas a density approaching that of the British Isles. Why, he won-dered, would anyone wish to induce migration given the po-tential problem of newcomers not fitting in? "May not our government be more homogeneous, more peaceable, more durable," he asked, if Americans relied on the fecundity of its citizens rather than importing others who had little understanding of the rights and freedoms America was testing?

Jefferson also was not convinced that blacks would fit into post-Revolutionary America. Though he advocated freedom for those held as slaves, he proposed sending them as far away as practical while simultaneously importing an equal number of whites to take their place. To his way of thinking, blacks and whites were so fundamentally incompatible as to make inevitable racial conflict that "will probably never end but in the extermination of the one or the other race."

Despite the fledgling nativism of some of America's founders, the New World needed workers and could scarcely afford to turn its nose up at those who came, even if they were the wretched of the earth. And that some were wretched was beyond dispute. The matter of African slaves and convicted criminals aside, even those who chose to emigrate from Europe were not generally of the highest classes. To escape poverty, many had come as indentured servants, and their status, for the period of servitude, was somewhere between that of a freeman and a slave. But despite their lack of aristocratic resources or polish, they represented the means to develop America's latent wealth. Consequently, both during and following America's colonial period, substantial effort went into promoting—in the British Isles and elsewhere in Europe—the opportunities across the Atlantic.

That promotion took many forms. The trading companies (chartered by the king to develop the colonies) and colonial proprietors advertised, distributed pamphlets, and sent recruiting agents to drum up enthusiasm for the voyage. Religious communities sought out the faithful, offering the opportunity to worship in peace. Would-be farmers and future squires capable of paying their way were promised title to uncultivated land. Those without funds were offered contracts that granted passage and ultimately freedom and property after the fulfillment of several years of service. What the colonies could not offer, however, was British citizenship to those aliens emigrating from outside the British domain. And for those eager to attract foreign labor to work America's fields, that was a problem.

Since only the Crown or Parliament could render one a British subject and the colonies had no national system of government, non-Englishmen wishing to immigrate to the New World had no assurance of the legal protections and rights granted the English-born. To receive comparable standing, they had to petition Parliament for naturalization or the Crown for denization—a status somewhat short of naturalization. A denizen had some, but not all, of the privileges of a native-born subject. He or she could purchase land, for instance, but not inherit it, and was barred from public office.

Individual colonies developed citizenship policies of their own. Some established procedures for naturalization by local courts. In others, royal governors and colonial charter holders granted denization. The policies, however, were inconsistent—requiring different periods of residency and different tests of religious faith. And none was formally recognized by England—which at the end of the seventeenth century flatly prohibited the issuance of colonial letters of denization valid outside any specific colony. The uncertain status of alien immigrants was a continuing exasperation for colonial leadership and was not resolved until 1740 when Parliament finally passed a naturalization act for America. The law granted citizenship to those who had been resident in the colonies for at least seven years (without an absence of more than two months), and who swore loyalty to the Crown and presented evidence of their Christianity. (Exemptions were made for Quakers and Jews, and Catholics were excluded from applying.)

After enactment of the new law, immigration to America remained constrained by continuing European conflicts; but the end of the Seven Years' War in 1763 (from which Great Britain emerged with greatly expanded colonial holdings, including Canada, Florida, and the American Midwest) was followed by a new wave of immigration. That surge continued until the eve of the Revolutionary War. After New Jersey and Pennsylvania passed new local naturalization acts in 1773, Great Britain forbade colonial awards of subjectship. The following year Parliament prohibited immigration to the colonies, leading the authors of the Declaration of Independence (in their bill of particulars against King George III) to proclaim: "He has endeavoured to prevent the population of these States; for that purpose obstructing the laws for naturalization of foreigners; refusing to pass others to encourage their migrations hither, and raising the conditions of new appropriations of lands."

After ratification of the U.S. Constitution, Congress quickly passed a naturalization law. Even during the Revolutionary War, however, Americans continued to encourage migration to the New World. Among the most famous advertisements was a book published in London in 1782 by J. Hector St. John de Crèvecoeur, a French-born aristocrat educated in England who had settled in America. The book, *Letters from an American Farmer,* was a celebration of the freedom, social equality, and opportunity available in America—a wide-open place unbounded by European conventions where men could own land, make their own laws, and start life anew. "It is not composed, as in Europe, of great lords who possess every thing, and of a herd of people who have nothing. Here are no aristocratical families, no courts, no kings, no bishops, no ecclesiastical dominion, no invisible power giving to a few a very visible one; no great manufacturers employing thousands, no great refinements of luxury. The rich and the poor are not so far removed from each other as they are in Europe."

The America he described was "not an easy place," but one where hard work and industriousness inevitably would be rewarded. In Europe, he wrote, the ill-born poor "were as so many useless plants . . . they withered, and were mowed down by want, hunger and war; but now . . . they have taken root and flourished!" In America, he exulted, "individuals of all nationals are melted into a new race of men, whose labours and posterity will one day cause great changes in the world."

Others who could not match Crèvecoeur's eloquence equaled his enthusiasm. An open letter composed by Welsh immigrants in Pennsylvania in 1800 lauded America as a great place to educate children, sell cattle and corn, and worship in one's own language. Several years later, a Virginia man wrote his brother in Great Britain insisting, "If you knew the difference

between this country and England you would need no per-
suading to leave it and come hither."

In the years following the American Revolution, such in-
vitations went not only to England but to all of Europe. After
such frustration with the English system, the founders wished
to make immigration and the subsequent acquisition of American citizenship as easy as possible and gave Congress power
"to establish a uniform rule of naturalization."

America's first naturalization act—passed in 1790—allowed
all "free white persons" who swore an oath of allegiance to the
Constitution to become citizens after a two-year period of residency in the United States (one of those spent wholly in one
state). Children under twenty-one automatically received naturalization with their parents.

Shortly thereafter, in the wake of the French Revolution
and Reign of Terror, Federalists began pushing for more restrictive immigration laws. They worried both about the likely
arrival of foreign extremists and about the growing political
clout of immigrants, who generally became Jeffersonians.
Congress extended the residency period to five years in 1795,
and also required that aliens declare their intent to become
citizens three years prior to naturalization. The new measures
did not satisfy the Federalists, who continued to fret over the
possibility of war with France and infiltration by subversives.
In 1798, they pushed through Congress a series of harsh new
laws that struck not only at suspected foreign agents but at all
immigrants and outspoken political rivals.

The centerpiece of the legislation was a new naturalization
act that required a fourteen-year residency period. In addition, prospective citizens were required to declare their intent
to become citizens five years before naturalization and to provide reports and certificates proving they had fulfilled the law's
terms. In the same session, Congress passed three other bills—
the so-called Alien and Sedition Acts—aimed at squelching insurrection. One empowered the president to disregard normal
due-process procedures during wartime in order to imprison
or deport aliens suspected of aiding the enemy. Another allowed him, even during peacetime, to imprison or deport those

foreigners believed to represent a threat to the nation. And the third imposed heavy fines and imprisonment for writing, publishing, or speaking anything of "a false, scandalous and malicious nature" about the government or government officials.

To Jeffersonians the new legislation seemed an assault on all they had fought for. Thomas Jefferson and James Madison wrote resolutions, given to and passed by the Kentucky and Virginia legislatures respectively, assailing the constitutionality of the measures. With the Sedition Acts, they felt, Congress had overstepped its bounds, granting the president authority so sweeping that he effectively assumed the powers of all three bodies of government. The Federalists were turned out of office in 1800, and the Jeffersonians quickly set about trying to restore some of the liberties they felt the nation had lost. As president, Thomas Jefferson ended all prosecutions under the Sedition Act and pardoned those already convicted. Congress reinstated the five-year naturalization waiting period.

The laws, however, had enduring impact, both politically and legally. The president retained the power to deport citizens of enemy nations and to exclude those believed to be a threat, and generally to deny suspect aliens due-process rights that American citizens would expect in similar circumstances. Perhaps most important, the episode elevated the practice of alien-bashing to an art, and one intimately linked to the promotion of partisan political agendas. For decades thereafter, Congress would not show much interest in controlling immigration, but as increasing numbers of newcomers arrived, the xenophobia manifested in 1798 would repeatedly reappear— particularly during times of war or economic distress.

America's initial post-1798 efforts at regulating immigration, however, were not aimed at discouraging aliens but at protecting them. The need for safeguards stemmed from the life-threatening conditions on many of the immigrant ships. One launched in Antwerp with five thousand passengers aboard arrived in America with only four thousand alive. Others lost half or more of their human cargo, or dumped diseased and half-starved survivors on ports ill equipped to minister to them.

Determined to prevent such outrages, Congress in 1819 passed the first of the steerage acts. The measure, aimed at preventing captains from cramming too many passengers aboard, forbade vessels from entering American ports with more than two persons for every five tons of the ship's weight. It also mandated the minimum amounts of food and water to be boarded and required the captain to report the number who had died en route and provide customs officials with a census of those brought in.

Those statistics ultimately would allow the government to determine the number and types of immigrants entering the country. Even without firm figures, however, cities with major ports could see that immigration was on the rise. The year of the steerage act's passage, the New York Society for the Prevention of Pauperism concluded that aliens were responsible for a large and growing proportion of the city's poverty. The society started a soup kitchen. State governments also focused on the problems caused by the inrush of immigrants, with some assessing fees from ship operators for immigrants landed, a portion of which was earmarked for various charity programs. Massachusetts charged ship captains two dollars for each passenger dropped off in Boston and required the posting of a one-thousand-dollar bond before allowing in invalids, professional paupers, and other undesirables, including "lunatics" and "idiots." New York levied fees and required ship captains to post bonds of up to three hundred dollars apiece for immigrants thought likely to end up penniless. Captains entering the city were also directed to provide biographical information on every passenger or to face a fine of seventy-five dollars for each person not reported.

The New York law was eventually challenged by a ship captain who argued that the Constitution barred states from regulating commerce. The Supreme Court ruled in 1837 that the state was not regulating commerce but exercising its legitimate police powers, adding, "We think it as competent and as necessary for a state to provide precautionary measures against the moral pestilence of paupers, vagabonds, and possibly convicts; as it is to guard against . . . physical pestilence." That ruling, which stood for nearly forty years, gave state governments a green light essentially to pass their own immigration regulations. And as immigrants continued to pour into America, states increasingly opted to do so.

The European migration had numerous causes: increased freedom to travel after the Napoleonic Wars, displacement traceable to the Industrial Revolution, and continuing economic and agricultural crises throughout the continent—especially in Ireland. Though large numbers came to America from all over Europe during the early 1800s, more came from Ireland than from anywhere else. In the 1820s, Irish made up 35 percent of a total 143,000 immigrants—twice as much as the English percentage. During the 1830s, the total number of immigrants quadrupled, reaching nearly 600,000. Again, Irish migrants predominated, comprising 35 percent, though Germans displaced Britons in the number-two slot. German migration, negligible in the previous decade, accounted for one fourth of those who came in the 1830s. The following decade, total immigration shot up to nearly 2 million and, again, it was dominated by Irish and Germans. The two groups together made up nearly three fourths of America's immigrants.

Since Napoleon's defeat in 1815, Ireland had been pounded by one setback after another. The end of hostilities reduced the need for Irish crop exports, and wheat prices plummeted. Widespread bank failures in the early twenties delivered another shock to the Irish economy, as did the British financial crisis of 1826. A series of poor potato harvests in the decades preceding the Great Famine of the 1840s made existence, for many, increasingly perilous. Worried that destitute Irishmen might stream into Great Britain, the government experimented during the 1820s with a scheme to settle several hundred poor Irish in Canada and subsequently decided that government-financed emigration was too expensive to practice on a large scale. Nonetheless, some parishes raised funds on their own to ship paupers abroad, and Parliament put few barriers in the way of those who could make it to America.

Americans greeted the European inflow with less than ecstasy, both because of the ever-increasing size of the migration and because its composition was jarringly different from earlier waves. Previously the majority of those from Ireland had been Scotch-Irish Protestants with an interest in staying in farming. The heavily Catholic newcomers gravitated toward urban areas. They also struck some Americans as less genteel and generally less desirable than those who had come before.

A series of violent clashes in the early 1830s between Irish laborers and railroad officials led to the deaths of two deputy superintendents of construction near the District of Columbia and drove one citizens' group to pass a resolution declaring "the present class of Irish laborers employed on the Baltimore and Washington railroad . . . a gang of ruffians and murderers." Around the same time, the Massachusetts legislature urged enactment of a federal antipauperism statute. A group of New Yorkers, fretting over the newcomers' religious orientation, established *The Protestant,* a weekly newspaper that later evolved into a magazine, for the purpose of inculcating "Gospel doctrines against Romish corruptions." Similar anti-Catholic publications sprouted in Philadelphia, Baltimore, and elsewhere.

The phenomenal immigrant-driven growth of the Catholic Church—from seventy thousand in the entire country in 1807 to one of the largest religious groups in the nation forty years later—fueled a growing sense of unease among many Protestant Americans. Rumors abounded concerning Catholic priests who allegedly raped nuns and committed other atrocities.

In 1834, a nun apparently suffering from overwork fled the Ursuline order in Charlestown, Massachusetts, and subsequently returned. Word soon spread that the woman was being held against her will, and a mob burned the convent to the ground. Eight were arrested, but no one was convicted of a crime. The following year saw publication of *Six Months in a Convent,* a best-seller that purported to be the memoir of one Rebecca Reed that detailed her escape from a life of Ursuline corruption. Shortly thereafter, the even more lurid *Awful Disclosures of the Hotel Dieu Nunnery of Montreal* was published by Maria Monk, a Protestant who had converted to Catholicism and then gone to a nunnery, where she supposedly discovered that nuns either submitted to priests' sexual demands or were murdered. The children of such assignations, said Monk, were killed, and their bodies disposed of in a huge hole in the basement of the nunnery.

Needless to say, such grisly tales buttressed anti-Catholic hysteria, lending crucial support to those who argued that the new immigrants would destroy U.S. institutions. And such crusaders were becoming increasingly visible. In New York in 1835, a Native American party (also known as the Native American Democratic Association) was formed to promote continued political dominance of the native-born and to act as a check on growing Catholic influence. Meanwhile, allied organizations went to work whipping up anti-Catholic sentiment. The following March, for instance, the New York Protestant Association convened a meeting to discuss whether "Popery" was compatible with civil liberty. The gathering was disrupted by enraged Irish Catholics; but the Native Americans, in coalition with the Whigs, carried New York's 1837 elections.

Though those first nativist efforts were short-lived and had little impact on the nation's political agenda, they foreshadowed more ambitious efforts to follow. The American Republican party, formed in New York in 1843, campaigned for barring the foreign-born from public office and increasing the naturalization waiting period from five to twenty-one years (the same amount of time native-born Americans had to wait before acquiring the right to vote). The party's candidates ran well in New York's 1844 elections, and American Republican offshoots quickly sprang up in Philadelphia, Boston, New Jersey, South Carolina, and elsewhere.

In addition to fighting in the political arena, the American Republicans and their confederates took the battle to the streets. In response to a complaint that Protestant Bibles were being forced on Catholic schoolchildren in Philadelphia, the school board ruled that parents could approve the Bible from which their children were read. Angered by the decision, the American Protestant Association held a huge public gathering in Philadelphia's Independence Square. Shortly thereafter, American Republicans convened a meeting in a largely Irish suburb of Philadelphia. That gathering was disrupted by neighborhood residents, but the party defiantly scheduled a second to protest "assaults of aliens and foreigners." A sniper fired upon the attendees, killing one and setting off several days of riots. Antipapists marched on the suburb, burning homes and torching two Catholic churches. Later that year, anti-immigrant activities set off a second round of riots that led to battles between Irish immigrants and the state militia and resulted in the deaths of two militiamen and numerous civilians.

Largely propelled by the potato-crop crisis of 1845, more Irish came to America during the 1840s than had left the island in all previous history. Most were poor. Irish nationals comprised two thirds of those receiving charity medical help through the New York City Dispensary and nearly half of those held in the state penitentiary. Massachusetts and Philadelphia amassed similar statistics, and assorted activists demanded that something be done to stanch the Irish deluge.

One of the loudest voices belonged to *Philadelphia Sun* editor Lewis C. Levin, who was elected to Congress in 1844 as a leader of the American party. As immigration from Ireland surged, he begged his colleagues to extend the naturalization waiting period to twenty-one years for the "protection of American institutions from foreign influence." "We stand now on the very verge of overthrow by the impetuous force of invading foreigners," argued Levin. "Europe can no longer contain the growing population that is swelling her to bursting. She must disengorge it at any price."

Despite Levin's impassioned orations, Congress declined to act. But two years later, when legislation was proposed to improve conditions on crowded and dangerous immigrant ships, Levin's tongue was sharper than ever. He denounced the proposal as "a bill to accommodate the paupers and criminals of Europe in their migration to the United States." And he insisted that both conditions in America and the quality of immigrants had changed. "If in the time of Mr. Jefferson it was deemed necessary, in self-defense, to pass a five-year [naturalization] law—when our western country was a wilderness, when educated and responsible men only came as emigrants, when only six or eight thousand annually landed at all ports of the United States, and when they melted into the mass of the American population—what ought to be the check now, in view of the deteriorated character of the foreign population?—in view of the fact that nearly two hundred thousand have landed at the single port of New York since the first day of March last and that instead of amalgamating with the mass of the American population, they stand out as a distinct political organization, under the control of foreign leaders?" Time had arrived, said Levin, to suspend naturalization altogether rather than "rally to the polls this living mass of moral putrescence and pitiable ignorance."

Again Levin's exhortations went largely unheeded. For America's open-door policy had by then achieved the standing of religious dogma. To reject it would have been, to many legislators, akin to rejecting the American Revolution. Also, despite the nativists' success in certain East Coast cities, they had not yet shown themselves to be a national political force— or to represent a politically advantageous approach. Moreover, the states—not Congress—were viewed as the first line of defense against unwanted immigrants. If, say, New York and Philadelphia were being deluged by lepers, lunatics, and paupers, their legislatures were perfectly within their rights to regulate them or keep them out.

Soon Levin's peers would become significantly less complacent. For uprisings in the German states would motivate hundreds of thousands of Germans to head for America even as the numbers pouring in from Ireland continued to increase. Gold discovered in California would draw thousands more—some from as far away as China. And a Supreme Court ruling in 1849 would begin chipping away at states' powers to regulate immigration by finding unconstitutional taxes imposed on immigrants by New York and Massachusetts. In the face of such events, nativists' arguments for federal intervention would receive a more serious hearing, as politicians previously flitting above the fray decided to get involved.

2

Years of Confusion, Days of Rage

For America, the decade and a half before the Civil War was a period of unprecedented expansion and immigration. The Mexican War, which ended in February 1848, gave the United States title to what is now Texas, California, Arizona, New Mexico, Nevada, Utah, and part of Colorado. Shortly after hostilities ceased, gold was discovered in California, news of which drew settlers not only from the East Coast but from Europe, South America, and China (from which the government had recorded the entry of only forty-six immigrants from 1820 through fiscal 1850). That influx filled a desperate need for manpower and precipitated an outbreak of nativism more virulent than any the nation had seen.

When large numbers of Chinese began arriving in the wake of the gold discovery, California initially welcomed them. Outgoing governor John McDougal hailed them in January 1852 as "one of the most worthy classes of our newly adopted citizens." His successor, John Bigler, disagreed. When a report prepared for the California Assembly found that Asians and others "dissimilar from ourselves in customs, language and education" were driving white immigrants away, Bigler sought special measures to check the "tide of Asiatic immigrants." The assembly responded by enacting a three-dollar-per-month foreign miners' tax (to be aggressively enforced against the Chinese) and a "commutation tax," which required ship captains to post a five-hundred-dollar bond for each immigrant landed. The tax would be commuted upon payment of a five-to-ten-dollar-per-passenger fee, the cost of which would be borne by Chinese travelers. Politicians rationalized their Sinophobia by portraying the Chinese as "coolies," in effect, as slaves—unfairly competing with whites—owned by a mysterious group of Chinese masters. Once the connection (however false or tenuous) to slavery was made, the identical arguments used to keep slaves out of the state could be used against the Chinese.

The anti-Chinese feelings stirred up by the politicians soon spread to the press and to the courts. San Francisco's *Daily Alta California,* the state's most influential newspaper, ran an editorial in 1853 arguing that Chinese, "morally a far worse class to have among us than the negro," were unfit for citizenship and should be permitted no more privileges than Africans or American blacks. A few weeks later, the paper ran a front-page condemnation of "semi-human Asiatics" who had brought about a "degradation and reduction of the price of labor" and suggested that eventually the Chinese might have to be removed by force. Around the same time, a state appellate court judge invalidated the conviction of a white man who had killed a Chinese, citing a recently enacted California statute that prohibited blacks, mulattoes, and Indians (and by extension, reasoned the judge, Chinese) from providing evidence against whites.

The following year, the foreign miners' tax was raised to six dollars per month (and scheduled to increase two dollars a year in perpetuity) for those not intending to become citizens. Since Asians were ineligible for naturalization, the law effectively targeted them without explicitly saying so. Shortly thereafter another tax was passed requiring fifty dollars from each immigrant landed—which was then more than the cost of passage from China.

Because six years earlier, the Supreme Court had abolished similar (and less onerous) immigrant taxes in New York and Massachusetts, California's legislators knew many of these laws were not likely to survive judicial scrutiny. The state's commissioner of immigrants found the legislation so constitutionally flimsy that he swore to enforce only those provisions he thought to be legal. That the lawmakers went ahead with the legislation anyway was an indication of the potency of its political appeal.

As Sinophobia swept through California, another brand of nativism was taking hold in the East, where record numbers of immigrants were spilling through the gates. Close to 3 million newcomers (including freethinkers and other refugees from Europe's failed democratic revolutions) entered America during the 1850s. At the time, America's major political parties were at a crossroads over slavery, and the Know-Nothing movement (represented by the American party) held out the promise of stability—or, at least, the promise of protection from foreign influence. Know-Nothings wanted the period for naturalization extended from five to at least twenty-one years. They also wanted political offices kept in the hands of native-born Protestants, reasoning that Catholicism's insistence on fealty to a foreign pope could endanger America's freedoms and institutions.

The movement had evolved from a collection of violently anti-Catholic, New York–based secret societies that venerated what they defined as native-Americanism. Membership was confidential in order to avoid political or economic reprisals from enemies. Each organization had secret handshakes and mysterious rituals. Some insisted that associates have at least two generations of American ancestors. When asked by the uninitiated about their membership, devotees would respond that they knew nothing and were consequently labeled "Know-Nothings" by *New York Tribune* editor Horace Greeley. At the height of the faction's influence, Know-Nothings and their allies dominated state legislatures in Massachusetts, Delaware, Pennsylvania, Rhode Island, New Hampshire, Connecticut, Maryland, and Kentucky.

Events seemed to corroborate Know-Nothing warnings of the foreign threat. The archbishop of New York, for instance, went on record describing the Catholic Church's objective as the conversion of "all Pagan nations, and all Protestant nations." A tour of America in summer 1853 by Monsignor Gaetano Bedini, apostolic nuncio to the United States, resulted in violent protests from immigrants who accused him of supporting the monarchy during the recent Italian uprisings—resulting in widespread condemnation of both the protestors and of the papal representative. The *New York Herald* editorialized shortly thereafter, "Had we no Irish or Germans or Italians in this country, the duties of a police officer would be a sinecure."

In addition to blaming foreigners for political violence, Know-Nothings also linked them to poverty and street crime. Nativist author Samuel Busey calculated that 1 in every 32 aliens was a pauper compared to 1 in every 317 Americans, and that 1 out of every 154 aliens was a criminal compared to 1 out of every 1,619 Americans. Foreigners were "the chief source of crime in this country," he concluded. Senator James Cooper demanded that an end be brought, once and for all, to European governments' practice of dumping paupers, criminals, and the diseased upon America. "In the great cities of the Republic, in New York, Philadelphia, Boston, Baltimore, St. Louis and New Orleans, the evils which have grown out of the admission of these classes of immigrants have become gigantic—frightful," he said.

Senator Charles Stuart insisted that undesirables were no more common among foreigners than among the native-born: "You may search the poorhouses and the prisons, and you will find there as many native Americans as foreigners. There is no . . . halo thrown around a man because he is a citizen of the United States." Nonetheless, the Know-Nothing view steadily gained converts, as Americans, particularly in major port cities, increasingly encountered examples of the foreign poor.

Despite the Know-Nothings' professed belief that native-Americanism transcended regional differences, adherents found the slavery question splitting them into northern and southern camps. When the Kansas-Nebraska Act, permitting the territories to decide through "popular sovereignty" (and in violation of the Missouri Compromise) whether they would be slave or free, was debated in (and passed) Congress in 1854, it created the same rifts in the Know-Nothing movement as it did in the rest of the country. Similarly, when the Homestead Act (to grant public domain land to those who settled on it) was proposed that year, Southerners fought it—reasoning the land offers would draw antislavery Northerners and Europeans to the West and ensure new political representation for antislavery forces. Though northern and western Know-Nothings also disliked the idea of Europeans getting American land, they generally supported the measure, viewing it as a way to assist native-born whites and to settle the largely barren West. The Homestead Act was defeated, along with the notion that Know-Nothings were any more united on such issues than the other political parties.

Even on proposals in which Know-Nothings were in agreement, regional differences in rationale surfaced. Senator Stephen Adams of Mississippi, in conformance with Know-Nothing orthodoxy, introduced a bill that would extend the naturalization period to twenty-one years. His major concern, however, was less with immigrants per se than with the fact that immigrants were neither pro-slavery nor likely to come to the South. Immigration, he argued at one point, had given the North twelve new congressional members during the 1840s—whereas without immigration the South would have gained representation relative to the North. In subsequent debate, he noted that if immigration continued at the same rate for another five years, "by the next apportionment the North will gain upon the South twenty-four additional members from immigration alone." In fifteen years, "the North will have a majority of more than two to one in the other branch of Congress; and . . . a similar majority in this body." That would be disastrous, said Adams. For the foreigners would vote for antislavery candidates and by so doing destroy the Union and the country.

Remarkably, for all the venom directed at the foreign-born,

no one was then seriously suggesting that they simply be turned
away at the border. The presumption was that America's traditions, Constitution, and sentiment all gave foreigners—at least
Europeans (excepting paupers, psychotics, and felons)—the
right to enter. At issue was whether, having arrived, they should
routinely be granted citizenship.

In arguing against the Know-Nothing program, author
Parke Godwin wrote in 1855: "Debar the half-million of emigrants who annually reach our shores from effective fran-
chise, and what would be the effect? Why, the growth, in the
very midst of the community, of a vast disenfranchised class—
of an immense body of political lepers." Because they were not
citizens, he said, they would have no attachment to society and
every reason to conspire against it. "We have already, in the
midst of us, one class of outcasts, in the poor and degraded
free blacks, and that, we should think, sufficient to appease
anybody's malignity, without striving to raise up another from
the Germans, the Irish, or any other nation." Know-Nothings,
on the other hand, saw disenfranchisement of those outcasts
as the only means of keeping them under control.

The 1854 elections left American party candidates and their
allies with forty-three votes in Congress, enough to be the balance of power on close issues, and more than enough to give
the Know-Nothing platform a thorough hearing. Even so, their
antiforeigner thrust was largely deflected by disputes over
slavery. Prodded by Southerners, the American party adopted
a plank at a national council meeting in summer 1855 urging
Congress not to legislate on slavery in the territories. Many
Northerners, finding the plank unacceptable, left the party. In
an attempt to mollify antislavery members, another national
council meeting in early 1856 removed the pro-slavery plank
and instead called for noninterference in territorial domestic
and social affairs—a compromise that pleased neither Northerners nor Southerners.

The party nominated former president Millard Fillmore
(who had lost the backing of his own Whig party) as its presidential candidate for 1856. By then, many northern Know-
Nothings had moved to the new antislavery Republican party,

which nominated former California senator and explorer John Charles Frémont as its candidate—launching him with the campaign slogan "Free Men, Free Soil, Frémont." Fillmore won only one fourth of the vote and carried only Maryland. Democrat James Buchanan won the race. The Know-Nothings, a party of people with only their distaste of foreigners in common, quickly faded into oblivion. In the end, it was little more than a distraction from the issue of slavery. And by 1856, it was clear to all sides that such distractions would not make the larger issue go away.

By the time Abraham Lincoln took office in early 1861, federal policy—or at least Lincoln's policy—was firmly on the side of immigration. Lincoln told an association of German-Americans that February, "In regard to Germans and foreigners, I esteem foreigners no better than other people, nor any worse. They are all of the great family of man. . . . And inasmuch as the continent of America is comparatively a new country, and the other countries of the world are old countries, there is more room here . . . and if they can better their condition by leaving their old homes . . . I bid them all God speed." The Civil War broke out two months later.

The Homestead Act—defeated in 1854 and vetoed by Buchanan in 1860, in deference to the South—was signed into law by Lincoln in 1862. The law granted 160 acres of public domain land to any settler who made improvements on it and farmed it for five years. Previously, under the Preemption Act of 1841, "squatters" had been permitted to buy such lands for a minimum of $1.25 per acre after living on it for fourteen months. Also in 1862, Congress chartered the Central Pacific and Union Pacific railroad companies to forge a rail link between the East and the West. Significantly, that same year, Congress prohibited importation of Chinese "coolies." The action was both a sop to those western states that had stayed in the Union and a further affirmation of the Union's antislavery stance. It was also the beginning of what would become several decades of federal legislation specifically aimed at curtailing immigration of Chinese.

Immigration of Europeans, however, was aggressively pro-

moted, with the Union caring little about their specific religion
or ethnicity—though individual displays of bigotry abounded.
In December of 1862, for instance, General Ulysses S. Grant
expelled all Jews from his Department of Tennessee domain,
apparently blaming them for illicit cotton trading through
Union lines. The order did not reflect official Union policy
but simply Grant's anti-Semitism, and it was soon rescinded on
Lincoln's instructions.

As the war continued to take its toll, Lincoln became more
emphatic in his endorsement of immigration, telling Congress
that workers were needed in mining, agriculture, and elsewhere in the U.S. economy: "While the demand for labor is
thus increased here, tens of thousands of persons, destitute of
remunerative occupation, are thronging our foreign consu-
lates, and offering to immigrate to the United States if essential, but very cheap, assistance can be afforded them." That
"noble effort," said Lincoln, deserved the aid of the United
States.

Even as Lincoln was calling for increased migration, British groups such as the National Colonial Emigration Society
were urging that the Irish and English poor be sent to America as a way of "not only rescuing many deserving persons
from impending misery, but at the same time permanently
lessening the burdens which have latterly pressed so heavily
on many classes of Her Majesty's subjects." Letters from U.S.
secretary of state William H. Seward, published in Irish newspapers and encouraging immigration to the United States, and
unfounded rumors that Ireland might soon pass legislation
barring emigration provided further incentives for the Irish
to hurry to America. *The Times* (London) questioned the United
States' intentions, publishing a warning in summer 1863 that
America's sudden interest in immigrants could merely be a
way of recruiting for the Civil War. Within twenty yards of
the emigration depot in America, reported *The Times*, were
two recruiting tents "with flaming placards offering large
bounties to young men who will take arms in the federal service."

The following March, Ohio senator John Sherman introduced a bill creating a commission of immigration to "encourage, facilitate and protect foreign immigration to and within the United States." The New York–based commissioner's job would be to distribute information about the United States throughout Europe informing prospective immigrants of America's manpower needs. Because of the dire need for labor in the West, noted Sherman, workers were being paid well, "and if it should be clearly shown to any intelligent person in Europe that it was his interest to come to America . . . there would be a great increase in the number of immigrants." Lincoln welcomed the initiative, calling immigrants "one of the principal replenishing streams which are appointed by Providence to repair the ravages of internal war," and signed the bill on July 4. Concerned about the charges that he was encouraging immigration in order to get troops for the war, Lincoln went on record opposing the drafting of foreigners.

In New York, previously the capital of anti-immigrant agitation, the new commissioner was accepted with a certain amount of equanimity. Mayor C. Godfrey Gunther argued that it was wrong to import men as "material for the army" during a civil war, and suggested that immigration should be allowed to take its natural course, but nothing approaching the hostility and consternation of the Know-Nothing era met the current crop of immigrants from Europe. As a group, however, Irish-Catholic immigrants still remained close to the bottom of the social and economic hierarchy, relegated for the most part to laboring jobs. They often were resented by unionists and the native-born, who believed immigrants were holding down wages and taking valuable jobs. At the same time, Irish immigrants resented free blacks, who they felt were restricting opportunities for them, and routinely opposed efforts to enfranchise blacks and supported efforts to push blacks out of many low-paying occupations.

Issuance of the Emancipation Proclamation early in 1863 had generated additional resentment, since it promised to increase competition from blacks. The military draft, enacted two months later, further angered New York's Irish immigrants, who were largely Democratic and hostile to the Repub-

lican ideas Lincoln represented. Though Congress had
exempted from military service those claiming foreign citizenship, it had not excused those in the process of naturalization.
Congress had, however, exempted blacks, which irritated those
who considered blacks responsible for the war. Many were also
outraged by a provision of the Conscription Act that allowed
the wealthy to avoid any military obligation. Though all men
up to age thirty-five (and all single men up to forty-five) were
eligible to be drafted for a period of three years, those who
paid three hundred dollars (or provided an acceptable substitute) did not have to go.

That June, an already edgy New York became even more
so, as three thousand longshoremen striking for higher wages
watched in anger as strikebreakers, many of them black, were
escorted in under police guard to take their places. Shortly
thereafter, New York's simmering racial and ethnic resentments came to a head and resulted in the most violent riot in
the nation's history.

On Saturday, July 11, draft officials set up operations in
New York. The following Monday, a crowd consisting of hostile (and, in some cases, merely curious) New Yorkers gathered to watch the lottery process. A pistol shot rang out from
an unknown source, and the crowd of onlookers quickly became a mob. The draft headquarters was torched, drafting
officers were attacked with stones and clubs, and the entire
block was soon consumed by fire. Upon spotting the police
superintendent, rioters took his watch, glasses, and gold-headed
cane. Most of the mob's anger, however, was directed at blacks,
whom protestors blamed not only for the war but for displac-
ing whites from jobs.

For several days, the predominantly Irish mobs roamed the
city, attacking blacks at random. The Orphan Asylum for Colored Children was set ablaze, and the several hundred children inside barely escaped before the building was enveloped.
A black man was hanged and then dragged through the street
by his genitals. Another had his fingers and toes cut off. Still
another had his throat slit before being tossed into the North
River, where he was discovered half-dead the following morn-

ing. A cart driver was set afire and hung from a tree. Total death estimates varied dramatically, with many placing the number in the thousands. No one placed it below one hundred. And no one was ever tried for the slaughter.

The rampage was a brutal reminder that the fading of Know-Nothingism had not erased the deep ethnic divisions in New York—or throughout America. Irish-Catholics continued to feel that their place in society was exasperatingly tenuous. And long after the Civil War, they (and similarly situated groups near the bottom of white society) continued to focus their most furious resentments on others even less able to win respect for their rights.

3

An Aroused West, an Excluded East

"The pressing want of our country is men," proclaimed Pennsylvania congressman William Kelley in the wake of the Civil War. The battle-ravaged South needed rebuilding, the thinly populated West needed settling, and the country's great mineral wealth needed to be mined. Hundreds of thousands arrived from Germany, Ireland, and England and, for the most part, were warmly received, but as increasing numbers of Chinese came to toil in America's mines and on the transcontinental railroad, anti-Chinese sentiment again began to rise.

Abraham Lincoln had signed legislation authorizing the necessary land grants and government bonds for the railroad in 1862, but plans had been largely on hold during the war, due as much to manpower, financial, and organizational problems as to the North-South conflict. Three years after congressional approval, less than fifty miles of the track between Sacramento and Omaha were completed. Unless progress picked up dramatically, the Central Pacific Railroad faced a financial fiasco. For in approving the project, Congress had, in effect, set up a race, issuing government bonds and granting land along the right-of-way in pace with the rate of work. The Central Pacific was building from the West (through the Sierra Nevadas), and the Union Pacific was building from the East; the two companies would meet somewhere in the middle—with the exact point determined by the speed of their respective workers. With the Union Pacific laying track eight times as fast as its Western rival, it stood to accrue substantially more bonds and land.

Charles Crocker, the Central Pacific director responsible for construction, was desperate for workers. In the final months of the war, he had even flirted with the idea of hiring Confederate prisoners or black Civil War veterans at military pay. In early 1865, he advertised for five thousand men to supplement his work crews of six hundred. Few appeared. To make matters worse, some of those already on board were talking about striking. Some fifty thousand Chinese were then in California—virtually all of whom were young males eager for work. When Crocker hit on the idea of using Chinese labor, his foreman, James Harvey Strobridge, resisted, but finally agreed to try out fifty Chinese for a month under white supervision. They did well. By the end of the year, an estimated seven thousand Chinese (and less than two thousand whites) were laying track for the Central Pacific. Additional workers were brought in direct from China.

The Chinese were cheaper than whites because they paid for their own food and housing while whites were cared for by the company. They were also considered more expendable, and would routinely be lowered from ropes into the rocks to drill holes for explosives and then race to get to safety before the charges went off. Sometimes they would not succeed. Scores of men of both races lost their lives in the tunnels and snow slides of the Sierra Nevada.

The new surge of Chinese immigrants soon drew fire from politicians and the press. When the Fourteenth Amendment was proposed in 1866—making citizens of all persons born in the United States and guaranteeing equal protection under the law regardless of race—Indiana congressman William Niblack reminded his peers that courts repeatedly had found blacks unacceptable as citizens and that California had found the same to be true of "Chinamen." "Let the white people . . . retain the power of the government in their own good hands and wield it for the good of all," he implored. With California preparing for statewide elections, the *San Francisco Examiner* urged support for the Democratic slate, portraying the opposition as a pro-Chinese, pro-Negro-suffrage "plunder league." "If . . . you are in favor of continuing this as a white man's government such as our fathers made it, and wish to reduce its expenses and taxation to such an extent that white men can live in it, then vote the ticket headed by H. H. Haight for Governor," advised the *Examiner* in 1867.

Henry Haight was elected governor, along with two congressmen and several members of the state assembly who had all run anti-Chinese campaigns. In a victory address repeatedly interrupted with applause, Governor-elect Haight called his election a "protest against corruption and extravagance in our State affairs, against populating this fair state with a race of Asiatics, against sharing with inferior races the government of the country, against the military despotism which now exists at the South under the last acts of Congress."

The following year, the United States negotiated the Burlingame Treaty, recognizing Chinese citizens' right to immigrate to America and conferring most-favored-nation status on China. Nonetheless, anti-Chinese agitation increased, due in part to the completion of the Pacific railway—which brought in settlers from the East. Many Chinese, because of their work with explosives on the railroad, were better qualified for quartz mining than the newly arriving whites, who, for the most part, were not at all eager to compete with Chinese; and politicians pandered to their fears. A California Democratic party platform statement suggested that giving Chinese the vote would not only "degrade the right of suffrage" but "ruin" the white laborer "by bringing untold hordes of pagan slaves . . . into direct competition with his efforts to earn a livelihood."

Representative James Johnson, of California, tried (without success) to get Congress to accept a resolution asserting that the Fifteenth Amendment (granting citizens of all races the right to vote) "never intended that Chinese or Mongolians should become voters." George Williams, of Oregon, proposed prohibition of Chinese contract labor, and read a newspaper account on the Senate floor about a Chinese resident of California who bought a female for six hundred dollars only to bemoan his lack of sufficient money to buy another. If prohibiting such outrages constituted discrimination, said Williams, "I suppose that the law prohibiting the African slave trade might be construed as a discrimination against Africans."

Several months later, when Massachusetts abolitionist Charles Sumner tried to strike all racial references from America's naturalization laws, Senator William Morris Stewart of Nevada argued that the measure would permit hundreds of thousands of "coolies" to be imported whose votes could be used to control the U.S. government. The likely result, he prophesied, would be armed revolt against the Chinese. "Because we did an act of justice, because we enfranchised the colored man, must we therefore necessarily abandon our institutions to the Chinese, or to the peoples of any country hostile to those institutions?" asked Stewart. When Sumner insisted that Chinese presented no great peril provided they pledged allegiance to U.S. institutions, the words fell on generally unreceptive ears. Sumner's amendment to remove "white" was rejected by a margin of more than two to one. An attempt by ally Lyman Trumbull to achieve much the same objective by adding "Chinese" was rejected even more overwhelmingly. Congress finally accepted wording that amended the 1798 naturalization act so that it applied to "aliens of African nativity" and "persons of African descent," but not to Chinese or any other nonwhite group.

As politicians whipped up animosity toward the Chinese, incidents of anti-Chinese violence cropped up. In 1867, a mob drove Chinese workers away from the Potrero Street railway in San Francisco and burned their barracks near the job site. In 1871, after a white man trying to stop a shooting duel between two Chinese in Los Angeles was accidentally killed, a mob of several hundred attacked Chinese bystanders, killing nineteen before running out of steam. West Coast legislators pointed to such incidents as evidence of the need to banish Chinese from America.

A federal court gave a boost to the campaign for federal involvement in 1874 by invalidating a California immigration statute allowing the state immigration commissioner to refuse admittance to certain objectionable aliens unless they posted a bond of five hundred dollars apiece. Among those subject to exclusion were the immoral, the lawless, "lunatic," "idiotic," "deaf," "dumb," "blind," "or crippled." Citing the law, the commissioner had barred twenty-two "lewd and debauched" Chinese women. In response to a suit filed on behalf of one of them, the circuit court revoked the law. The provisions were so broad, noted the judge, that they failed to distinguish between prostitutes and merely boisterous women. Moreover, he suggested, the law effectively abrogated the U.S. treaty with China. Though he was "aware of the very general feeling prevailing in this state against the Chinese," the solution could not be found in state legislation: "If their further immigration is to be stopped, recourse must be had to the federal government."

The following year, the U.S. Supreme Court struck an even more serious blow against state immigration regulations (and reversed its own 1837 ruling) by nullifying New York and Louisiana statutes that sanctioned taxation of foreign passengers. Such taxes—even if they were not called such, said the Court—were a regulation of foreign commerce, which was a power prohibited to states: "The laws which govern the right to land passengers in the United States from other countries ought to be the same in New York, Boston, New Orleans, and San Francisco." By "providing a system of laws in these matters, applicable to all ports and to all vessels," suggested the Court, Congress could settle "a serious question, which has long been matter of contest and complaint."

The ruling made doubtful the constitutionality of all state immigration laws and added the High Court's weight to politicians' demands that Congress accept responsibility for keeping undesirables out. As usual, Californians led the chorus, but others, including President Ulysses S. Grant, also called for federal intervention. Nearly a year before the Supreme Court decision, Grant had asked for legislation to curb trafficking in Chinese coolies and prostitutes, claiming that "the great proportion of the Chinese immigrants who come to our shores do not come voluntarily." Congress responded by enacting a law in March 1875 that prohibited transporting subjects of China, Japan, or other Asian countries to America against their will. It also barred immigration of those convicted of nonpolitical crimes and women imported "for the purposes of prostitution." (A woman subsequently convicted under the statute for paying a prostitute's passage from Copenhagen to New York appealed—without success—on the grounds that the law banned only those whores who came from the Orient.) The measures did not add up to an immigration policy, but they were the beginning of a system of broad federal restrictions. California's lawmakers, however, demanded more.

In 1876, California Democratic congressman William Piper proposed a resolution urging renegotiation of the Burlingame Treaty with China to "prevent any further immigration of the subjects of that empire to the United States." Shortly thereafter, the state's Republican senator, Aaron Sargent, offered a similar resolution. Neither passed, but they spurred Congress to appoint a joint House-Senate committee (to which it appointed California's leading anti-Chinese legislators) to go to the West Coast and investigate the Chinese problem. Around the same time, California's state senate conducted its own inquiry and, after hearing testimony from an array of witnesses hostile to the Chinese, concluded that at least three thousand Chinese women were being held in the state as sexual slaves. The legislators also determined that Chinese were unsanitary, unassimilable, and prone to criminality, and that they reduced wages below the level at which Americans could live. Congressional investigators came to much the same conclusions and recommended amending the Burlingame Treaty to arrest "the great influx of Asiatics into this country." Anti-Chinese planks were included in both 1876 state party platforms and in the national party platforms as well.

The presidential race that year pitted Republican Rutherford Hayes against Democrat Samuel Tilden and ended with disputed returns in Florida, Louisiana, Oregon, and South Carolina. An electoral commission named to resolve the controversy awarded the White House to Hayes. In return, however, the South was assured that Reconstruction would end. Federal troops were withdrawn and carpetbaggers sent home—a turn of events that strengthened the coalition between the anti-black South and the anti-Chinese West.

Meanwhile, Chinese settlers tried—through letters, newspaper articles, meetings with lawmakers, and countless lawsuits—to allay whites' fears and protect themselves from whites' resentment, but the anti-coolie campaign had achieved such momentum and the political benefit (for white politicians) had become so clear that there was little relief to be had. All problems—including falling wages—in the then-sluggish California economy were laid at the feet of the Chinese; and the result was an upsurge in anti-Chinese violence—much of it organized by militant labor organizations. In Chico, a small town north of San Francisco, several invaders stormed into a home occupied by six Chinese men in March 1877 and held the men at gunpoint before killing two of them and wounding two others. As the assailants fled, they set the home afire. Later in the week, more men raided Chinatown, setting fires to a washhouse and soap factory. Eleven Californians subsequently were arrested for murder and arson. Some two hundred outraged Chinese came out to watch the men marched to jail, and many subsequently contributed funds to aid the prosecution. During the trial, the men revealed that they had been acting on instructions from a secret labor society called the Council of Nine that supposedly ordered killing and intimidation as a method of protesting against and frightening the Chinese. Five were found guilty.

The Chico murders stirred the indignation of the *San Francisco Examiner,* which covered the events with relative compassion. That compassion, however, only went so far. A few weeks following the Chico incidents, the *Examiner* noted that the drought sweeping the region had put white men out of work and urged all employers to fire their Chinese help. "There is now no good reason why they should not do so and hire white men in their place."

That summer the anti-Chinese movement reached a new peak. The evening of July 23, a crowd assembled in a sandlot near San Francisco's city hall to hear pro-labor orators. Much of the crowd was already in a foul mood because of an aborted attempt by the Central Pacific to cut wages. One speaker fanned the anger by claiming that a steamship company had contracted to deliver twenty-five thousand Chinese to the state by October. Either the whites or the Chinese would have to leave, he said. Other equally incendiary remarks were made, igniting an eruption of violence that went on for three days. Chinese homes and businesses were burned in various parts of town. The wharf and a lumberyard known to hire Chinese were torched, and numerous Chinese were killed.

The rampage led the Committee of Vigilance, comprised of San Francisco's business elite, to call for federal measures to halt Chinese immigration. The Workingmen's Trade and Labor Union of San Francisco headed by Denis Kearney was also agitating against the Chinese. The organization, also known as the Workingmen's party of California, was dominated by Irish immigrants, like Kearney, who saw Chinese workers as the enemy. The party's manifesto was unmistakably clear: "Before you and the world we declare that the Chinaman must leave our shores. We declare that white men, and women, and boys, and girls, cannot live as the people of this great republic should and compete with the single Chinese coolie on the labor market. . . . To an American, death is preferable to life on a par with the Chinaman."

A Kearney-led Thanksgiving Day parade drew an estimated seven thousand marchers. His candidate, Isaac Kalloch, became mayor of San Francisco, and his associates swept elections to the constituent assembly charged with rewriting the state constitution. That constitution, adopted in 1879, explicitly denied the vote to the criminal, the insane, and those born

in China. It also denied Chinese aliens the right to own property, to testify against whites, to bear arms, to engage in mer-
cantile businesses, or to be employed in California public works.
While ratifying the new constitution, California's voters also
approved—by a vote of 154,638 to 883—a referendum endorsing Chinese exclusion. The ballot had been designed in
such a way that in order to reject the measure a voter had to
scratch out the word "against" and write in "for." In touting
the results of the referendum, California politicians conve-
niently left out the details of the ballot's design, but pointed
to the vote as evidence that—in the words of Senator George
Perkins—"Men of all parties and creeds . . . agree that they
[Chinese immigrants] are a blight upon our industries and citizenship, and an injury to our people."

As California rewrote its laws and remade its constitution
with an eye toward persecuting and excluding Chinese, the
state's congressmen (joined by legislators from Oregon, Nevada, and other western states) inundated their colleagues with
resolutions and statements demanding federal anti-Chinese
legislation. Congress responded in 1879 by passing a law limiting to fifteen the number of Chinese passengers (government officials excepted) allowed on any vessel bound for the
United States. Rutherford Hayes vetoed the bill, maintaining
that only the president—not Congress—could abrogate a treaty
with another nation.

The following month, a federal court dashed any hopes
Chinese immigrants may have entertained of still qualifying
for naturalization under existing law. "Neither in popular language, in literature, nor in scientific nomenclature, do we ordinarily, if ever, find the words 'white person' used in a sense
so comprehensive as to include an individual of the Mongolian
race," noted the circuit-court judge. Revisiting the 1870 Senate debate in which Charles Sumner had unsuccessfully tried
to have "white" stricken from U.S. naturalization laws, the judge
concluded, "It is clear, from these proceedings, that Congress
retained the word 'white' . . . for the sole purpose of excluding the Chinese from the right of naturalization."

A year later, the Burlingame Treaty was renegotiated. The

Chinese government agreed to provisions barring criminals, contract laborers, prostitutes, and the diseased from migrating to the United States. The most significant Chinese concession, however, was language that gave America the right to suspend but not "absolutely prohibit" immigration, for a limited period, of skilled or unskilled laborers who "endanger the good order of the said country [meaning the United States] or of any locality within the territory."

Fully aware of Congress's escalating anti-Chinese crusade, the Chinese negotiators apparently thought the careful wording would protect Chinese nationals from capricious and unwarranted debarment. They underestimated both the depth of U.S. Sinophobia and the lengths to which politicians, particularly in an election year, would go to cater to it.

In the months following ratification of the treaty, a blizzard of Chinese restriction resolutions and bills rained down on both houses of Congress—among them one from California senator John Miller that would exclude Chinese laborers for twenty years. He noted that both 1880 party platforms had called for stronger controls on Chinese immigration, and he rehearsed what had by then become standard charges against the Chinese. They were a "servile people," he railed, in eternal bondage to the Six Companies who had imported them; and they lived so cheaply—"like swine in the sty"—that whites could not compete with them. In an unmistakable allusion to the Civil War, he asserted: "An 'irrepressible conflict' is upon us in full force, and those who do not see it in progress are not so wise as the men who saw the approach of the other 'irrepressible conflict' which shook the very foundation of the American empire upon this continent."

After prolonged debate, the bill passed the Senate by a two-to-one margin in March 1882. The House passed it two weeks later by an even larger margin, but President Chester Arthur vetoed it because it violated the recently renegotiated treaty. Almost immediately, several new bills were proposed that got around Arthur's primary objection by shortening the exclusion period. By the end of April both houses had passed a measure providing for a ten-year period of exclusion of all

Chinese laborers (including miners) and that commanded, "hereafter no state court or court of the United States shall admit Chinese to citizenship; and all laws in conflict with this act are hereby repealed." Those Chinese nationals who were not laborers thenceforth would need a special certificate from the Chinese government to enter the United States. Those already present could remain; but those who wished to leave and return would be required to present a certificate proving they had originally come to the United States before November 1880. Ship captains who transported Chinese in violation of the law were subject to a five-hundred-dollar fine or a one-year prison sentence for each person landed and the possible loss of their vessel. President Arthur signed the bill in May. That same year Congress passed a general immigration act barring paupers, criminals, the insane, and others likely to become public charges.

The general act was merely the next natural step in the ongoing transfer of responsibility for immigration from the states to the federal government. The anti-Chinese legislation, however, was a direct repudiation of what formerly had been a hallowed U.S. tradition deeming that all nationalities could enter—even if all could not be citizens. It was also the first law to specifically deny naturalization to an ethnic group as opposed to designating those—whites and persons of African ancestry—who could be naturalized.

In the years following passage of the act, anti-Chinese violence flourished. In September 1885, near Rock Springs, Wyoming, twenty-eight Chinese were killed by whites wielding rifles and handguns and determined to eject Chinese workers from the mines. Though many of the victims were shot running from structures set afire by the mob, no one was indicted for the slaughter. Shortly after the Wyoming uprising, three Chinese miners in Seattle were murdered. When that failed to dislodge the Chinese population, several hundred were forcibly removed from their homes. Such actions took place with striking regularity and rarely were seriously punished.

Meanwhile, Congress—with White House cooperation—endeavored to shut the door entirely on Chinese immigration by passing several measures in succession (generally in election years). In 1884, Congress broadened the definition of "laborers" who were excluded and tightened identification procedures, requiring all Chinese travelers headed for the United States to carry official documents setting forth their profession, status, and exact destination. Four years later, Congress tightened the laws again, barring from reentry any Chinese laborer and former U.S. resident who did not have a wife, children, parents, or property valued at one thousand dollars within the United States. The act passed even as the Chinese government balked at signing a treaty that sanctioned the exclusion acts, prompting President Grover Cleveland to call the legislation an "act in self-defense." The mixing of Chinese and American workers, said Cleveland, had proved "to be in every sense unwise, impolitic, and injurious to both nations."

In 1892, Congress extended the period of exclusion for another ten years and ordered all Chinese laborers within the country to get certificates of residence. Those without the documents necessary to obtain the certificate were required to produce "at least one credible white witness" to authenticate their right to residency. In a display of goodwill (or, more likely, simple pragmatism—since no one desired to pay the cost of deporting those who did not comply), Congress amended the "white witness" provision the following year to permit testimony by "one credible witness other than Chinese" and extended the registration period to accommodate those who had waited and hoped—in vain—that the law would be declared unconstitutional.

As the exclusion acts neared expiration in 1902, Westerners again lobbied for extension. Oregon senator John Mitchell called Chinese exclusion "one of the great policies of the country." Senator Clarence Clark of Wyoming argued that just as white Southerners best understood blacks, white Westerners best understood the Chinese: "The Chinese question is the race question of the Pacific Coast." Congress followed the Westerners' lead and, with amendments later that year and in 1904, extended the exclusion statutes indefinitely while outlawing Chinese immigration from any U.S. territory to the mainland.

Chinese immigrants, who lacked standing to fight Sinophobia at the polls, vigorously fought it in federal courts, filing one suit after another to combat the laws that allowed only a select few Chinese into the nation and even prohibited the reentry of those who had lived in America for much of their lives. The judicial results were mixed at best.

In 1884, the U.S. Supreme Court ruled that one Chew Heong could reenter the United States after taking a trip to Honolulu and returning without the reentry certificates then required of Chinese nationals. Chew Heong, a laborer who had originally come to America in 1880, had moved to Honolulu the following year. He had tried to return to the mainland in September 1884, shortly after enactment of the second Chinese restriction act, but, possessing no reentry certificate, had been detained aboard ship in San Francisco Harbor and subsequently ordered deported. Chew Heong had sued for his right to stay, claiming the 1882 and 1884 acts did not bar laborers who were residents of the United States at the time of the 1880 treaty between the United States and China. Since he had left the country before passage of the first exclusion act, said Chew Heong, he had been in no position to obtain a reentry certificate. The Court agreed, reasoning that to deport him would be tantamount to violating the treaty, which could not have been Congress's intention. "It would be a perversion of . . . language," concluded Justice John M. Harlan, to exclude "Chinese laborers who had left the country with the privilege, secured by treaty, of returning, but who, by reason of their absence when those legislative enactments took effect could not obtain the required certificates."

A California circuit court applied similar reasoning the following year to admit Ah Ping, a San Francisco–based merchant who had been on business in British Columbia when Congress had passed the first of the Chinese exclusion laws. Consequently he had been stuck abroad without a reentry certificate. As a merchant, Ah Ping did not likely belong to the excluded classes at any rate, said the court, but certainly, given the Supreme Court's decision on Chew Heong, there were no grounds to bar an otherwise legal resident who simply had not had an opportunity to acquire documentation.

A few years later, however, as federal regulations became ever more restrictive, the courts became less indulgent. In 1889, the U.S. Supreme Court refused to admit Chae Chan Ping, a laborer who had lived in San Francisco for twelve years before traveling to his native China in summer of 1887. Before leaving, he had obtained the required reentry certificate. While he was abroad, however, Congress passed the 1888 act barring the return of Chinese laborers who had left the country. On returning, Chae Chan Ping presented his certificate but was refused permission to set foot on U.S. land. Instead, he was held captive in San Francisco Bay aboard the steamer that had brought him there. While the Court agreed that the statute abrogated part of the treaty with China, it ruled that Congress was within its right to do so: "To preserve its independence, and give security against foreign aggression and encroachment, is the highest duty of every nation, and to attain these ends nearly all other considerations are to be subordinated," wrote Justice Stephen J. Field.

Field (who had dissented from the previous decision permitting Chew Heong to stay) compared the exclusion of the Chinese to the exclusion of "paupers, criminals and persons afflicted with incurable diseases" whose presence was likewise "deemed injurious or a source of danger to the country." If Congress had decided "the presence of foreigners of a different race in this country, who will not assimilate with us, to be dangerous to its peace and security," reflected Field, the Court could not dispute that judgment. The Chinese government or Chinese travelers had no recourse, he suggested, but to appeal to America's politicians.

The courts were equally hard-nosed in 1893, following passage of the 1892 law requiring all Chinese laborers to carry certificates of residence or face deportation. In one case involving Ah Fawn, an alleged gambler and "highbinder" (professional criminal), the circuit court in California was faced with deciding whether Ah Fawn's professions made him a "laborer"—and therefore subject to deportation for not carrying the required certificate. The court concluded that "laborer" applied to "all immigration other than that for teaching, trade, travel, study, and curiosity," and as such even covered professional gamblers and murderers. The effect was to make virtually all Chinese immigrants in America—including doctors and other professionals—"laborers" under the law and therefore liable to be deported if they did not obtain the certificates.

That same year, the Supreme Court reviewed the cases of three men arrested for not carrying their papers. Two had refused to get the certificates, and the third had been unable to obtain one since he had only Chinese witnesses to attest to his legal residency. Following the earlier reasoning of Field in the Chae Chan Ping case, Justice Horace Gray concluded that the United States could deport all three. "The right of a nation to expel or deport foreigners . . . rests upon the same grounds, and is as absolute and unqualified as the right to prohibit and prevent their entrance into the country," he wrote. ". . . Congress, having the right, as it may see fit, to expel aliens of a particular class . . . has undoubtedly the right to provide a system of registration and identification of the members of that class within the country, and to take all proper means to carry out the system which it provides."

One major concession granted by the courts concerned persons of Chinese extraction who were born in America and who therefore were citizens of the United States. That decision came in the case of Wong Kim Ark, a San Francisco–born man of Chinese descent who had spent his entire life in the United States with the exception of two brief visits to China. Upon returning from his second visit at the age of twenty-two in 1895, he was refused entry. Since he was Chinese, reasoned custom officials, he could not also be a U.S. citizen; and since he was a laborer, he was barred by the Chinese exclusion acts.

Justice Gray rejected the reasoning, pointing out that the Fourteenth Amendment granted citizenship to *all* persons born in the United States, and that Congress could not, by statute, negate that. "The power of naturalization, vested in Congress by the Constitution, is a power to confer citizenship, not a power to take it away." The exclusion acts, he added, could not keep out U.S. citizens, even if those citizens were laborers of the "Chinese race."

The decision was an important one, for it meant that American-born children of Chinese immigrants were protected against certain indignities that would be visited on their parents. They could travel without restriction and without the need to carry around the widely hated residency certificates. The collective decisions and attendant legislation also meant, however, that Congress had largely achieved its goal: Chinese immigration to the United States was virtually halted. And those Chinese who did remain were subject to deportation at the slightest congressional whim.

4

Radicals, Race,
and New Restrictions

Whlie Congress was choking off immigration from China, many American intellectuals were exploring political radicalism and scientific racism. The two movements attracted adherents from opposite sides of the ideological spectrum and sought fundamentally different objectives, but both fueled America's fear of foreigners. Together they would justify, to the federal government's satisfaction, a fundamental reshaping of U.S. immigration policies. For many legislators, the beginning of that decades-long process was with the labor unrest of the 1870s.

The rail strike of 1877 erupted following an attempt by four eastern lines to impose a 10 percent pay cut. The work stoppage quickly mushroomed into a huge and violent event that set laborers against state militias and local police. President Rutherford Hayes sent federal troops into several cities to put down the uprising, which ultimately resulted in more than one hundred deaths, and which German and French socialists were widely blamed for igniting. That same year, some twenty alleged members of a secret predominantly Irish-

American organization known as the Molly Maguires were hung for their involvement in murder, robbery, beatings, arson, and numerous other crimes stemming from labor disputes in the eastern Pennsylvania coal mines. The incident again made explicit, for many Americans, the connection between foreigners and organized mayhem.

Nearly a decade later, a full-fledged red scare broke out in the wake of a bomb explosion in Chicago's Haymarket Square. The bomb was tossed during a rally called to protest police violence precipitated by a general strike for an eight-hour workday. In the ensuing confusion, an unknown number of civilians and seven police officers were killed (or mortally wounded)—most, apparently, from police gunfire. The bomber was never identified, nor was anyone ever directly linked to him. Nonetheless, eight local anarchists—seven of whom were immigrants—were convicted of murder at a trial during which the prosecutor denounced them as "godless foreigners." Seven were given the death sentence. Two of those condemned to die were granted clemency by the governor, one committed suicide, and four were subsequently executed. Six years after the executions, Illinois reform governor John Peter Altgeld pardoned the three who remained in jail. Feelings against the anarchists still ran so high that Altgeld's political career was ruined.

Shortly after the Haymarket incident, Congressman Melbourne Ford's Select Committee on Investigation of Foreign Immigration recommended that anarchists be barred from entering the country. Congress took no immediate action. In September 1901, President William McKinley was assassinated in Buffalo, New York, by Leon Czolgosz, a self-declared anarchist and the American-born son of Russian Poles. "[W]hat started the craze to kill was a lecture I heard . . . by [anarchist] Emma Goldman. . . . She set me on fire," confessed Czolgosz. The murder spurred congressional action. A new immigration act, passed eighteen months after the slaying, excluded anarchists from immigrating to the United States, along with "persons who believe or advocate the overthrow by force or violence of the government of the United States, or of all government or all forms of law, or the assassination of public officials."

Until the final years of the century, most immigrants continued to come from Northern and Western Europe—primarily from Germany, England, Ireland, and Scandinavia. The direction of the change, however, was unmistakable. Though only 26,000 Italian immigrants came to America from 1820 through 1870, more than a million more had arrived by 1900. Simultaneously emigration from Russia jumped from less than 4,000 to more than 750,000. From Portugal, it went from slightly over 5,000 to nearly 60,000. From Poland, it increased from less than 4,000 to well over 160,000. As immigration shifted, many Americans wondered whether the peril posed by foreign blood was every bit as real as that posed by foreign anarchists.

The Slavic and Mediterranean newcomers came for much the same reason as did their Western and Northern European counterparts: They were fleeing hard times and seeking a better life. In Russia, the assassination of Czar Alexander II in 1881 had led to savage anti-Jewish riots and, shortly thereafter, severe restrictions on Jewish settlement and commerce. In Italy, agricultural workers had been devastated when their citrus fruits were squeezed out of the U.S. market by California and Florida production, at the same time as French tariffs blocked importation of Italian wine.

Some of the hostility toward the new immigrants had little to do with their ethnicity. During the early wave of Italian migration, many came as contract workers bound to a *padrone* who would handle their passage to America and hire them out for whatever the market would bear. Labor organizations were outraged at the low-price competition—and in 1885 prodded Congress into passing a statute forbidding anyone from assisting, encouraging, or paying transportation costs for alien contract laborers.

Ethnicity, however, was clearly a factor when, in 1891, a New Jersey glass works' hiring of eleven Russian Jews touched off a riot—as it was in New Orleans that same year when a jury's refusal to convict Italians accused of murdering the police superintendent led a mob to kidnap and kill eleven of the suspects still being held. Two years before those incidents, Congressman Ford's Select Committee on Investigation of Foreign Immigration concluded that the new immigrants did not measure up to the old stock. A much larger proportion of them seemed to be criminals, paupers, or insane. The House Judiciary Committee came to much the same conclusion, reporting that at least half the criminal, insane, and paupers in America's largest cities were foreign-born.

The reports mobilized Congress to tighten admission procedures. A new immigration act, passed in 1891, took back many duties of inspection and regulation that had been contracted out to the states. It also authorized the appointment of a superintendent of immigration, provided for medical inspection of immigrants before they were allowed to land, and added new classes of aliens to the list of those excluded. In addition to the paupers, lunatics, idiots, felons, prostitutes, and contract workers proscribed by earlier measures were added polygamists, "persons suffering from a loathsome or a dangerous contagious disease," and those convicted of a "misdemeanor involving moral turpitude."

Almost immediately, some legislators questioned whether the new measures would be enough to keep all undesirables out, and Senator Henry Cabot Lodge of Massachusetts and his allies began exploring options for curbing, in Lodge's words, "the wholesale infusion of races whose tradition and inheritances, whose thoughts and whose beliefs are wholly alien to ours." A literacy test, Lodge reasoned, would restrain such groups as Italians, Russians, Poles, Hungarians, and Greeks while leaving Western and Northern Europeans largely unaffected.

The Boston-based Immigration Restriction League, organized in 1894, became an effective lobby for that idea, as well as for the general proposition that such ethnic groups represented inferior and unassimilable races. Ethnic animosity, of course, was nothing new to America—or even to immigration legislation. The Chinese exclusion and coolie acts had already established a strong precedent for considering race as a factor in admitting immigrants. Never before the 1890s, however, had Congress seriously considered the idea that whites might belong to an inferior race—and that an immigration policy might be crafted to favor Europeans of better blood.

William Z. Ripley's *The Races of Europe,* published in 1899, provided an intellectual foundation for such policies by dividing contemporary Europeans into three distinct races: tall, blond, blue-eyed "Teutonic"; stocky, chestnut-haired, hazel-eyed "Alpine"; and dark, slender "Mediterranean." Ripley, an assistant professor of sociology at the Massachusetts Institute of Technology and lecturer in anthropology at Columbia University, expounded at length on such characteristics as stature, complexion, head shape, and nose type. He was reluctant, however, to endorse an "ethnic explanation" for observed differences in ambition, intelligence, artistic ability, and disposition toward suicide, finding the arguments "too simple." "With the data at our disposition," noted Ripley, "there is no end to the racial attributes which we might saddle upon our ethnic types."

David Starr Jordan, president of Stanford University, had no such reluctance. To Jordan, the lighter Teutonic types represented a higher stage of development than their darker cousins, and in a 1902 book that celebrated "noble and royal" Anglo-American blood, he hinted at possible disaster ahead: "In the red field of human history the natural process of selection is often reversed. The survival of the unfittest is the primal cause of the downfall of nations." While neither Jordan nor Ripley explicitly called for excluding Eastern and Southern Europeans, many of their intellectual successors did. For once the proposition of genetically discrete European races was accepted, the scientific theories of the age demanded no less. Darwinism, after all, extolled survival of the fittest, and Mendelian genetics provided a framework for understanding the harm inferior gene pools could cause.

Darwin's cousin and eugenics' founder Francis Galton had credited genes for a wide range of human traits—from genius to feeblemindedness to promiscuity—in his 1869 classic, *He-*

reditary Genius, in which he complained, "Much more care is taken to select appropriate varieties of plants and animals for plantations in foreign settlements than to select appropriate types of men." The ancient Greeks, said Galton, had been a superior race—as superior, on average, to nineteenth-century Europeans as "our race is above that of the African Negro." Years of immigration, however, had relentlessly driven down the quality of the once-great Greek tribe. Galton's disciples in America feared that much the same could happen here.

For American eugenicists, protecting the nation from inferior gene pools effectively boiled down to two tasks: keeping out those races (Slavic, Mediterranean, and all nonwhites) whose genes were hopelessly substandard and keeping out those who exhibited traits (alcoholism, pauperism, insanity) that stemmed from tainted genes; and those tasks were lent urgency by the steep upsurge in American immigration.

In 1900, America's percentage of foreign-born was nearly 14 percent—as high as it had been at any point since the colonial age—and climbing. Total immigration for the century's first decade approached 9 million—exceeding, by 3.5 million, immigration in any previous decade. The great majority of the newcomers were from Eastern and Southern Europe. Immigration from Asia—though tiny compared to the total—was also increasing. Whereas twenty-six thousand Japanese settled in America during the 1890s, five times that number came the following decade. Similar increases occurred in the traffic from Turkey and India.

For restrictionists of every stripe, the numbers added up to a disaster—particularly in light of testimony from such presumed experts as Francis Amasa Walker, who had directed the 1870 and 1880 U.S. censuses, that immigrants were breeding faster than native-born Americans. Generating remedial legislation, however, was not a simple task, as America had no real experience discriminating against European "races." In contrast, the nation's treatment of blacks and Chinese provided ample precedents for moving against the Japanese. Moreover, Asian stereotypes were already widely accepted and did not require the invention of new racial categories, as

America's commissioner of immigration, W. M. Rice, demonstrated in 1898 by pronouncing Japanese to be "tricky, deceitful, immoral, and un-Christian."

As the Russo-Japanese War progressed in 1905, many Californians feared Japanese immigration would soon rise beyond endurance. That February, the *San Francisco Chronicle* launched a preemptive strike with a series documenting the "Japanese Invasion: The Problem of the Hour." The war with Russia, concluded the *Chronicle,* could result in an "inundating torrent" of Japanese at a time when America was already dealing with the "negro question" and having to absorb a flood of immigrants—Bohemians, Lithuanians, Poles, Croats, Slavs, and Italians—who were "in the bulk, neither the fittest nor the best." "There is no room upon American soil for another race problem," declared the *Chronicle,* and accused the Japanese of instigating a crime wave in San Francisco, selling their daughters into prostitution, taking jobs from white men and women, and coming to America "solely for the purpose of learning methods by which they will fight us in future years."

In the climate of hysteria generated by the *Chronicle,* both houses of the state legislature voted unanimously for a resolution that pronounced the Japanese "wholly undesirable" by dint of their character and "race habits" and called upon the federal government to block further Japanese immigration. A bill to bar Japanese laborers was offered by California congressman Duncan McKinlay. The House took no immediate action, but Californian politicians continued to push the idea, and in late 1906, San Francisco politicians stepped up their anti-Japan campaign to such an extent that the White House finally took notice.

A major scandal was then unfolding in the city growing out of political boss Abraham Ruef's control of city hall, the city commissions, the police force, and the school board. Ruef and his protégé, Mayor Eugene Schmitz, were being pummeled in San Francisco's newspapers for running an administration based on graft. In need of a political diversion, Schmitz and assorted Ruef allies latched on to the Japanese issue. As its contribution to the campaign and under prodding from the

Exclusion League of North America, the school board directed principals to send all Japanese children to the Oriental Public School—giving, among other reasons, the fact that Japanese were crowding whites out of school. At the time, ninety-three Japanese students were attending school with American children in San Francisco. The Japanese government, offended by the school board's action, protested diplomatically and prodded the U.S. government into threatening a federal suit to force San Francisco to back down. Meanwhile, Ruef and Schmitz were indicted for extorting money from restaurants. Soon thereafter, they were charged with numerous other crimes—including receiving kickbacks from city contractors and bribes from bordellos. The following February, with the charges still pending, President Theodore Roosevelt summoned Mayor Schmitz and the school board to Washington.

Roosevelt, who desired cordial relations with Japan, had even advocated permitting the naturalization of Japanese residents. As a pragmatist, however, Roosevelt realized that growing anti-Japanese sentiment in the West had to be satisfied. For him, the meeting with Schmitz and company was an opportunity to iron out a diplomatically embarrassing situation with the San Francisco schools while demonstrating his willingness to move against the Japanese. For Schmitz, the tête-à-tête was a godsend, giving him a chance to enhance his prestige despite the corruption charges hanging over him. In the course of the meeting, San Francisco officials agreed to withdraw the plan, and Roosevelt promised to do what he could to restrict Japanese immigration.

To carry out his part of the bargain, Roosevelt sought authority from Congress to limit Japanese immigrants who did not come directly from Japan. A cooperative Congress passed a provision giving the president authority to bar passport holders from countries (or territories) whose citizens were entering the United States by routing their voyage through nearby countries or U.S. possessions. Citing the authority of the new law, Roosevelt issued an executive order that March cutting off migration of Japanese and Korean laborers (skilled and unskilled alike) from Mexico, Canada, and Hawaii. The Japa-

nese government objected to the order and subsequently exacted a promise from the Roosevelt administration that America
would enact no new embarrassing restrictions on Japanese immigration. In return, under the unwritten accord known as
the Gentlemen's Agreement, Japan promised to prohibit Japanese laborers from migrating to the continental United States.

The deal put the "Oriental problem" (temporarily) to rest,
but European immigration showed no signs of slowing. To help
Congress come to grips with the issue, the 1907 immigration
act authorized a massive study. The resulting forty-two-vol-
ume report, issued in 1911, confirmed Congress's anxieties
about Eastern and Southern Europeans. The new immigrants,
concluded the Dillingham Commission (named for the legislation's author and the commission's chairman, Senator William P. Dillingham of Vermont), were, in fact, more likely to
be unskilled, unsettled, and generally undesirable than Western and Northern European immigrants. Later experts would
dispute those conclusions, but they were an important part of
the justification for the new restrictions Congress continued to
write into law.

In 1903, while prohibiting anarchists, Congress had broadened its list of excludable aliens to encompass epileptics and
"persons who have been insane within five years previous" or
who "have had two or more attacks of insanity at any time
previously." In 1907, it added feebleminded persons, those with
tuberculosis, and those whose physical or mental defects hin-
dered their earning a living. The ever-expanding list of exclusions, however, was proving to be not much of an obstacle for
the vast majority of those pouring in from Eastern and Southern Europe. The literacy test was promoted as a better screen
by legislators and lobbyists who were evidently convinced that
few Poles, Russians, or Italians could read.

Persuaded by Henry Cabot Lodge's argument, Congress
had passed the literacy requirement in 1896, only to have it
vetoed by Grover Cleveland, who thought a reading test a poor
criterion for citizenship. Similar bills passed in 1913, 1915, and
1917, and were vetoed for much the same reason. By early
1917, anti-immigration forces were considerably stronger. The

United States was on the verge of entering World War I, and many believed America should barricade the doors. Despite arguments that the literacy test was little more than a way of favoring the affluent and educated, both houses overrode Woodrow Wilson's veto and barred all sighted aliens over sixteen years of age who could not read either in English "or some other language or dialect, including Hebrew or Yiddish." The act also expanded the list of excluded classes, adding chronic drunks and those suffering from "constitutional psychopathic inferiority." The latter condition referred to those whose blood carried genes for a bizarre and incurable psychosis described by one House document as "a congenital defect in the emotional or volitional fields of mental activity which results in inability to make proper adjustments to the environment."

The law's most sweeping prohibition, however, was aimed at Asians. Though Chinese and Japanese had been effectively barred by the Chinese exclusion acts and the Gentlemen's Agreement, access had remained open for others from the Orient. Various congressmen had periodically attempted to remedy that with proposed legislation barring Asians, Hindus, or other nonwhite groups. In 1913, a bill prohibiting immigration of aliens ineligible for citizenship (i.e., Asians) had passed both houses, but had been vetoed by President William Taft because it also contained the literacy requirement. In overriding the veto in 1917, Congress created a zone from which immigration was to be barred that covered India, Burma, Siam, most of the East Indian and Polynesian islands, and parts of Russia, Arabia, and Afghanistan.

Having acted on immigration, Congress turned its attention to the war, which the United States formally entered less than two months later, and which would help justify immigration policies markedly more restrictive than any America had yet enacted.

5

A War Ends,
an Era of Isolation Begins

T he outbreak of World War I intensified America's already strong suspicions of foreign radicals. Two months
before the United States entered the conflict, Congress
authorized deportation of any alien "found advocating or
teaching the unlawful destruction of property, or advocating
or teaching anarchy . . . or the assassination of public officials." A month before the war's end, Congress broadened the
statute to include any foreigner who believed in anarchy, or
violent overthrow of government, or was opposed to "all organized government," or was affiliated with any organization
holding such beliefs—regardless of whether the alien was actively promoting such ideas.

Previously the Labor Department (then responsible for deportations) had resisted deporting members of the Industrial
Workers of the World unless they did something more antagonistic than merely belong to the organization. The new law
was Congress's way of overcoming that reluctance. In June 1920,
nearly two years after the war ended, the anti-anarchist act
was expanded yet again—to cover all aliens who wrote, pub-

lished, commissioned, distributed, printed, circulated (or even possessed with intent to circulate) any materials advocating violent overthrow of the government or "all forms of law." The burst of legislative activity was propelled not only by war worries but by the Russian Revolution. The laws proved to be of no demonstrable value in weeding out violent foreigners, but they kept Labor Department officials and Justice Department agents extremely busy planning thousands of arrests and deportations.

The most famous deportee was Emma Goldman, who had made a career out of preaching anarchism, pacifism, free love, and feminism. Along with 248 other foreign-born American residents—all but two of them men—Goldman was forced aboard a U.S. warship anchored in New York Harbor and expelled four days before Christmas, 1919. "I do not consider it a punishment to be sent to Soviet Russia," she said upon departing. "On the contrary, I consider it an honor to be the first political agitator deported from the United States." Many of her fellow passengers were banished for belonging to an organization called the Union of Russian Workers. Scores of others would subsequently be deported for membership in the Industrial Workers of the World or various communist organizations.

At the time, Justice Department officials boasted of plans to deport a total of sixty thousand radicals, and Attorney General A. Mitchell Palmer was lobbying Congress for additional funds to carry out the mission. The goal was never reached, but not for lack of effort. J. Edgar Hoover, then director of the Justice Department's Radical Division, pursued an extremely aggressive arrests policy. Agents, generally working with local police, invaded meeting halls and private homes and carted off books, papers, and other belongings that might contain evidence of membership in tainted organizations. In many instances, they did not bother to produce arrest or search warrants—or even to separate aliens from citizens—but merely took anyone present into custody. As a result, hundreds of innocent men and women were hauled before hearing officers and treated as traitors by government officials who demanded to know whether they believed in sabotage, anarchy, communism, or the American government. Many of the common laborers caught in the government's net had little understanding of the ideas they were accused of holding. That was no bar to their deportation. Nor was the fact that some had spouses and young children who knew no country other than America.

One of the largest operations took place January 2, 1920. Agents, coordinated from Washington, simultaneously hit locations in thirty-three towns across the country and made twenty-five hundred arrests. (The Chicago raid took place a day earlier because the local state's attorney was a Republican and didn't want to share the glory with the Democratic administration.) That January, roughly ten thousand suspected radicals were arrested, and most of the cases were subsequently dismissed (either by the Labor Department or in federal courts) for lack of due process, insufficient evidence, or similar reasons. Of the nearly six hundred deportations ordered in the first six months of 1920, none of the deportees was convincingly linked to bombs or other instruments of terror.

As federal agents waged war on foreign extremists, many state legislatures waged war on foreign languages. Nebraska passed a statute in 1919 making teaching in any tongue other than English illegal. Fourteen other states followed suit, and several declared English or "American" to be their official language. Nebraska officials claimed their objective was "to create an enlightened American citizenship in sympathy with the principles and ideals of this country, and to prevent children . . . from being trained and educated in foreign languages and foreign ideals before they have had an opportunity to learn the English language and observe American ideals." The U.S. Supreme Court soon struck down the laws forbidding foreign-language instruction in schools, saying they were in conflict with the Fourteenth Amendment prohibition against depriving "any person of life, liberty, or property, without due process of law." Liberty, said the Court, included the right "to acquire useful knowledge."

Concerned about a possible labor shortage immediately following the war, the federal government had approved a plan whereby otherwise inadmissible workers from Canada and Mexico could come to America for short periods of time. As immigration rose, officials realized that no special programs were needed to attract foreign workers, and increasingly focused on ways to keep them out. The need for doing so was underscored by the increasingly urgent utterances of racial demagogues—and by statistics the war had helped to provide.

Those statistics came from the recently developed IQ test, which had been administered to 1.7 million U.S. Army recruits. Results from more than one hundred thousand of those examinations were analyzed in depth by tester Carl C. Brigham, whose analysis purported, among other things, to refute "the popular belief that the Jew is highly intelligent." It also showed that blacks, Poles, Italians, and Russians were dimwits in comparison to Germans, Britons, and Danes. And it suggested that those numerous northern blacks who were apparently smarter than many whites were so largely because they had some white genes. Most ominously, however, the report concluded, "American intelligence is declining, and will proceed with an accelerating rate as the racial admixture becomes more and more extensive." The solution, as the army's examiners saw it, was to take measures to preserve the nation's "pure-bred races" and ensure the nation's survival and "upward evolution."

For those who had little patience for wading through pages of analysis of army test results, eugenicist Madison Grant's *The Passing of the Great Race* offered much the same argument without the statistics. The book, published in 1916 and revised and reissued in 1918, had become required nativist reading by the 1920s. Its thesis was laid out in a foreword by Columbia University zoologist Henry Osborn, who said the gravest current danger to the American republic was "the gradual dying out among our people of those hereditary traits through which the principles of our religious, political and sound foundations were laid down and their insidious replacement by traits of less noble character." Grant, expanding on William Ripley's racial theories, strongly warned against "mongrelization"—the mixing of "primitive" and Anglo-Saxon blood. The traits of the "higher races," explained Grant, were recently developed and highly unstable. Breeding WASPs with Jews, Italians,

Hindus, Negroes, and other "lower" types would inevitably produce offspring possessing the brutish qualities of the primitive but none of the redeeming characteristics of the superior race. Grant recommended excluding inferior races from America, explaining that when the Founding Fathers spoke of equality, they "meant merely that they were just as good Englishmen as their brothers across the sea."

The 1920 Republican party platform statement recommended new immigration restrictions, including a "higher physical standard" and more complete exclusion of criminals and mental defectives. Commissioner of immigration Frederick A. Wallis went substantially further, suggesting that an amendment to the Constitution might be needed to keep European rabble out. More than 10 million European nationals "are now waiting in various ports of war-stricken Europe to swarm to the United States as soon as they can obtain transportation," claimed Wallis, who added, "I would rather send back a thousand good men than let one bad man come into the country." The *Literary Digest* echoed Wallis's concern, fretting over the loss of the "American type" if the nation had to absorb the 15–25 million Europeans eager to enter.

Meanwhile, California politicians lobbied for stronger prohibitions against Japanese immigration. At congressional hearings held in the state in the summer of 1920, U.S. senator (and former San Francisco mayor) James Pheland contrasted the status of Japanese with that of other acknowledged undesirables: "If urging their exclusion from California is regarded as persecution, then the same would apply to the Chinese; it would apply to the reds and the anarchists and the unfit of all races and classes. It is not persecution; it is preservation." At those same hearings, Governor William D. Stephen complained that Japanese growers already controlled several crops—including tomatoes, potatoes, and asparagus—and fretted, "The fecundity of the Japanese race far exceeds that of any other people that we have in our midst." The *Los Angeles Times,* the *Sacramento Bee,* and other leading California newspapers pummeled the Japanese with such headlines as IMPERIAL VALLEY IS AROUSED OVER THE JAPANESE MENACE and JAPANESE PLAN INVASION OF INDUSTRIAL FIELDS.

Spurred on by such relentless propaganda, the House overwhelmingly passed a bill that December authored by immigration committee chairman Albert Johnson that would suspend immigration—immediate relatives excepted—for fourteen months. Instead of following the House lead, however, the Senate substituted a bill the following February to restrict immigrants by quota. The maximum number of immigrants to be admitted annually from each country would be calculated by taking 3 percent of the tally of each nationality present at the time of the 1910 census. Several years earlier, Senator William Dillingham had proposed the concept but subsequently abandoned it in favor of the literacy exam. In 1918, its first full year of operation, however, the literacy test had kept out fewer than sixteen hundred aliens. ("Most of the . . . anarchists that we had penned up here a few days ago could read and write," groused Commissioner Wallis at one point in 1920.) With the literacy test proving to be so undiscriminating, Congress was receptive to more extreme measures. The House accepted the Senate bill, and four days later Congress adjourned. The legislation died when a seriously ailing (and lame-duck president) Woodrow Wilson neglected to sign it.

That April the California state assembly and senate passed a resolution demanding "absolute exclusion . . . of all Japanese immigration, not only male but female, and not only laborers, skilled and unskilled, but 'farmers' and men of small trades and professions." Though few were insisting on total prohibition of Europeans, the clamor for an end to unlimited immigration was becoming overwhelming. During Senate debate in early May over a new quota bill, George Henry Jackson maintained that if so many foreigners were not crowding in, Americans could have more children. The notion that America was a melting pot was "tomfoolery," added Jackson. "It has not melted any of them. They are either Germans or Irish or Italians or Poles or Magyars or Austrians." Senator J. Thomas Heflin of Alabama charged that recent immigration had left the United States "face to face with the greatest evil that has confronted us in a century. We have reached the point where alien power and influence dare to challenge that of the native stock in our country." Because immigration had been beneficial in the past, said Heflin, was no reason to welcome foreigners who would destroy America: "Choose you this day whom you will serve, the god of good government in the United States or the mammon of immigration agents and steamship companies."

Later that day, the Senate accepted the quota bill by a vote of seventy-eight to one—with seventeen abstaining. The business of reconciling it with a similar measure passed by the House proceeded quickly, and Warren Harding signed the legislation May 19, 1921. The 3 percent quota (calculated from the 1910 census) did not apply to tourists, diplomats, minor children of citizens, aliens from Asian countries excluded by prior legislation, and those whose access was regulated by treaty (such as the Japanese). Nor did it cover the Americas, from which immigration remained unrestricted. Though immigration from Canada was averaging close to one hundred thousand per year, Congress had no desire to create friction with its northern neighbor by attempting to change the rules, and no one expected huge numbers to come from Mexico, the Caribbean, or Central and South America.

Under the law, 357,803 immigrants would be permitted to enter America each year, of which 197,630 would come from Northern and Western Europe and 155,585 from Southern and Eastern Europe. Immigration from the non-European world (the Americas excepted) would be inconsequential. The legislation, considered a temporary measure, was scheduled to expire the following year—in the interval Congress presumably would thrash out a permanent solution—but was subsequently extended through June 1924.

As the 1924 expiration date for the quota legislation approached, activists, academic theorists, and politicians inundated Congress with advice. Nativist Lothrop Stoddard insisted that Eastern and Southern Europeans were so fertile that, if allowed to enter in substantial numbers, they would soon overrun the country. He calculated, for instance, that in two centuries one thousand Harvard graduates (presumably all WASPs) would have only fifty descendants while one thousand Romanians would have one hundred thousand. American interests would be best served, argued many, by adopting a quota based on a census that predated the large Eastern and Northern European migration. That view was succinctly summed up in a 1922 *Scientific Monthly* article by Harvard professor Robert Ward:

"We are facing a permanent tendency toward rapidly increasing and steadily deteriorating immigration, and millions of prospective immigrants overseas are impatiently waiting for the 30th of June, 1924, when they will rush in, in a seething chaotic mob, unless Congress takes steps to stop them. . . . It cannot be strongly enough emphasized that, while the original argument in favor of 3 percent was economic, the real, fundamental, lasting reason for its continuance is biological. . . . If we want the American race to continue to be predominantly Anglo-Saxon-Germanic, of the same stock as that which originally settled the United States, wrote our Constitution, and established our democratic institutions; if we want our future immigration to be chiefly more of kindred peoples . . . easily assimilable, literate, of a high grade intelligence, then the simplest way to accomplish this purpose is to base the percentage limitation upon an earlier census than that of 1910 . . . i.e., before southern and eastern Europe had become the controlling element in our immigration."

Though Western and Northern Europeans already had been apportioned a majority of the quota slots, they were taking only 47 percent of those allotted. Eastern and Southern Europeans, however, were using virtually every opening available. The commissioner general of immigration nonetheless advised cutting back even further on visas assigned to Eastern and Southern Europe, insisting, "If immigrants are not permitted to come from the new sources, they certainly will come from the old."

Even the Supreme Court provided ammunition for exclusivist arguments with a series of decisions that sanctioned anti-alien legislation and racially discriminatory policies. In 1922, the Court considered the case of Takao Ozawa, who was born in Japan but had lived in the United States for twenty years and had sued for the right to be naturalized. Ozawa con-

tended that the 1790 language permitting naturalization of only
"free white persons" referred merely to persons neither Indian nor black. Subsequent acts, he argued, had made clear
that U.S. policy was to welcome aliens, with the exceptions of
those "morally, mentally and physically unfit for citizenship
and the Chinese." In annexing Hawaii and other territories,
he noted, America had made citizens of numerous races, including "Mongolians" and Puerto Ricans—who were "as dark
as the Japanese." Clearly stretching the bounds of credulity,
Ozawa also contended that the dominant strains of Japanese
were "white persons" who spoke an "Aryan tongue" and had
"Caucasian root stocks."

The U.S. Justice Department disagreed, asserting, "The men
who settled this country were white men from Europe . . .
and it was to men of their own kind that they held out the
opportunity for citizenship in the new nation." Justice George
Sutherland, writing for the Court, sided with the Justice Department: "The intention [of the original naturalization stat-
ute] was to confer the privilege of citizenship upon that class
of persons whom the fathers knew as white, and to deny it to
all who could not be so classified."

A similar case came before the Court the following year.
Bhagat Singh Thind, a high-caste Hindu, claimed to be a
"white" Aryan and therefore eligible for naturalization. Justice
Sutherland differed, declaring, "It may be true that the blond
Scandinavian and the brown Hindu have a common ancestor
in the dim reaches of antiquity, but the average man knows
perfectly well that there are unmistakable and profound differences between them today. . . . It is a matter of familiar
observation and knowledge that the physical group characteristics of the Hindus render them readily distinguishable from
the various groups of persons in this country commonly recognized as white. The children of English, French, German,
Italian, Scandinavian, and other European parentage quickly
merge into the mass of our population and lose the distinctive
hallmarks of their European origin. On the other hand, it cannot be doubted that the children born in this country of Hindu
parents would retain indefinitely the clear evidence of their

ancestry." The Court went on to observe that Congress had prohibited immigration from Asian countries and added, "[I]t is not likely that Congress would be willing to accept as citizens a class of persons whom it rejects as immigrants."

That same year, the Court evaluated a Washington state law making ownership of (or investment in) land illegal for those who had not made a good-faith declaration of intent to become a U.S. citizen. The law—like those in California, Florida, and a few other states—effectively prohibited Asians from owning property. A white couple who wished to lease their land to a Japanese farmer had sued to prevent the state from confiscating it if they did so. The plaintiffs argued that the law violated their right to lease their property and that of the alien to practice his profession. They also contended that the law discriminated against those aliens who were not allowed to declare in "good faith" that they would become U.S. citizens. Pierce Butler, who wrote the Court's decision, saw the matter differently.

Congress had the right to decide who could be citizens, said Butler. He acknowledged that, in exercising that right, Congress had singled out Asians for exclusion. The grounds for doing so, however, had been "substantial and reasonable." And since Congress had properly denied Asians the right of naturalization, the state acted no less properly in denying them property—since those who could not be citizens could not be trusted to protect state interests: "It is obvious that one who is not a citizen and cannot become one lacks an interest in, and the power to effectually work for the welfare of, the state, and, so lacking, the state may rightfully deny him the right to own and lease real estate within its boundaries." Such was emphatically not discrimination against Asians because of their race and color, because "all persons . . . who have not declared their intention in good faith to become citizens are prohibited from so owning agricultural lands."

In holding that it was "reasonable" to decide naturalization rights by race, and by agreeing to the basic unassimilability of certain races, the Supreme Court sanctioned the eugenic theories guiding congressional debate on immigration. By suggesting that aliens could not be trusted to safeguard U.S. interests, the Court legitimized the antiforeign (and, in particular, the anti-Asian) sentiment that had swept through the nation. And by giving its blessing to the myriad laws that discriminated against Asians on the basis of their ineligibility to citizenship, the Court all but invited new discriminatory legislation.

When Congress returned to immigration legislation in 1924, the anti-Asian contingent felt free to wage attack on the so-called Gentlemen's Agreement. The original agreement had allowed the parents, wives, and children of American residents to come to the United States. Americans had not anticipated, however, that "wives" would be taken to mean those committed to marry—sight unseen—Japanese men in the United States, an observance of Japanese custom permitted by U.S. officials. The practice had become such a source of irritation to West Coast politicians that the Japanese government, in 1920, had stopped issuing passports to the so-called picture brides. Nevertheless, those determined to stop Japanese immigration decided to keep the issue alive. California senator Samuel Shortridge spoke—with gross exaggeration—of the "hundreds of thousands of Japanese women known as picture brides" who had swarmed into the country. As a result of the arrival of so many women, Japanese were reproducing at a rate three or four times that of whites, claimed Shortridge. They had already "Japanized" Hawaii, and were well on the way to doing so with California. Shortridge advised treating the Japanese precisely like the Chinese, whose exclusion "has been wholesome and entirely beneficial to this country."

In response to the pressure, the House and Senate readied provisions barring all aliens "ineligible for citizenship" from immigrating to the United States. The House report on its bill asserted that the measure was simply following the recent Supreme Court, reasoning: "The Supreme Court . . . has decided that the nationals of oriental countries are not entitled to be naturalized. . . . Clearly there should not come to the United States, beyond the exemptions necessary, persons who cannot become citizens and must continue in the United States to owe allegiance to a foreign government."

Secretary of State Charles Hughes wrote Congress warning that the restrictions under consideration would violate diplomatic agreements and "be deeply resented by the Japanese people." He also suggested that they were unnecessary, since including Japan among the quota nations would mean admitting fewer than 250 Japanese a year. The Japanese government subsequently complained to the State Department that passage of the exclusion bill would mean "an open declaration on the part of the United States, that Japanese nationals as such, no matter what their individual merits may be, are inadmissible into the United States, while other alien nationals are admissible on certain individual qualifications equally applicable to them all." Despite the complaints, congressional action proceeded on the bills. And after the Japanese ambassador wrote yet another letter to the State Department decrying the measure, which would bring "grave consequences . . . upon the otherwise happy and mutually advantageous relations between our two countries," anti-Japanese congressmen chose to read the words as a "veiled threat" and, with much patriotic saber rattling, pushed the House and Senate into accepting the controversial amendment—an act that would poison U.S.-Japanese relations up to and beyond World War II.

Following acceptance of the measure to exclude Japan, Congress's attention shifted back to Europe, and to the proposal specifying use of the 1890 (pre–"new source" immigration) census as a basis for quotas. Senator LeBaron Colt of Rhode Island denounced it as a hypocritical subterfuge: "For what reason is it proposed to go back to the census of 1890? The reason is the desire to exclude southern and eastern Europeans. If you are going to do that, do it openly." Colt went on to call "the adoption of an immigration law based upon racial discrimination" the "most dangerous and un-American principle ever propounded in the American Senate." Few agreed. The House passed the bill 323 to 71, the Senate passed it 62 to 6, and President Calvin Coolidge signed it in May. That same session, Congress created and appropriated a million dollars for the Immigration Border Patrol.

The Immigration Act of 1924 set the per-country quota at 2 percent of the foreign-born population of the 1890 census (instead of 3 percent of the 1910 census as designated by the 1921 law). Total European immigration under the new formula would be restricted to 164,667 a year, with a minimum per-country quota of one hundred. Immigration from the Americas would be unlimited. Asians would continue to be excluded, and wives and unmarried minor children (under eighteen) of U.S. citizens would be admitted outside of quota constraints.

After July 1, 1927, the "national origins" system was projected to replace the revised plan. Quotas would no longer be calculated as a percentage of the foreign-born but as a proportion of the "national origins" of Americans. ("Descendants of slave immigrants," "descendants of American aborigines," and "aliens ineligible to citizenship or their descendants" were excluded from the count.) Americans' "national origins" were to be determined by classifying surnames of the white population (as of 1920) and calculating the percentage that each ethnic group comprised of America's population. Immigrants (150,000 total) would then be selected in ethnic proportion to those already present, excepting those from the "Western Hemisphere" (the Americas), who could continue to come in unrestricted (unless they, as individuals, were considered undesirable).

For two years' running, Congress delayed full implementation of the "National Origins" Law as statisticians tinkered with the methodology for determining per-country quotas. So many Americans had Anglicized their names that England would receive most of the available visas if the previously agreed-on process was followed. In the end, officials shifted some of the English numbers to other Western and Northern European countries. The program was fully implemented in mid-1929—with 82 percent of the visas earmarked for Northern and Western Europe, 16 percent for Southern and Eastern Europe, and 2 percent for the rest of the world.

With "national origins" in place, racial isolationism—which had begun with the Chinese exclusion act of 1882—became the cornerstone of U.S. immigration policy. America, if Congress had its way, would be a nation ethnically frozen in time. That such might not be possible for a country already irremediably heterogeneous—or might have tragic implications for refugees in search of sanctuary, or might not even be in America's best interest—was never seriously entertained.

6

A Second War,
Some Second Thoughts

The Great Depression, which began as the National Origins Act was implemented, provided yet another reason to exclude those who would drain the economy or take American jobs. In late 1930, President Herbert Hoover ordered vigorous enforcement of the 1917 statute barring anyone likely to become a public charge, meaning only those of considerable means would be admitted as immigrants (until Franklin Roosevelt rescinded the order in 1936). Hoover administration officials also launched a massive program of Mexican repatriation—and deported many who did not return voluntarily. Such policies, in combination with the economic crisis, brought immigration to a virtual halt. In several years during the 1930s, more people left than came. Total immigration for the decade—528,000—was lower than at any point since the 1820s.

Even as Adolf Hitler's army marched across Europe and hundreds of thousands tried to flee Nazi atrocities, immigration to America remained low, for the quota legislation made no special provision for asylum for those at risk. Franklin Roosevelt found a small loophole around those laws in late 1938 and announced that his labor secretary would temporarily extend the visas of 12,000–15,000 Germans who had come as visitors. They "must not be forced to return to Germany to face the concentration camps and other forms of punishment that they believe await them," said Roosevelt. At the same time, he relaxed application procedures for immigration visas. Strict adherence to the law would force thousands of Jewish refugees to wait in Nazi-threatened (or occupied) territory until a quota number came up. Roosevelt ordered the State Department to allow such applicants to move temporarily to safer countries (the United States excepted) without losing their place in the national-origins quota line. He did not seek congressional action to change the law, however—apparently accepting the advice of Martin Dies, chairman of the House Committee on Un-American Activities, that such a proposal "would not receive more than a hundred votes."

The following May, events focused attention on America's restrictive policies when a refugee ship—the S.S. *St. Louis*—carrying more than nine hundred German Jews arrived in Cuba. Most of those aboard had intended to wait on the island for American visas, but the Cuban government reversed its previous policy and refused to accept the passengers' landing permits. For a week and a half, with the international press monitoring its every move, the ship sat anchored between Havana and Miami, as the émigrés sought permission to land in either place. Their efforts failed, and the dejected captain finally turned back toward Europe. As the ship neared the Florida coast, shortly before steaming away, it was briefly followed by a U.S. Coast Guard patrol boat seeking "to prevent possible attempts by refugees to jump off and swim ashore." (Ultimately the passengers were offered sanctuary in Great Britain, Belgium, France, and the Netherlands.)

The month the S.S. *St. Louis* gave up on America, a bill to admit twenty thousand German refugee children was dying in congressional committee. The legislation's sponsors—Senator Robert Wagner, a New York Democrat, and Congresswoman Edith Nourse Rogers, a Massachusetts Republican—had lined up an impressive array of supporters, including Albert Einstein, John Steinbeck, and Herbert Hoover. Concerned about anti-Semitism, advocates stressed that the bill would help not only Jews but children of all persuasions. They also emphasized that it would cause no unemployment or other hardship in America since sponsors were assured for the children. Nevertheless, the Daughters of the American Revolution, the American Legion, and others argued that America's resources should go to Americans and that no German immigration should be permitted above the quota. Facing such opposition, much of it blatantly anti-Semitic, Wagner and Rogers conceded that their bill's chances for passage were nil.

Americans seeking refugee admissions above those permitted by the quotas repeatedly faced such frustration; for in the early days of World War II, most politicians were less concerned about refugees than about keeping sinister aliens at bay. In June 1940, Congress passed the Alien Registration Act, which made it unlawful to "attempt any form of subversion of the Armed Forces" or "advocate in any way the overthrow of the . . . United States." The law also authorized deportation of aliens convicted of carrying semiautomatic or automatic weapons or who refused to register and be fingerprinted.

With the bombing of Pearl Harbor in December 1941, anti-alien (and, in particular, anti-Japanese) sentiment exploded. The day after the attack, the *Los Angeles Times* reported that the FBI had already rounded up two hundred suspected Japanese "subversives" and was seeking more. Meanwhile, police were ordered to "stop all cars bearing Japanese and to confiscate maps and binoculars or radios." That month *Time* magazine ran a feature titled "How to Tell Your Friends [the Chinese] from the Japs," observing, "Those who know them best often rely on facial expressions to tell them apart: the Chinese expression is likely to be more placid, kindly, open; the Japanese more positive, dogmatic, arrogant. . . . Japanese are hesitant, nervous in conversation, laugh loudly at the wrong time . . . walk stiffly erect, hard-heeled. Chinese, more relaxed, have an easy gait, sometimes shuffle."

In February, congressmen and senators from the West Coast

convened two special committees to deliberate on defense and on alien nationality and sabotage. After hearing testimony from government officials and others, the committees jointly recommended "immediate evacuation of all persons of Japanese lineage and all others, aliens and citizens alike, whose presence shall be deemed dangerous or inimical to the safety of the defense of the United States from all strategic areas." That Valentine's Day, Lieutenant General John L. DeWitt, commander of the Western Defense Command, wrote a letter to Secretary of War Henry Stimson describing the Japanese as an "enemy race" and warning that Japanese-Americans were apparently "organized and ready for concerted action," awaiting a favorable opportunity: "The very fact that no sabotage has taken place to date is a disturbing and confirming indication that such action will be taken."

Five days later, President Roosevelt issued Executive Order 9066 empowering military commanders—"as protection against espionage . . . and sabotage"—to designate military areas from which anyone could be excluded and within which residents were subject to "whatever restrictions" the military decreed. The following week, the *Los Angeles Times* trumpeted a federal roundup of several hundred Japanese, German, and Italian aliens as the "first triumph of the war in the Pacific Coast states." The *Times* added, "Among suspicious circumstances encountered by the agents were Japanese using the citizenship of their American-born children to control land near vital aircraft plants. Others were said to be clinging to 'farming' land near defense areas—land obviously unsuited for the purpose." In early March, Lieutenant General DeWitt declared the entire Pacific Coast "particularly subject to attack, to attempted invasion . . . and . . . subject to espionage and acts of sabotage." With massive parts of the West Coast designated "military areas," DeWitt ordered curfews for those of Japanese descent and, soon thereafter, compulsory evacuations. Congress quickly passed legislation making it a crime for those in military zones to disobey military commands. Eventually more than one hundred thousand persons of Japanese extraction—most of whom were U.S. citizens—were uprooted and transported to internment camps in Arkansas, Arizona, California, Colorado, Idaho, Utah, and Wyoming.

The same war-fueled fears that had led to anti-Japanese panic soon spurred Congress to reconsider its proscriptions against the Chinese—who were, after all, allies in battle. In 1943, several bills were put forward seeking repeal of the Chinese exclusion acts. They were presented, in effect, as a bouquet to the Wellesley-educated Madam Chiang Kai-shek, whose tour of America that year, capped by a speech to a joint session of Congress, had warmed congressional feelings. One of the repeal bills, sponsored by Congressman Martin Kennedy of New York, was introduced the day before Madam Chiang's congressional address.

No action was taken on those bills, but a small cadre of congressmen sympathetic to China decided that time was ripe to bring the issue to a head. That group, including Martin Kennedy and Walter Judd of Minnesota (who had been stationed in China as a missionary doctor), worked closely with a small circle of influential private citizens (among them, American Civil Liberties Union founder Roger Baldwin and *Asia and the Americas* editor Richard Walsh) who organized themselves into the Citizens Committee to Repeal Chinese Exclusion. Proponents concluded early on that full repeal would not be possible, that fear of the "yellow peril" was so pervasive that the best they could hope for was the assignment of token Chinese quotas. They also realized that only by selling the issue as part of the war effort would they be able to mobilize public support.

To drive home the point that China was an ally, the Citizens Committee launched a massive public campaign to commemorate the July anniversary of China's six years of combat with Japan. To demonstrate that they were not on the radical fringe, committee members tried to enlist the aid of key groups previously in opposition. They scored an important victory when the formerly Sinophobic San Francisco Board of Supervisors endorsed repeal of exclusion. Equally significant was the about-face of the Congress of Industrial Organizations—a reversal achieved in large measure through the work of Monroe Sweetland, a Citizens Committee founder who was also director of the CIO's National Committee for American and Allied War Relief. Both organizations justified their switch by noting the tiny number of visas to go to China, explaining that the admission of 105 or 107 Chinese annually was a small price to pay to help win the war.

To avoid alarming Americans, the committee advised Chinese organizations not to lobby Congress in support of legislation but only to offer "gratitude" for any actions Congress might take. Likewise, the Japanese American Citizens League was told their advocacy would be counterproductive. The committee also quietly urged Jewish and black groups not to become involved, in the belief that anti-Semitic or southern congressmen might be antagonized by such organizations. In contrast, the CIO, the Catholic Church, and others with strong mainstream credentials were encouraged to make their views known.

That June *The New York Times* joined those urging repeal of exclusion. Like many others, the *Times* focused on the small numbers of Chinese who would be entering and on the importance of the gesture as a way to "thank the Chinese for what they are doing for our common cause." In early October, President Roosevelt made an appeal to Congress. "I regard this legislation as important in the cause of winning the war and of establishing a secure peace," said Roosevelt, adding, "China's resistance does not depend alone on guns and planes. . . . It is based as much in the spirit of her people and her faith in her allies. We owe it to the Chinese to strengthen that faith. One step in this direction is to wipe from the statute books those anachronisms in our law which forbid the immigration of Chinese people into this country and which bar Chinese residents from American citizenship. . . . We must be big enough to acknowledge our mistakes of the past and to correct them." Advocates coalesced around a bill sponsored by Congressman Warren Magnuson, a Democrat from Washington State, who—as a Westerner, a member of the American Legion, and someone generally identified as anti-immigration—was considered the perfect defender of a pro-Chinese bill.

The need to combat Japanese propaganda and shore up

Chinese morale were big selling points for the bill. Congressman Ed Gossett, a Texas Democrat who was generally conservative on immigration issues, made the argument in blunt language: "To date we have been more considerate of the vicious, treacherous Japs than we have of the kindly, heroic Chinamen." After also pointing out the pending proposal would admit only 105 Chinese a year, he added, "This . . . is not an immigration bill. This bill is a war measure and a peace measure."

Despite strong misgivings expressed by numerous legislators—one of whom denounced the Chinese as "opium smokers"—the bill cleared the House that October. The Senate passed it the following month, and Roosevelt signed it December 17. As legislators had assured nervous supporters, the act allocated only 105 slots for Chinese immigrants—including any immigrants of Chinese extraction who might migrate from countries other than China. The law also made Chinese immigrants eligible for naturalization—meaning that, for the first time ever, America had put a group of Asian immigrants on an equal citizenship footing with whites; and for the first time since 1882, Congress had passed legislation that strove to increase rather than inhibit immigration from an Asian country. Though both gestures were largely symbolic, they opened the door—as opponents had feared—for more expansive gestures to follow. For once the concession was made that Chinese were not only allies but human beings worthy of considerate treatment, blanket discrimination against other Asians became more difficult to defend.

Several months before passage of the 1943 act, the first in a series of cases concerning treatment of Japanese-Americans came before the U.S. Supreme Court. Two American-born men of Japanese descent—one in Seattle and the other in Portland—had defied the military curfew on persons of Japanese extraction, maintaining that they were entitled to the same rights and freedoms as white Americans. The Court saw no merit in their argument, unanimously concluding that the order (aimed at preventing sabotage and espionage) made a reasonable racial distinction but did not discriminate against Japanese-Americans since the military had no means of quickly distinguishing between loyal and disloyal Japanese.

In December of 1944, two new cases were decided. In the first, the Court upheld the conviction of Fred Toyosaburo Korematsu, an American-born man of Japanese descent who defied a military evacuation order by refusing to leave San Leandro, California. Writing for the majority, Justice Hugo Black equated the evacuation order with the curfew policy, saying both derived from the need to quickly neutralize potential saboteurs and had nothing to do with racial prejudice: "Korematsu was not excluded from the Military Area because of hostility to him or his race. He was excluded because we are at war with the Japanese Empire, because the properly constituted military authorities feared an invasion of our West Coast and felt constrained to take proper security measures, because they decided that the military urgency of the situation demanded that all citizens of Japanese ancestry be segregated from the West Coast temporarily, and finally, because Congress, reposing its confidence in this time of war in our military leaders—as inevitably it must—determined that they should have the power to do just this." This time, however, the decision was not unanimous, but drew three spirited dissents, the most biting from Justice Frank Murphy, who wrote: "This exclusion of 'all persons of Japanese ancestry, both alien and non-alien,' from the Pacific Coast area on a plea of military necessity . . . goes over 'the very brink of constitutional power' and falls into the ugly abyss of racism."

That same day, in a companion case brought by a Japanese-American woman imprisoned in an internment camp, the majority sided with Murphy and ruled that America had no business imprisoning demonstrably patriotic Japanese-Americans, bringing an end to the detention policy. "Loyalty is a matter of the heart and mind, not of race, creed, or color. He who is loyal is by definition not a spy or a saboteur. When the power to detain is derived from the power to protect the war effort against espionage and sabotage, detention which has no relationship to that objective is unauthorized," wrote William

Douglas for the Court. Struggling to explain the seemingly contradictory reasoning employed in the two decisions, Black drew a distinction between upholding a conviction for resisting evacuation and upholding the detention policy itself. The Korematsu case, he insisted, was really not about the relocation camps since, even had Korematsu gone along with the evacuation order, he might not have been sent to one.

The Court's willingness to grant freedom to those held in internment camps was made easier by the favorable progress of the war and by the fact that the widely expected sabotage had failed to materialize. Moreover, the Allied struggle against Nazism and German racial theories made American racial theories increasingly difficult to justify. Realizing that, legislators proposed a rash of new immigration bills to relax—if ever so slightly—the 1924 act's rigid racial and ethnic restrictions. The so-called War Brides Act of December 1945 allowed veterans to bring in alien spouses and children above the numbers permitted by the quotas. A bill passed the following summer permitted aliens engaged to veterans to enter. Another authorized immigration and naturalization for natives of India and the Philippines. That August, a statute was enacted admitting (outside of the quota structure) Chinese wives of American citizens. Despite the flood of new legislation, no one was seriously suggesting that immigration from Asia be put on an equal basis with immigration from Europe. Like the quota for China, the numbers assigned to India and the Philippines were tiny, and Japanese continued to be excluded. The largely symbolic legislation nonetheless indicated incipient congressional embarrassment with the racial prohibitions in immigration and citizenship law.

Because the numbers of Asians authorized to immigrate were so small, they were not seen as posing any material threat to the quota system's goal. Europe, however, was teeming with refugees displaced by the war, many of whom wished to come to America. Only by setting aside the quota system could substantial numbers be taken into the United States. While many legislators were quite willing to try to help, they were not willing to abandon the quota system to do so.

Previously the White House had tried simultaneously to satisfy the letter of the quota laws and the dictates of human compassion. An order signed by Franklin Roosevelt had allowed a ship carrying nearly one thousand European refugees to land in America in 1944. Those aboard had been placed in a detention camp in Oswego, New York, to await the end of the war—after which they were to leave the country, even if they subsequently intended to seek American residency. In December 1945, Harry Truman had signed an executive order enabling forty thousand displaced persons to receive preferential consideration for visas within the limits set by current law. However, the president and much of the press soon lost patience with the quota restrictions. In 1946, *The New York Times* urged that America take more refugees: "We can speak most convincingly for freedom when we have done our fair share." *Life* magazine called the failure of the U.S. government to extend a welcoming hand "shocking." Truman complained, in his 1947 State of the Union Message, that only about five thousand displaced persons had entered the United States since May 1946 and said he felt hobbled by the quotas: "The fact is that the executive agencies are now doing all that is reasonably possible under limitations of the existing law and established quota." He asked for legislation to help "those thousands of homeless and suffering refugees of all faiths."

Several bills were introduced that year, but none left congressional committee. Truman continued to focus on the issue in 1948, stressing that he was not asking for permanent immigration reform but solely for a measure to deal with the aftereffects of the recent war. He pointed out that one million of those liberated by Allied forces remained in limbo in West Germany, Austria, and Italy, afraid to return to their homes in Eastern Europe. Leaving them indefinitely in refugee camps was unthinkable. "The only civilized route is to allow these people to take new roots in friendly soil," said Truman.

That June, just before adjourning, Congress passed the Displaced Persons Act of 1948. The bill was less than Truman had sought, and he signed it reluctantly, criticizing the measure as "flagrantly discriminatory" and anti-Semitic and lambasting Congress for endlessly dragging its feet. "If Congress were still in session, I would return this bill without my approval and urge that a fairer, more humane bill be passed. It is a close question whether this bill is better or worse than no bill at all." Truman further noted that, while the law would, in the next two years, admit two hundred thousand of those languishing in displaced persons' camps as well as two thousand Czechoslovakian refugees and three thousand orphans, it would give preference to persons from the Baltic states and (through various technicalities) exclude more than 90 percent of displaced Jews. Also, instead of admitting evacuees outside of the quota system, the act simply mortgaged future quotas to accommodate them—appropriating (per country) up to 50 percent of visas that would otherwise go (in succeeding years) to regular immigrants. "This is a most begrudging method of accepting . . . people and will necessarily deprive many other worthy people of an opportunity to come to the United States," scolded Truman.

The first displaced persons' ship, from Bremerhaven, Germany, reached New York Harbor that October 30. The 813 men, women, and children aboard were greeted by a banner reading WELCOME TO AMERICA and by a roster of luminaries led by Attorney General Tom Clark, who called their ship "the vanguard of a fleet . . . that will transform the victims of hatred, bigotry, religious intolerance and wars into happy and peaceful souls."

Two years later, Congress eliminated most of the features Truman had found so discriminatory and made the bill's numbers more generous. Those admitted, however, would continue to be deducted from the regular quota allocation. Eventually more than four hundred thousand came under the act whose rigid adherence to quota limits stood in stark contrast to the generosity of spirit undergirding the resettlement program. As new refugee crises loomed, succeeding presidents again and again found themselves struggling to find a way around those restrictions.

In addition to producing European refugees, World War II spurred a migration much closer to home. After American employers had requested help coping with war-induced labor shortages, Congress had approved highly regulated programs for employment of Mexican laborers (too poor to qualify as regular immigrants) in America's fields and on her railroads, and employment of natives of British Honduras, Barbados, and Jamaica in U.S. factories. Between 1943 and 1946, some 200,000 Mexican farmhands were admitted, as well as 130,000 railway workers. Along with the officially sanctioned farm workers (or braceros) came an inflow of illegal entrants (commonly called wetbacks). By 1946, use of "wetbacks" had become so widespread that the head of the Immigration and Naturalization Service office in Los Angeles observed that their removal, "particularly during harvest seasons, would have brought disaster to the agricultural enterprises employing them."

Neither the bracero program nor the illegal traffic had ended with the war. Many employers preferred the so-called wetbacks because they came without paperwork (or minimum-wage) requirements. As the illegal force grew, the U.S. government winked at it, seeing Mexico as a needed and temporary source of laborers who would quietly depart when their work was done—at no cost to America. By the 1950s, however, officials realized the Mexicans were not behaving exactly as expected. Instead of coming and going with the crops, many were staying; and instead of stabilizing at some comfortable number, the migrant population was growing apace. Some communities—particularly near California's southern border—began to feel swamped. Federal policymakers, once complacent about the Mexican influx, began to ponder ways to bring it under control. That search would lead to a massive Mexican repatriation program, as federal policy increasingly focused not only on controlling legal migration but on curtailing the illegal traffic across America's southern border.

7

Keeping Them Out

I n no previous decade in U.S. history had the world seemed
quite so threatening as it did to Congress during the 1950s.
In the East loomed communists eager to wreak havoc. Just
over the border was the menace of millions of Mexican peasants. And throughout Europe, revolutionaries, saboteurs, and
the culturally or genetically undesirable lay ready to destroy
or defile the United States. Motivated by tension and para-
noia, Congress proceeded to reevaluate its policies governing
immigration, border control, and internal security.

In 1950, after reviewing the impact of the 1924 National
Origins Act, the Senate Judiciary Committee concluded that
the law had not quite worked as expected but, on balance, had
"served its purpose well." Since July 1929, when the legislation
was fully implemented, Western and Northern Europe, which
had been counted on to contribute 79 percent of total immigrants, had contributed little more than half that. The saving
grace, however, as seen by the committee, was that *all* immigration had been exceedingly low. Only 836,085 quota-re-
stricted immigrants had been admitted, while nearly four times

that number had been eligible. "It would appear that the numerical restrictive feature of the formula, the economic depression, and the turmoil of war, have so limited immigration that there has been no significant effect on the homogeneity of our population," said the committee's report, concluding that "adoption of the national origins formula was a rational and logical method of . . . restricting immigration in such a manner as to best preserve [America's] . . . sociological and cultural balance."

Congress's continued preoccupation with maintaining America's ethnic composition conflicted with congressional discomfort over explicitly racist provisions in U.S. law. Such embarrassment led Congress that August, in legislation establishing a civil government in Guam, to eliminate the racial impediment to American citizenship for Guamanians—making all persons born on the island since early 1899 (when the territory was occupied by America) citizens of the United States. In the end, Congress resolved the conflict by keeping the quota system intact but increasingly granting token quotas (one hundred or so visas a year) to non-European countries. By so doing, Congress could claim that it was no longer practicing discrimination but at the same time receive credit for keeping out those considered "un-American" or dangerous.

With the Internal Security Act of September 1950—passed three months after President Truman ordered troops into Korea—Congress declared, in effect, that anyone even remotely considered a threat was to be kept out. Passed over Truman's veto, it banned a wide range of aliens, including those who would enter America to engage in activities "which would be prejudicial to the public interest, or would endanger the welfare or safety of the United States." The law also barred (or permitted deportation of) members of the U.S. Communist party and those belonging to "any totalitarian party of the United States, or of any state, or of any foreign country, or of any affiliate or subdivision of any such party," and anyone else the government suspected might eventually engage in activities "subversive to the national security" or advocate opposition to the U.S. government by nonconstitutional means.

Truman subsequently denounced the act's sweeping provisions as "thought control." Senate Judiciary members who had opposed the legislation issued a report calling some of its features "obviously unconstitutional" and others "so thoroughly impracticable as to be useless as a means for achieving the end which the sponsors of the bill contemplate." The commission responsible for implementing the Displaced Persons Act of 1948 complained that the law established "a virtual block on all persons who had lived behind the Iron Curtain or in Hitler's Germany or Mussolini's Italy." Nevertheless, its strict anticommunist, antiradical prohibitions were subsequently incorporated into the Immigration and Nationality Act of 1952 (also passed over presidential veto), which repealed and comprehensively recodified the scores of immigration laws that had evolved, helter-skelter, over the years.

That legislation, known as the McCarren-Walter Act, retained the basic quota structure of the 1924 law. The Senate rejected an attempt by Senator Hubert Humphrey to substitute the 1950 census for the 1920 census in computation of national origins and to allow unused quota slots to go to oversubscribed countries. Congress did accept some less sweeping reforms. It removed all remaining racial prohibitions against naturalization and immigration (Japan was given a quota of 185) and allowed alien husbands of American citizens to claim the same quota-exempt status previously limited to alien wives.

Because of growing anxiety over Mexican migration, the law included a so-called wetback provision, making it a felony to bring into or induce to come to the United States aliens who were ineligible for entry. The measure also prohibited transporting undocumented entrants within the country—if done in support of an illegal entry. To cut black immigration, the act set token quotas for colonies—such as the British West Indies—whose residents had formerly been able to qualify under the European parent-country quotas. The law also put in place a preference system to enhance the collective quality of immigrants: the first 50 percent of visas within each country's quota would go to those with skills or training considered valuable to the United States. The remaining visas were to be distributed among a variety of relatives of U.S. citizens and residents.

In his veto message, President Truman condemned the legislation as an insult to the Italians, Greeks, and Turks (all received low quotas) with whom the United States had formed the NATO alliance. He found the idea of protecting America against Eastern Europe abhorrent and absurd: "The countries of Eastern Europe have fallen under the Communist yoke— they are silenced, fenced off by barbed wire and minefields— no one passes their borders but at the risk of his life. We do not need to be protected against immigrants from these countries." Other proponents of liberalization chose to focus on the few good things they saw in the law. The Japanese American Citizens League supported the bill—despite its restrictive tone and the tiny quotas allocated to Asia—because, in making all races eligible for naturalization, it opened a critically important door. Once basic citizenship rights were won, the battle over quotas could be more successfully fought—or so reasoned Mike Masaoka, JACL's Washington representative, who endured the "demeaning process" of lobbying Washington's anti-Asian politicians by convincing himself that more could be accomplished through cooperating than through attacking Congress head-on.

Truman, of course, felt no such constraint. Three months after the McCarren-Walter Act passed, he appointed a presidential Commission on Immigration and Naturalization, chaired by former U.S. solicitor general Philip Perlman, to evaluate America's immigration laws. The commission's treatise, *Whom We Shall Welcome* (released in January 1953), said America's immigration policies had "frustrated and handicapped . . . American foreign policy" and called racially discriminatory quotas a "major disruptive influence." The commission recommended increasing the numbers allowed to immigrate and replacing the present quota system with one that did not discriminate on the basis of race, ethnicity, or creed. Dwight Eisenhower, in his first State of the Union Message the month after the report's release, made much the same request. Current law, he said, "contains injustices. It does, in fact, discriminate. . . . I am therefore requesting the Congress . . . to enact a statute which will at one and the same time guard our legitimate national interest and be faithful to our basic ideas of freedom and fairness to all." Inspired by presidential rhetoric and the commission report, a number of legislators—including Massachusetts senator John F. Kennedy—proposed bills to repeal or radically modify McCarren-Walter, but congressional leadership refused to take action.

Congress proved less intractable on the question of refugee assistance. The Refugee Relief Act of 1953 authorized 214,000 new visas, designated primarily for victims of Nazism and Soviet expansionism. Unlike the 1948 act, the new relief measure did not take numbers from any country's quota but distributed visas that otherwise would not have been issued. In a sense, the new act was a major—if belated—victory for Truman, who had made no secret of his disdain for the practice of mortgaging future generations' visas. It was also, however, a reminder that, despite the 1952 recodification of immigration law, Congress had yet to come up with a consistent approach to handling refugees.

For many Washington immigration officials, the refugee problem was minor compared to that of illegal Mexican migration. "Before 1944 the illegal traffic on the Mexican border . . . was never overwhelming in numbers," noted the President's Commission on Migratory Labor in 1951, but in the past seven years, "the wetback traffic has reached entirely new levels," constituting at least 40 percent of the migratory farm work force: "In its newly achieved proportions, it is virtually an invasion."

Such alarm accounted for the so-called wetback provision in the McCarren-Walter Act. In 1953, with the new law in place, agents continued to apprehend an average of one hundred thousand illegal entrants from Mexico every month. The United States, concluded the border patrol chief, was suffering "perhaps the greatest peacetime invasion ever complacently suffered by any country under open, flagrant, contemptuous violation of its laws."

During a fact-finding tour of California, Attorney General Herbert Brownell found local officials reporting an epidemic of venereal disease, vandalism, tuberculosis, and violent crime attributed to illegal migrants. Eager to take action, Brownell sought out General Joseph Swing, a West Point graduate and career army officer who was then training troops to go to Korea. The gist of the conversation, as recalled by Swing, was "that he [Brownell] had a check for two million dollars in his pocket to help pay Army expenses, to put the Sixth Army down along the border to fend off the wetbacks." An astounded Swing dissuaded Brownell from pursuing that idea any further, explaining that to station troops along lonely stretches of the border would be to risk countless Mexican deaths. In the meantime, Eisenhower announced his approval of Brownell's drive against illegal Mexican entrants.

Brownell and acting Immigration and Naturalization Service commissioner Benjamin Habberton launched a colossal lobbying and publicity campaign, portraying "wetbacks" as savage sellers of dope and sex, who were filling up America's hospitals, jails, and relief rolls. "Their depredations range from harvesting food crops at night for subsistence, to robbery and rape," Habberton told legislators. Catering to Congress's obsession with communism, Habberton also claimed that about one hundred members of the Communist party crossed daily into the United States around El Paso and that about fifteen hundred former and present party members resided just across the border.

A group of women's organizations in El Paso responded to the campaign by requesting a "crossing-card plan" to assure them a supply of domestic servants. In general, however, Brownell elicited the public outrage that he sought. CBS radio's *The Wetbacks,* in April 1954, featured a series of prominent Californians attesting to the "wetback" disaster. "Imperial County has the highest tuberculosis rate, the highest venereal disease rate, and the highest infant mortality rate of any county in California," claimed a county medical officer who saw "a definite tie-in between the influx of Mexican people into our county and our public health problems." Around the same time,

The Reporter magazine ran an exposé claiming that some two hundred children in Imperial County were on relief because Mexican fathers had deserted them and that illegal entrants were costing the county at least a quarter of a million dollars a year. "No one could guess," added *The Reporter*, "how many Communist agents, saboteurs, and international smugglers were infiltrating the country through the mesh of holes in the border, but it was plain that the border was no effective barrier against them."

That no one rose to the migrants' defense was not surprising. Religious organizations and social-welfare workers inclined to be sympathetic to foreign farm workers thought exploitation of illegal immigrants could best be ended by shipping them home. Even Mexican-American organizations generally looked on the undocumented migrants with disfavor. One Hispanic veterans group, the American GI Forum of Texas, blamed the federal government for inadequately patrolling the border and thereby providing a "cheap labor subsidy for southwestern farmers and ranchers." Mexico's foreign minister pointedly urged the United States to punish employers who hired undocumented Mexicans.

The only interest group willing to embrace the illegal entrants was comprised of influential growers—and they did so as unobtrusively as possible, by lobbying for constraints on the border patrol. Boasting no constituency except those wishing to exploit them, "wetbacks" were the perfect threat against which to wage war for a low-profile, little-respected agency in search of a budget-enhancing cause.

In testimony before the House Appropriations Committee, acting INS head Habberton made much of the need for increased border-patrol activity, while noting that Congress planned to cut $3.25 million from his budget. Brownell spoke at length of the likely need for costly special equipment (including two-way communications systems and watchtowers) to better defend the frontier. The appeals had their intended effect, rallying previously flagging congressional support for the INS—and for Brownell's planned antiwetback war.

"I want the Senate, here and now, to put the executive

branch on notice that we want illegal immigration stopped, at whatever cost," proclaimed Senator Herbert Lehman as he proposed an amendment doubling the border patrol's budget. Brownell recruited General Joseph Swing, who had retired from the army only weeks earlier, to head the antiwetback campaign and the INS. Swing promptly hired two retired generals to help coordinate "Operation Wetback," which was launched in June 1954. The objective was to secure the southern border, and the mind-set was straight out of GI Joe. Nearly five hundred INS officers were transferred from the Canadian perimeter and from large cities in the U.S. interior, joining the more than 250 patrol agents already along the California-Mexico border. Agents conducted a furious string of raids—swooping down on factories and farms, arresting anyone who appeared not to belong. Ranchers and others who had recruited undocumented workers assisted the INS effort by identifying "wetbacks" among their own employees. In some areas, small airplanes were used to spot suspected aliens and to direct jeeps in rounding them up. Planes were also used to transport migrants to so-called staging areas from which they were shipped down to Mexico. The U.S. Army supplied logistical support.

Thirty days after the operation began in California, the main INS force moved to Texas. Meanwhile, mopping-up operations were mounted in the interior, as INS officers descended on Chicago, Kansas City, St. Louis, and other cities. In late 1955, Swing bragged, "The 'wetback' problem, which some said would 'never be solved' has been dealt with vigorously and effectively, bringing new gains to the Southwest border area through increased employment and decreases in disease, crime, and welfare unemployment case loads." He estimated that—thanks to "Operation Wetback"—at least thirty thousand Texans who normally migrated in search of work would be able to find jobs at home.

Eventually federal officials were to claim that "Operation Wetback" had resulted in the departure of well over a million illegal entrants. One scholar, however, concluded that the boast was impossible to verify since the largest part of that figure consisted of those supposedly scared into returning to Mexico by the publicity campaign that preceded the actual operation. Whatever the actual numbers, the effort was a public-relations success. The INS border patrol, previously imperiled, was given a new lease on life. Politicians, satisfied the wetback problem was solved, focused on other matters; and legislation making the employment of illegal immigrants a punishable offense died for lack of interest.

Following "Operation Wetback," admissions of legal agricultural workers from Mexico rose sharply: from 222,000 in 1954 to 351,000 in 1955, and to 432,000 in 1956. The INS interpreted the increase as a sign of its success in curtailing the illegal flow and redirecting part of it into legal channels. The American labor movement, however, could see only that Mexicans were still taking American jobs; and much of the religious and social-service community could see only that migrant workers continued to be easily exploited. Like the refugee problem, the Mexican migration problem awaited a more permanent solution.

8

A Reluctant Reform

Two paradoxes haunted Dwight Eisenhower and John F. Kennedy: that America, which considered itself a refuge, had no ongoing policy for accepting refugees; and that a country founded on the concept of human equality would choose immigrants principally on the basis of ethnicity and race. Eisenhower hammered at those inconsistencies as he lobbied Congress for a less parochial immigration policy; and when frustrated by legal limitations on America's ability to take in Hungarians following the Soviet invasion of 1956, Eisenhower bent the law. He did so through emergency parole (a discretionary power granted the attorney general as part of the 1952 immigration act) and brought in—from 1956 through 1958—more than thirty thousand persons who otherwise would have been excluded. Parole authority was intended for individual emergencies, not mass admissions, but lacking anything better, Eisenhower employed it as an alternative refugee program.

Kennedy was to follow Eisenhower's lead, both in lobbying for immigration reform and in using the parole power as a

partial substitute, but his strong interest in immigration predated his election as president. As a senator, he had published
a book (*A Nation of Immigrants*) in 1958 in which he had rewritten several lines from Emma Lazarus's poem to reflect his
view of the message sent by U.S. statutes: "Send me your tired,
your poor . . . as long as they come from northern Europe,
are not too tired or too poor or slightly ill, never stole a loaf
of bread, never joined any questionable organizations, and can
document their activities for the past two years." The following year, Kennedy proposed a bill to eliminate much of the
bias in the current quota system and to provide for regular
admissions of refugees. The bill never got out of committee.
Any plans he may have had of quickly focusing on immigration reform as president were preempted by events.

Days before Kennedy's inauguration, the United States
broke relations with Cuba over a series of provocations cul-
minating with Fidel Castro's decision to cut America's diplomatic staff. Shortly thereafter came the Bay of Pigs debacle.
The following year brought the Cuban Missile Crisis. Meanwhile, thousands of Cubans were trying to escape the chaos
that had swirled around them since Castro's ascension in 1959.
The Kennedy administration paroled nearly sixty thousand of
them into the country in 1962—more than fourteen times the
number admitted during the previous two years. While Cubans were fleeing their homeland, legions of Chinese were doing
the same. An estimated 1.5 million Chinese emigrants had
poured into Hong Kong over the past decade. Countless more
were being refused entry. Many in Congress were demanding
that the United States do something "to end the spectacle of
the West turning back 'refugees from Communism.' " The administration again used its parole authority—admitting several
thousand exiles who (because of the small Chinese quota) could
not otherwise have been admitted. The continuing refugee
crises led in mid-1962 to the Migration and Refugee Assistance Act, a Kennedy-requested measure to facilitate resettlement of Cubans and to coordinate assistance to (and increase
funding for) international refugee programs. In mid-1963,
Kennedy was finally ready to propose a general program of
immigration reform.

The mood in Congress had changed considerably since 1952. The incessant need for emergency measures to admit refugees had convinced many legislators that the time had come to update the law. The civil-rights revolution sweeping America had persuaded others that racially determined quotas had to go. Even before Kennedy submitted his proposals in July 1963, a number of legislators had offered reform bills of their own.

Kennedy called for phasing out the national-origins program over a five-year period and replacing it with one that would put countries on a more equal basis. First priority for visas would be given to those individuals with skills America needed and second to various categories of family members. Asian and African countries would no longer be limited to token quotas. No one country would be permitted to receive more than 10 percent of the total slots; and up to 20 percent of unallocated visas could be used for refugees or other emergency cases. Under the current system, three countries—England, Ireland, and Germany—were allocated more than 70 percent of America's visas, with less than 1 percent going to all of Africa and less than 2 percent to Asia.

The day Kennedy sent his proposals to the Hill, school-desegregation talks were collapsing in Los Angeles, civil-rights crusaders were storming Florida restaurants and lunch counters, and hundreds of protesters—advocating construction jobs for blacks and Puerto Ricans—were on their way to New York jails. In Cambridge, Maryland—where National Guard troops were stationed—Attorney General Robert Kennedy was negotiating a truce between white politicians and blacks demanding. an end to Jim Crow. A month earlier, President Kennedy had sent Congress a civil-rights bill that still awaited action.

With the ongoing civil-rights crisis and test-ban treaty talks with the Russians commanding center stage, Congress was not inclined to focus on immigration. Also, Michael Feighan of Ohio, the new House Immigration Subcommittee chair, was hostile to the bill, as was James Eastland of Mississippi, under whose purview the legislation would fall in the Senate. Hill insiders predicted that the bill would go nowhere. Reformers, however, were counting on the president to marshal public opinion behind his ideas. They were also counting on a new attitude in Congress. Hawaii had gained statehood in 1959, giving Congress its first Asian and Pacific American members—including Daniel Inouye, an authentic war hero. Unlike in years past, congressional advocates of anti-Asian legislation would have to face, as colleagues, those who were the target.

Kennedy's death seemingly made such strategic concerns irrelevant. For Lyndon Johnson had never shown much of an interest in the subject, and without a champion, the Kennedy bill was dead. To the surprise of much of America—including his former colleagues in Congress—Johnson took up the immigration-reform banner, along with the rest of Kennedy's unfinished legislative business.

In his first State of the Union Message, Johnson beseeched Congress, "Let us carry forth the plans and programs of John Fitzgerald Kennedy, not because of our sorrow or sympathy, but because they are right." He invoked the fallen president's name three times in an inspirational address that declared war on poverty, embraced a sharp tax cut, and strongly linked immigration and domestic civil rights. "Americans of all races stand side by side in Berlin and in Vietnam. They died side by side in Korea. Surely they can work and eat and travel side by side in their own country," said Johnson, calling in the next breath for an end to discrimination against those trying to immigrate to America: "A nation that was built by immigrants . . . can ask those who now seek admission: 'What can you do for our country?' But we should not be asking: 'In what country were you born?' "

Afterward, Johnson sent word to Democrats on the House Judiciary Committee that he wanted Kennedy's immigration proposals passed intact. If compromises had to be made, they would be made in the Senate—where Johnson, a former Senate majority leader, felt completely at home. The public backed the president—at least according to a Louis Harris poll published in January of 1964 that found nearly two out of every three Americans wanted the deceased president's legislative initiatives enacted into law. Harris reported that congressional inaction on Kennedy's proposals "has now become the principal point of criticism by the public."

Despite Johnson's oratory and Harris's poll, the immigration bill died, but the president revived it in 1965. He reminded Congress that every president since Harry Truman had called for immigration reform and denounced the laws on the books as discriminatory, hypocritical, and "incompatible with our basic American tradition . . . that a man is to be judged—and judged exclusively—on his worth as a human being." So determined was Johnson to push the bill through that he had Congressman Jack Brooks of Texas temporarily placed on the immigration subcommittee to nudge a reluctant Feighan and to provide an extra vote to get the bill to the floor.

As Johnson pulled strings from the White House, the Kennedy brothers waged their own campaign. Robert Kennedy, who had lobbied for the bill as attorney general, did so again as a senator from New York, arguing that human decency and the tide of history dictated an end to the old ways: "Everywhere else in our national life, we have eliminated discrimination based on national origins. Yet this system is still the foundation of our immigration law." Edward Kennedy presided over hearings in the Senate and led the battle on the Senate floor.

In the interim, another Harris Poll came out—which asked not about Kennedy's programs in the abstract but specifically about immigration. The public (by a two-to-one margin) said the law should not be changed. Other responses seemed to endorse the thinking behind the national-origins concept. Asked which nation's immigrants they preferred, 28 percent of respondents named Canada first. England or Scotland followed, with 22 percent. Scandinavia and Germany completed the top four. Among those areas scorned were Russia (a reflection, presumably, of the Cold War), Asia, the Middle East, and Mexico. "Just ride New York's subways and you'll find the immigrants smell and are dirty and impolite, push you around, have no respect. Keep them out," elaborated one poll respondent.

Many witnesses who testified before Congress exhibited similar feelings. Originally immigrants came to make "a contribution," insisted the Daughters of the American Revolution,

but nowadays they sought only to escape unpleasant situa-
tions. New York, added the DAR, had paid "a very sizable
sum to take care of those groups [alluding to Puerto Ricans]"
who "do not meld in." Kentucky congressman Frank Chelf
fretted over provisions in the new legislation that would permit more immigration from recently liberated, predominantly
black Caribbean countries. Perhaps it would be all right to allow more "colored folks . . . if we need them," he said, but
given the United States' problems finding jobs for American-
born blacks, Chelf doubted that the country could accommodate those from outside. Others worried about danger from
pagan religions, or about communist infiltration from Eastern
Europe and Asia, or migration of primitives from Africa. "Take
the English speaking people, they gave us our language, they
gave us our common law, they gave us a large part of our
political philosophy. . . . With all due respect to Ethiopia—I
don't know of any contributions that Ethiopia has made to the
making of America," huffed Senator Sam Ervin of North Carolina.

Such qualms were eased by proponents who insisted that
eliminating national origins would, in fact, not much change
things. One expert after another drove home the point that
the 1924 system was already all but dead, that roughly two
thirds of those who came to America were being paroled in
through the Department of Justice as refugees, were benefi-
ciaries of special legislation, or were coming to reunite with
parents or spouses (and were thereby exempt from quota restrictions). Meanwhile, the huge quotas for England and a
handful of other favored countries—a total of sixty thousand
a year—were not being used.

Advocates likewise made clear that though the bill was an
equality measure—something of a companion to the Civil Rights
Bill of 1964 and the Voting Rights Act then moving through
Congress—it was not intended to primarily benefit Asians and
blacks. Italy, for instance, had a national-origins quota of just
under six thousand a year. Another seven thousand Italians
arrived annually outside of the quota—principally those joining family in America. Under the new legislation, Italy would

receive an annual quota of 16,500, and perhaps another 7,000 would enter as family members or special cases. Other restricted European countries would similarly benefit, whereas the increase from Asia would be minimal. "The bill will not flood our cities with immigrants. It will not upset the ethnic mix of our society," promised Edward Kennedy. Robert Kennedy estimated that the increase from the so-called Asia-Pacific triangle—an area covering most of Asia and the Pacific islands—would amount to roughly five thousand the first year, "but we do not expect that there would be a great influx after that."

In the House, Immigration Subcommittee chairman Feighan altered the administration's preference system to lessen even further the chance of ethnic change. Under President Kennedy's plan (which Lyndon Johnson had retained), first priority for visas was to go to those boasting skills or training that America needed—those "with the greatest ability to add to the national welfare." Under Feighan's, the vast majority would go to family members. The revision in the view of many changed the proposal from one based on merit to one based on nepotism, and from an immigration-reform and civil-rights bill to a family-reunification measure. Nonetheless, once the bill became perceived as a means to reunify families, selling it became much easier. For far from making a revolution, legislators would be bringing in people much like those already in America; they would be acting "more or less like an extended family," observed Congressman Peter Rodino. The bill passed the House in late August—318 to 95. The measure had a rougher time in the Senate, where legislators worried it might lead to more minority immigration.

Upon receiving their independence from Great Britain, Jamaica, Trinidad, and Tobago had been assigned token quotas instead of being permitted unlimited immigration (like other countries in the Americas or "Western Hemisphere"). The administration's plan to remove the quotas induced visions of hundreds of thousands of blacks coming from the Caribbean. In addition, lawmakers feared the bill might lead to fewer restraints on Asians. At present, persons of Asian ethnicity were regulated under the quota assigned to the country of their supposed racial origin—regardless of their actual place of birth. Children of Chinese immigrants to Canada or South America, for instance, were charged to China's tiny quota instead of being allowed to come as Canadians or South Americans. If Asians were treated as whites, one doomsayer estimated, perhaps a million would slip in. Senators were also disturbed at the prospect of reduced quotas for certain European countries while immigrants could stream in from El Salvador, Paraguay, Nicaragua, and other nations of South and Central America. With migration from Mexico growing apace, many thought it time to restrict—not encourage—Western Hemisphere immigration.

In return for abolishing the national-origins structure, Sam Ervin, Everett Dirksen, and fellow conservatives on the Senate Judiciary Committee insisted on a quota of 120,000 per year for countries of the Western Hemisphere. The administration gave in. The measure passed the Senate on September 22 by a seventy-six to eighteen margin. By the end of the month, a compromise measure—incorporating the new Senate restrictions—was back on the floor of the House. Congressman Henry Gonzalez of Texas rose to oppose the new Western Hemisphere quota, insisting it would torpedo U.S. relations with Latin America. His objections were dismissed, and the House-Senate compromise was overwhelmingly endorsed in both houses of Congress. "Before we knew it . . . we had a ceiling," recalls Raúl Yzaguirre, a young Latino activist who had recently moved to Washington and was later to head the National Council of La Raza.

The bill that passed was not what Kennedy had envisioned. Any intention of rethinking refugee policy or of removing provisions barring persons for political beliefs was forgotten as Congress made the bill into a welcome mat for American's extended families. As one of Kennedy's former lieutenants complained, a large dose of parochialism had replaced the flexible and "internationally oriented" provisions that the late president had recommended.

Still, the administration's primary goal had been achieved.

The national-origins system had been abolished—or would be following a three-year transition period—repudiating more than eight decades of legislation whose principal purpose had been to keep outsiders away. Under the new law, total quota immigration would be limited to 120,000 for the Western Hemisphere and 170,000 for the rest of the world. No country outside the Americas was to be permitted more than 20,000 quota positions. Though skills would still count in the system of quota preferences, three fourths of the new quota numbers were assigned to various categories of family members. The law reserved a small number of slots—6 percent of the total—for refugees. It also included a labor-certification provision to ensure that new immigrants would not take jobs from native Americans; permitted temporary employment of foreign laborers if domestic manpower was not available (a provision included to appease growers concerned about the expiration of the bracero program the previous year); and created a Select Commission on Western Hemisphere Immigration to study the impact of imposing the Western Hemisphere ceiling—due to take effect in July 1968.

In the end, reformers were surprised at how easily they had won. Yet, because of their concessions, they were also unsure of how much they had lost. Not much sleep was missed over the matter. As Senate staff member Dale S. deHann observed, "There was a sense that there would be time to look at the immigration bill again." In later years, the extent to which Congress had deluded itself would finally become clear.

Knowing that most Americans hailed from European stock, legislators had assumed that the generous family numbers would almost all go to Europeans; but an unforeseen flood of Asian refugees (who, once settled, could sponsor family members as regular immigrants) would eventually result in numbers intended for Europeans increasingly going to Asians, and the good feelings that had swept through Congress as the 1965 statute gathered steam—when all assumed that the egalitarian new law was little more than a generous gesture—would gradually give way to grave concern.

As Lyndon Johnson prepared to sign the new law that Oc-

tober at a special Liberty Island ceremony, such worries were
in the future. In that autumn of its naïveté, Congress's self-
confidence was without limit—as was its belief in the goodness
of its act. Both Kennedy brothers attended the celebration, as
did Governor Nelson Rockefeller, Senator Hubert Humphrey,
New York mayoral candidate John Lindsay, and several
hundred others who had helped to pass the bill—and who rel-
ished their success in rewriting the rules for new generations
of would-be Americans.

Under a clear sky, silhouetted against the Statue of Liberty, lighted by the sun of a warm and hopeful day, Johnson
spoke passionately of justice and reaffirmed America as sanctuary for the world's oppressed. "The bill that we sign today
is not a revolutionary bill. It does not affect the lives of millions. It will not reshape the structure of our daily lives, or
really add importantly to either our wealth or our power. Yet
it is still one of the most important acts of this Congress and
of this administration. For it does repair a very deep and pow-
erful flaw in the fabric of American justice . . . and . . . will
really make us truer to ourselves both as a country and as a
people." His words rang like an anthem, as Johnson there-
upon divulged his big news of the day, which dealt not with
the law he was in New York to ratify but with Cuba. "I declare
this afternoon to the people of Cuba that those who seek refuge here in America will find it."

Johnson revealed that he had already ordered the Department of Health, Education and Welfare to facilitate Cuban arrivals and was sending Congress a request for $12.6 million
for aid to Cuban escapees. The new initiative stemmed from
Castro's recent announcement that those whose families had
already fled Cuba would be allowed to join them abroad. Fidel
Castro's declaration was interpreted as a direct challenge to
the United States, to which commercial flights from Cuba had
ceased following the missile crisis of 1962. With the cessation
of flights, the torrent of Cuban refugees had quickly dwindled
to a trickle, consisting for the most part of those willing to
cross the sea in small boats. Castro's newest edict could mean
thousands of Cuban emigrants. Ironically, the new immigra-

tion law authorized such small numbers for political refugees that, even as Johnson signed it, he underscored one of the bill's inadequacies by opting to use the attorney general's special parole powers to bring the Cubans in.

The New York Times applauded the president's initiative but questioned whether Castro would allow a mass departure. The Cubans began arriving by boat later that week. By the middle of October, some seven hundred had come to America. By December (with the help of the Swedish embassy), an airlift had been organized providing for the transport of four thousand Cubans a month.

LBJ's face-off with Castro eclipsed the news that the United States had fundamentally transformed its immigration law. Johnson, appreciating America's ambivalence on the subject, could hardly have minded. And if he had to give immigration a human face, he could have done much worse than to make it Cuban. Cuba was, after all, a small place from which emigration was strictly controlled—which defused any concern about a Cuban deluge. Also, Cuban refugees came wrapped—so to speak—in the flag of anticommunism. In the shadow of the Cold War, that made them rather special.

In 1968, the Select Commission on Western Hemisphere recommended extending the date for imposing the ceiling on immigration from the Americas to allow for further study. Congress rejected the extension, and the new restrictions were set in place. Unlike the rest of the world, however, the Western Hemisphere was given no preference system. Though the law set an overall numerical limit, it provided no means—within that limit—for ranking the desirability of different types of immigrants; nor did it provide a system for determining whether one country should be allowed more immigration than the next. Theoretically one country could be awarded all the visas for the region, leaving everyone else with none.

In opposing the ceiling, Representative Gonzalez had argued, "Canada could entirely preempt the quota for any one year by sending into the United States 120,000 immigrants. . . . Who is to say that the persons administering the new law would not permit this? And what would be the effect on the Latin nations?" In fact, few of his colleagues were worried about Canada dominating the numbers. Instead, congressmen fretted over the nations to the south—especially Mexico. Those concerns were aggravated by the appearance of huge backlogs in Latin American countries as would-be immigrants took their place in the queue.

In 1973, Pennsylvania congressman Joshua Eilberg introduced legislation to bring the Western Hemisphere into line with the rest of the world. By allowing no more than twenty thousand quota immigrants from any one country, the statute would halve such admissions from Mexico. The bill passed the House but died in the Senate. Three years later, Eilberg—then chairman of the House Immigration Subcommittee—put forth his measure again. By then, total (including nonquota) immigration from Mexico had grown to more than sixty-two thousand persons annually, compared to just over seven thousand from Canada. In the midst of a campaign season, however, few legislators were focusing on those numbers. Eilberg's new bill might have died like the first had he not chanced upon Hispanic issues lobbyist Manny Fierro at a Washington social function. Fierro told Eilberg that if rules for the Americas were to be changed at all, they should be liberalized—not used as a weapon against Mexicans; and he suggested that maybe Eilberg should simply admit defeat and give up the fight for a Western Hemisphere preference system.

Eilberg reacted to the advice with fury. The last Wednesday evening in September, while the Hispanic opposition was elsewhere and as Congress prepared to adjourn for the year, he brought the bill up for immediate consideration. The visa backlog, he said, was creating a crisis—and preventing the most deserving from coming to America. "It may be," he declared, "that a neighbor in Canada is waiting in line behind a neighbor in South America." The House responded by passing the bill, whereupon Eilberg headed to the other side of the Capitol to urge the Senate to do the same.

The Senate was in chaos. To protest a bill granting fees to lawyers in certain civil-rights cases, James Allen of Alabama had used procedural ploys to immobilize the chamber for a week. The controversial bill had eventually passed, but scores of others were stacked up behind it. Weary, irritable, and raring to get home, senators were in no mood to consider immigration-law amendments. Nevertheless, that Friday evening— the last night the Senate would be in session—Eilberg convinced Acting Majority Leader Robert Byrd to bring his proposal up for consideration. Meanwhile, bills whizzed by at a bewildering pace; one reporter counted the passage of seventeen in thirteen minutes. Much of the Senate had only the foggiest notion what many contained. Byrd temporarily withdrew Eilberg's legislation (after a senator objected, mistakenly believing it had something to do with government ·land in Alaska) until a colleague who could explain its contents returned to the floor. Presently Byrd brought the bill up again, and Eilberg remained until it passed.

Gerald Ford conceded the need for regulation in the Western Hemisphere, but wished to avoid offending Latino voters or alienating a neighboring country. He signed the bill, while declaring his intention to submit legislation to Congress to increase the quota numbers for Mexico. The next time Congress convened, of course, Ford was leaving the White House.

Even without Eilberg's pyrotechnics, some form of legislation to curb the traffic from Mexico eventually would have passed. Congress felt an overwhelming need to regain control of the border. For a great many legislators, ending hemispheric discrepancy was coming to be seen as the unfinished business of the 1965 act. That the bill passed sooner rather than later, however (unchanged and virtually without debate), was due entirely to Eilberg. That a law so affecting Latinos could pass without significant Latino input was viewed by many activists, in retrospect, as outrageous. They vowed never to let such a thing happen again.

9

A Legacy of Vietnam

Richard Nixon promised withdrawal from Vietnam with honor, and he was true to at least part of his word. In early 1973, the United States declared that, for America at least, the war was over. At the Paris cease-fire ceremony marking the end of U.S. involvement, the mood was far from celebratory. "The Vietnam cease-fire agreement was signed," one correspondent reported, ". . . in eerie silence without a word or a gesture to express the world's relief that the years of war were officially ending. . . . The cold, almost gloomy atmosphere at two separate signing ceremonies reflected the uncertainties of whether peace is now assured."

In the months that followed, Vietnam gave way to the headlines and heartache of Watergate; and in a valedictory, delivered with quaking voice on a sticky and overcast August day, Nixon called on Americans "to rediscover those shared ideas that lie at the heart of our strength." Gerald Ford picked up the theme in his Inaugural Address. Sounding more like a priest than a president, he talked of ending the national nightmare with prayer, of binding "the internal wounds of Watergate, more painful and more poisonous than those of foreign wars." A sympathetic and solicitous Congress agreed, unanimously, to help him—voting a formal pledge of cooperation with the nation's new president.

In March 1975, the fall of Da Nang, South Vietnam's second-largest city and former headquarters of the U.S. Marines, brought new attention to an area of the world many had assumed America had left forever. As Da Nang succumbed to the Viet Cong, former residents streamed south, many having pawned priceless heirlooms to finance their escape. For thousands, that mad dash became the first leg of a grisly odyssey that would end for some at the bottom of the ocean and for others in the United States.

Publicly Ford insisted on optimism, declaring, "I still think there is an opportunity to salvage the situation." But two weeks later, the American embassy in Cambodia closed its doors—a result of the collapsing military situation all around. And as the embassy in Saigon prepared to shut down, politicians debated the fate of thousands of Southeast Asians tainted, so to speak, by association with the United States.

A Pentagon contingency plan called for using a marine division and air support to evacuate them. But torn between a sense of obligation and a fear of being pulled once more into war, Congress questioned the wisdom of sending American troops to rescue Vietnamese. Senate Foreign Relations Committee chairman John Sparkman spoke of the need to balance humanitarianism with realism. Senator Thomas Eagleton asked that military assistance be limited to "the minimum necessary to rescue Americans." Others argued that troops be used to save both American and Vietnamese lives. Many wondered whether America could possibly cope with so many refugees— one estimate placed the total number at six hundred thousand—who had hopes of escaping to the United States.

Like an anxious mother with a terminally ill child, America stood by as Vietnam withered, obsessed with the thought that maybe—through neglect or misconduct—she was, at base, to blame. South Vietnam's refusal to absolve the United States of responsibility intensified the deeply felt guilt. In a resignation tendered as his country crumbled, President Nguyen Van Thieu reproached his superpower friend. "When the Americans saw the loss of . . . vehicles and weapons, why did you not come and replace them?" he wailed. "When you saw our people being lost, why did you not come in and help our people? . . . The Americans promised us—we trusted them. But you have not given us the aid you promised."

For most American politicians, dealing with feelings of culpability did not mean supporting a renewal of the war. It only meant trying to disengage without disaster while holding out a glimmer of hope to those Vietnamese who had placed their faith in the United States. Shortly after Nguyen's emotional resignation, President Ford spoke in New Orleans at Tulane University. America would regain her pride again, Ford reassured his audience, "But it cannot be achieved by refighting a war that is finished—as far as America is concerned." Better, he said, to look to the future to bind the nation's wounds.

At the end of April, Saigon finally fell. Before the airport there closed, about forty thousand Vietnamese were evacuated by air. In the final days of the war, planes loaded with émigrés landed in Guam every eighteen minutes, and Navy Seabees worked twelve-hour shifts setting up thousands of tents to house them.

Nearly one hundred thousand refugees fled into the South China Sea. Many were picked up by U.S. Navy ships off the coast of Vietnam and taken to processing facilities in Guam and in the Philippines—creating pandemonium in an evacuation program that could barely keep ahead of the flow. The flood of Vietnamese into U.S. military facilities in the Philippines so alarmed the Philippine government that it demanded each person be processed and sent away within three days.

Exactly where the Vietnamese would be sent was not at first clear. The Ford administration—which quickly authorized parole for 130,000 Vietnamese, Cambodians, and Laotians—had no coherent plan. Early in the process, federal officials asked California to consider housing the refugees. Governor Edmund Brown, Jr., citing the state's nearly 10 percent unemployment rate, replied that California could not afford to do so. Shortly thereafter, the Defense Department decided on three military bases as reception centers: Camp Pendleton in southern California, Fort Chaffee in Arkansas, and Eglin Air Force Base in Florida. Later, a fourth center was added at Indiantown Gap, Pennsylvania.

Americans, in general, were not enthusiastic. A Gallup Poll found 54 percent opposed to resettling the Vietnamese in the United States, with only 33 percent in favor. Legislators—considering Ford's request for $507 million to underwrite Vietnamese migration—reflected their constituents' misgivings. House Immigration Subcommittee chairman Joshua Eilberg worried about burdening the United States with so many newcomers when the nation faced a housing shortage, rising costs, and the highest unemployment rate in decades. "We must strive to insure that the presence of large numbers of refugees does not disadvantage the American people," said Eilberg. He was also uncomfortable with refugees coming directly into the United States, without being screened in another country first. Only once before, observed Eilberg, had the United States been a country of first asylum—a decade earlier with refugees from Cuba. Since then, some six hundred thousand Cubans had come to America—something he thought the country should consider before extending a similar invitation to the Vietnamese. House speaker Carl Albert rejected that line of thought: "Given the small number in comparison with the refugees from Cuba, I think this is what the American people want us to do." Shortly thereafter, Congress appropriated $405 million—making available a maximum of $455 million—for the transport, shelter, and settlement of Southeast Asian émigrés.

In the first few days, as evacuees arrived, few sponsors emerged to offer them employment and shelter. Some officials wondered whether the camps might turn into long-term settlements and the Vietnamese into permanent wards of the state. But sponsors eventually appeared, and inhabitants began leaving the camps at the rate of one thousand or so a day. By year's end, all 130,000 had departed, with every state in the union taking at least a few, leading *U.S. News & World Report* to rejoice, CHRISTMAS BRINGS HAPPY ENDING FOR VIETNAM REFUGEES.

"I guess nobody believed the American people would be as

open and forthcoming as they have," exulted the head of the federal task force responsible for resettlement. Getting the refugees situated, however, was merely the first step in a complex process of adjustment—for America and for the Indochinese.

Some difficulties stemmed from the newcomers' status. Having been brought in under the U.S. attorney general's emergency parole authority, they were neither citizens nor permanent residents; they were "parolees," which meant they could not hold certain jobs or even be sure they would be allowed to stay. Many also had to cope with a devastating change in social status. Largely English-speaking, middle class, and members of South Vietnam's elite, thousands went on welfare. Others took jobs they considered far beneath them. Even years after arriving, only a tiny number managed to achieve a comparable status to that enjoyed in Vietnam. Instead, ex-generals became taxi drivers and middle-class matrons became maids, all the while coping with communities loath to embrace a population of Southeast Asians.

Some Americans were worried about competition for jobs; others harbored bitterness over the Vietnam War and blamed the Indochinese for the loss of American lives; others simply were not convinced that Asians made good neighbors. One Arkansas woman grumbled, "I hope they all catch pneumonia and die." Numerous communities went through three distinct phases: apprehension at news of the émigrés' coming, anger when they arrived, and acceptance—though often of a begrudging or tentative nature—once the refugees began to fit in. Getting from the first to the third stage often took years. In Fort Smith, Arkansas, four years after arriving (along with two thousand other Southeast Asians), one Vietnamese woman confessed that rejection sometimes still occurred: "From time to time, people talk and it hurts us. But not often."

Many Vietnamese never adjusted to their first American environment; they simply moved somewhere else, mainly to California. Despite the government's policy of spreading refugees around, 50 percent of all Southeast Asians in America ultimately wound up in one of three states: California, Texas, or Washington—with California housing 40 percent of the total.

In 1977, as Vietnam's communists consolidated control and as border conflicts intensified with Cambodia and China, thousands of Vietnamese in small boats took to the South China Sea. Many either perished in the waters or drifted from port to port—unable to find one that would take them. A Burmese ship that rescued ninety Vietnamese waited a month for permission to dock at Hong Kong Harbor. An Israeli vessel that saved sixty-six from a sinking boat was unable to unload them anywhere in the region—and eventually took them to Israel. Night and day, refugees kept coming—not only from Vietnam, but increasingly from Cambodia and Laos.

Unable to ignore the crisis, President Jimmy Carter authorized Attorney General Griffin Bell to use his parole authority. Late in 1977, thousands of "boat cases" began arriving in the United States; also coming were refugees from camps in Thailand—primarily Laotians, Cambodians, and Vietnamese who, for the most part, had associations with (or relatives in) the United States and were deemed to be in danger because of that. In all, twenty-three thousand Indochinese were paroled into American in 1977. President Carter also signed legislation that year allowing Indochinese refugees to become permanent resident aliens, thereby opening the door to U.S. citizenship.

Bell's use of his emergency authority renewed a running battle with Congress. Early in 1976, after the Ford administration acted to accept eleven thousand additional Indochinese, Congressman Joshua Eilberg had requested a moratorium on paroles while Congress considered comprehensive refugee legislation. Bell, however, argued that the law did not require him to seek the consent of Congress but merely suggested that he consult; to him, and to the White House, the Southeast Asian situation had seemed sufficiently serious for unilateral action. Eilberg was not satisfied with that response. Nor were several members of Congress who felt that by using parole so freely, the White House had totally usurped their role in refugee policy.

That the refugees were Indochinese instead of European

was also a factor—at least with Eilberg, who criticized the administration for bringing in Southeast Asians and yet pleaded with the White House to parole in five thousand Soviet émigrés stranded at the processing center in Rome. Edward Kennedy, then head of the Senate subcommittee on refugees, was so incensed at Eilberg's favoritism that he refused to back Eilberg unless Eilberg also endorsed bringing in Indochinese. Still, no one was happy with what the parole process had become. Kennedy thought it an invitation to discrimination on racial or ideological grounds; Eilberg believed it placed too much unregulated power in the hands of the executive branch; and Attorney General Bell complained that since the parole power required an emergency to trigger it, "Refugees are hostage to a system that necessitates that their plight build to tragic proportions so as to establish the imperative to act."

In late 1978, the United Nations estimated that 175,000 Laotians, Cambodians, and Vietnamese were crowded into camps throughout Asia—principally in Thailand and Malaysia. The Thai government—unwilling to continue housing them—began pushing émigrés back to sea. Malaysia eventually did so as well—leaving untold numbers to perish at the hands of pirates or to quietly vanish in the ocean.

One group of twenty-five hundred Vietnamese—primarily ethnic Chinese—was reportedly forced to pay for their passage in gold and then launched, by a hostile Vietnamese government, on a voyage to nowhere. Their small freighter—the *Hai Hong*—ended up on the south coast of Malaysia, but the government refused to let the occupants disembark. For several months, the exiles drifted, as news of their predicament flashed around the globe. West Germany, the United States, and other Western nations ultimately stepped forward to offer the vagabonds a home. The last of the group was airlifted out some six months after the ordeal began.

Others were not so fortunate. Thousands died—some spectacularly so. Two hundred émigrés drowned off the coast of Malaysia after police towed their fishing boat out to sea. Equally horrible incidents finally induced the Malaysians to suspend the policy of turning boats away. George Bush assailed Jimmy Carter in an opinion piece for *The Washington Post:* "For President Carter, who professes a strong belief in Christian ethics, it should be a tormenting thought that by his hand, the United States has put an entire people adrift in a cruel, hostile sea—and for scarcely any purpose." The article was directed at Carter's China policy, but in bringing up the tragedy of the boat people, Bush, in effect, drove home another point: that the cataclysm whipping through Southeast Asia was, in large part, America's fault.

In 1978, the attorney general paroled in eighty-one thousand Southeast Asian refugees. The next year, he brought in more than twice that—and nearly ten times the number sanctioned by U.S. immigration law for *all* refugees. Unlike the first wave of Southeast Asians, who were overwhelmingly Vietnamese, the second contained numerous Laotians and Cambodians; and whereas the first had consisted of an educated and—to a large extent—English-speaking elite, the second contained many peasants with only the vaguest understanding of U.S. society. They arrived at a time when Americans—never eager to accept hordes of poverty-stricken strangers—had grown weary of sacrificing for the huddled masses of Vietnam. Sister Ann Wisda, head of the United States Catholic Conference in Oklahoma, called the new Vietnamese arrivals "parasites" planning to "sponge off the American people." Ninety percent of those who had arrived since mid-1978, she said, "have no intention of obtaining a job until they are forced to do so."

Violence broke out in several places. Attacks on Vietnamese living in a housing project on the outskirts of Denver forced many of the families to move. And a bitter feud between Vietnamese and American fishermen in the Texas coastal town of Seadrift led to the shooting death of one of the whites. Several Vietnamese fishing boats were burned in retaliation, and the owner of a local crab-processing factory that employed mainly Vietnamese temporarily shut down for fear of violent vendettas. "As long as there's one gook left in a fishing town on this Gulf Coast, there's going to be trouble," fumed one native. The feeling that refugees were disrupting a way of life was not at all unique to Seadrift. A local Louisiana official, com-

plaining that Vietnamese were eating the pets of other fishermen, threatened to deny the refugees a place to dock their
boats. "What we have here is a group of people who have been
dumped in our area who are totally unaccustomed to our ways,
our manner of living, our mores and our laws," grumbled the
president of the Plaquemines Parish Commission Council.

Many communities blamed Washington for the assimilation problems, faulting the federal government for dumping
refugees on them without adequate social-service support. Some
within the administration agreed. The Department of Health,
Education and Welfare acknowledged that, despite the fact that
most Indochinese refugees were unable to speak English and
had few marketable skills, virtually no job training or English
instruction was available to them; in most cases, they received
little orientation in dealing with Americans or U.S. culture.

A large part of the problem, argued Attorney General Bell,
lay with the way refugees were generally admitted—through
the emergency parole procedure that rendered the U.S. government incapable of planning, and thereby incapable of co-
ordinating with voluntary agencies, with state and local officials,
and even with its own bureaucrats. The time had come, he
said, to go back to the drawing board.

Previously bills introduced to improve the refugee process
had never got through Congress; but the retirement of Senate
Judiciary Committee chairman James Eastland at the end of
1978 promised to change that. For years, Eastland had blocked
virtually all immigration legislation that came before him,
though occasionally he would step aside and let Kennedy pre-
side—as he had during the reform battles of 1965. With South
Vietnam falling in 1975, he had again indulged Kennedy, allowing the younger senator—in his capacity as chair of the
subcommittee on refugees—to send two staff members to
Vietnam to assess the situation firsthand. "Sure, kid," he had
said, when Kennedy got him on the phone. "You can send
your boys out there to Vietnam." Then he had added that he
needed a tractor driver and that maybe Kennedy's boys could
find him one in Southeast Asia. No one knew whether the
request was serious or not, but it underscored for Kennedy's

staff how cavalier Eastland's approach to the whole subject of immigration could be.

In contrast, Kennedy saw reforming national refugee policy as a critically important cause. Shortly before succeeding Eastland as full committee chairman, he wrote to several administration officials soliciting their cooperation. He also had his staff meet with counterparts in the administration to co-ordinate the details of legislation. In March 1979, he introduced his bill—with endorsements from the attorney general and the secretaries of state and of health, education and welfare. Elizabeth Holtzman and Peter Rodino sponsored companion legislation in the House. The act was signed into law the following year.

The Refugee Act of 1980 sanctioned substantially higher numbers than the 1965 law. It provided routine admission for fifty thousand refugees annually. This yearly "normal flow" was roughly one-sixth the figure for all restricted classes of immigrants, and the number could be raised following consultation with Congress. Much as he had done with the 1965 legislation, Kennedy minimized the new bill's impact: "This . . . does not really increase our annual immigration flow, since by the use of the parole authority over the past several decades, the United States has accepted, on an average, some 40,000 refugees each year." The act also rewrote America's definition of a refugee. Previously the United States had only recognized those fleeing communism or the Middle East; the new law followed the lead of the United Nations—designating as a refugee anyone who fled because of a well-founded fear of persecution due to race, religion, nationality, political opinion, or social-group membership.

Even those qualifying under the new definition, however, would not automatically be allowed to enter. In most cases they would also need to be deemed of "special humanitarian concern to the United States." The words, Kennedy acknowledged, were impossible to define; but he noted that in the past the United States had tilted toward refugees from those countries where "the United States has had strong historic or cultural ties, or where we have been directly involved or had treaty obligations." That tilt was expected to remain—despite the new law's self-conscious nod in the direction of fairness. During the first six months of fiscal 1980, only 120 of 114,284 refugees came from Africa, and (excluding Cuba) only 64 from Latin America. Carter administration projections promised no substantial change.

Unlike 1965's legislation, the new act did not ignite an orgy of self-congratulation because, though it was fairer than the one it replaced, it was largely perceived as dealing with turf (a more significant role for Congress) and administrative neatness (a more coherent process for admitting—and a clearer definition of—refugees). The final version barely squeaked through the House—passing by a vote of 207 to 192. Even those who strongly supported the legislation did not go out of their way to call attention to it. For the bill was precipitated, in large measure, by the plight of émigrés from Vietnam; and many Americans were far from convinced that the United States was where those exiles belonged, or that America could afford to absorb more—from Vietnam or from anywhere else. Unlike regular immigrants, who have to demonstrate a means of financial support, refugees typically come with little more than rags and hope. They have to be resettled and often given financial assistance. As one study of Vietnamese refugees concluded, "Virtually all . . . relied on cash assistance during the early months in the U.S., and we find no evidence of 'bootstrappers' who made it on their own."

In 1965, legislators had essentially averted their eyes and pretended that refugees would fade away—or at least that not many would turn to America. Hungary, Chile, China, Cuba, were all seen as aberrations. And in the beginning, Vietnam was as well. The new law was an acknowledgment that, even if Vietnam's exiles vanished, others eventually would be knocking at the door, that refugees were not an aberration but an inevitable result of the way the world worked, and that their acceptance was an unavoidable responsibility of the U.S. role in international affairs.

At the height of the Vietnamese refugee explosion, with public attention already riveted on immigration, INS commis-

sioner Leonard Chapman had launched a crusade against illegal aliens—portraying them as usurpers of American welfare
checks and American jobs. Not coincidentally, Chapman was
also campaigning for more manpower and a higher budget
for the INS, and the press fell in line behind him.

In five years, the numbers of illegal aliens had grown from
4 million to between 8 and 12 million, claimed *Business Week*
in 1975, adding, "With 10-million unemployed Americans
scrambling for jobs in the same labor market, the U.S. must
find a way to stop the influx of illegal aliens." Two years later,
the magazine updated its statistics, asserting that illegal entrants held 3.8 million American jobs and were sending $2.5
billion a year out of the country. *The Washington Post* noted
that a new federal program providing 2 million jobs "would
just about compensate for the lowest estimated number of jobs
held by illegal aliens in this country." *U.S. News & World Report*
warned, "The problem of the illegal aliens grows more critical
every day. They are everywhere, in swollen numbers. Perhaps
6 million Mexicans . . . are now scattered throughout the U.S.
Hardly a city anywhere does not have its share, not only of
illegally entered Mexicans, but Dominicans, Pakistanis, Guate-
malans, Chinese. . . . In another 10 years, today's illegal entrants will have given birth to possibly 15 million offspring. . . .
The old refrain about illegals' doing 'stoop-and-carry labor'
that Americans scorn as beneath their dignity may carry some
historic truth—but it rings rather hollowly when 6.7 million
American citizens are unemployed." The Texas legislature was
so alarmed at the projected growth of the undocumented population that it voted in 1975 to withhold funds from local school
districts for children not "legally admitted" into the country.

Sundry others hopped onto the anti-illegal-alien bandwa-
gon. In 1977, the Ku Klux Klan announced a border watch
by its members aimed at curtailing migration from Mexico. In
1978, James H. Scheuer, chairman of the House Select Committee on Population, called for a "firm, hard sealing" of the
U.S.-Mexican border. In addition, he recommended helping
Mexico develop better birth-control methods and deporting
any immigrant who received welfare within five years of entering the United States. John Tanton, a Michigan ophthal-

mologist and former national president of Zero Population Growth, urged ZPG to involve itself in the issue. ZPG subsequently kicked off a fund-raising appeal with a letter denouncing illegal immigration as a "human tidal wave . . . depressing our economy and costing American taxpayers an estimated $10 billion to $13 billion a year." Many inside ZPG, however, were uncomfortable with Tanton's approach. Some thought it smacked of racism; and Tanton was urged to find another forum for his zealotry. In 1979, he organized the Federation for American Immigration Reform, which soon became a leading advocacy organization for restrictions on immigration.

Despite the rising anxiety over the supposed increase in illegal immigration, no one really knew how many illegal immigrants existed—much less how many jobs they were taking. Before Chapman arrived, the INS estimated the number at slightly over a million. At one point Chapman concluded it might be as high as 12 million. Later, a figure of 8.2 million was arrived at by consultants employing a technique—the Delphi method—that had six experts make independent guesses of the numbers of undocumented immigrants and, through indirect communication, arrive at a collective opinion. U.S. Census experts dismissed the INS figures because they could find no basis for them. Pressed to make an estimate of their own, the census experts reckoned the number of undocumented Mexicans in the United States at something under 3 million and concluded that, contrary to popular belief, Mexicans made up less than 50 percent of those illegally present.

The INS numbers were not manufactured in a total vacuum. Seizures of illegal migrants had been steadily rising— from 344,000 in 1970 to 767,000 in 1975 and to 1.076 million in 1979—but only a tenuous connection existed between those statistics and estimates of the total undocumented population. The statistics, for instance, did not differentiate between those arrests that resulted from more aggressive law enforcement and those reflecting a real increase in illegal immigration; nor did they distinguish between the same individual arrested at different times and different individuals. The statistics did provide politicians, however, with a crisis to resolve. Gerald Ford established a task force to study the issue and ended up endorsing penalties for employers who hired the undocumented. Jimmy Carter not only supported sanctions against employers but also amnesty for many undocumented immigrants who had sunk roots in the United States. Congress acted on neither proposal. In 1980, however, thousands of Cubans and Haitians pouring into Miami would bring the immigration crisis vividly alive, and Congress, sensing public patience had run out, would scramble to take charge.

10

From Mariel to Miami

W hen Fulgencio Batista fled Cuba on New Year's Day, 1959, he set off a chain of events that would utterly transform South Florida's politics, culture, and economy. At the time, as revelers swarmed through the streets of Havana, setting hotels, casinos, and *El Tiempo* newspaper aflame, few Cubans could envision anything other than the glorious new era to come; and in Florida—as elsewhere in America—people generally took the coup to mean that the corruption, the gangsters, and the gambling would go, Cuba's potential would be fulfilled, and the United States would continue importing sugarcane and tobacco and be little affected by the island's revolution.

For many Cubans, disenchantment came almost instantly. "My revolutionary fervor," one expatriate recalled, "lasted about a week." After hearing Fidel Castro's first televised address, he became convinced the savior was a demagogue. Others—particularly those who had fled or had gone to jail for their beliefs—were enchanted by Castro's vision a good deal longer. Roberto Suarez, an expatriate with a degree in finance from

Villanova University, returned to Cuba from New York and was made head of a bank. But as he watched Castro's growing fascination with communism, Suarez—and thousands like him— became alarmed. In 1961, with his wife and seven children, Suarez fled and found work in a Miami mailroom. Droves of others did much the same. In the beginning, they were—from Washington's perspective—not so much immigrants or even Latin Americans as ornaments of American democracy and refutations of the communist way of life.

In 1965, when Castro opened the port of Camarioca, Lyndon Johnson was pleased to offer asylum to any Cuban who came. More turned up in South Florida (particularly Dade County) than anywhere else. Between 1960 and 1970, Dade County's population of ethnic Cubans increased nearly eight-fold—from 29,500 to 224,000—of which 85 percent were foreign-born. In the beginning, Florida politicians enthusiastically welcomed the newcomers, counting on them to reinvigorate the local economy. County commissioners even declared Dade to be officially bilingual. But by the middle-1970s, some Miamians had grown resentful. A school-board candidate won election in 1974 by pledging to halt the expansion of bilingual education—even though one third of Dade County's students spoke Spanish as their first language. "Many non-Latin Miamians bridle at their city becoming bilingual," reported *Business Week*. "They feel outnumbered in the streets and in the stores."

Such feelings were kindled not only by Cubans but by the influx of others—most conspicuously from Haiti—seeking haven in Florida. In 1972, when sixty-five Haitians (some claiming to be escaped political prisoners) landed on a ritzy beachfront condominium community after nineteen days aboard a leaky, rudderless sailboat, they were more objects of wonder than dismay. Their dramatic story of survival amid high winds and violent seas—and of their rebuff in Cuba where they had landed but refused to declare themselves communists—made for fascinating front-page reading. Even though local officials fretted that more Haitians might come, and immigration officials pointed out that the Haitians would likely be deported, beachfront-property owners put on a cordial face, providing blankets, food, and water for the famished émigrés.

Six years later, when thirty-three Haitians landed at Key Biscayne (the onetime winter residence of former president Richard M. Nixon), politicians complained that they might harbor tuberculosis and venereal disease, and some suggested tossing the Haitians into quarantine. Unlike the Cubans, who were largely white and well-to-do, the Haitians were black and poor. From the perspective of U.S. immigration officials, they had little to offer America. Nor could the Haitians be used in political propaganda, since the Duvaliers—François "Papa Doc" and son Jean-Claude (who succeeded his father as Haiti's ruler in 1971)—were considered friends of the United States. During the 1970s, 99 percent of Haitian applications for asylum were rejected.

Initially the middle-class Haitian expatriate community—some of whose members were embarrassed by the impoverished boat people—took little active interest in the peasants' predicament. But as boats continued to come and more and more Haitians were turned away (on the grounds that they were "economic migrants," not real refugees), many Haitian expatriates grew indignant. Some came to Miami to help set things right. Lawyers, religious workers, and social reformers also converged on Miami, seeing, in the city's tinderbox of refugees and racial trepidations, an opportunity to participate in one of the great evolving moral crusades of the day and to resolve some fundamental questions of refugee rights.

What protections were owed a person who had landed in the United States and was pleading for asylum? Why was America's first major group of black refugees being treated so differently from Cubans or Russians? Such questions demanded not only legal answers but political and moral ones; and for some, they made Miami an irresistible intellectual and ethical challenge.

Ira Kurzban, a New Yorker who had attended law school at UC Berkeley, came down in early 1977—with financial support from the National Council of Churches and Church World Service. The spectacles that greeted him upon arrival struck him like scenes from hell: a Haitian child held for several weeks in a West Palm Beach jail; Haitian families split up without reason—a mother sent to a camp in West Virginia, a father shipped to Texas, and a child sent somewhere else. The Haitians would be herded together, given mass asylum hearings—sometimes without benefit of translators—and deported. When Kurzban complained to one judge that such treatment reminded him of slavery, the judge dismissed the words as the hyperbole of a fanatic. The legal work, however, was getting results: Judicial rulings came down forcing the U.S. Immigration and Naturalization Service to give Haitians the right to work, the right to a full hearing for asylum, and the right to information to support their claims.

But though Haitians were winning in court, they were losing the battle for South Florida's heart. In Delray Beach, residents protested a decision by World Harvest for Christ to build a residence for Haitian refugees. When the home was constructed anyway, shots were fired into it. Eventually the structure was burned to the ground. In Miami scores of Haitians (along with their belongings) were tossed out of a church that had been providing food and temporary shelter, following an argument between a Haitian refugee and the pastor, James Jenkins. Jenkins, head of Friendship Baptist Church, said he was tired of providing for the Haitians when they were so uncooperative and when so little help was forthcoming from federal and local agencies. T. Willard Fair, head of the Urban League of Greater Miami, was even more hostile, contending that the Haitians had no right to be in America. Left to their own devices, Haitian advocates might have struggled for years, trying to get the public aroused over their charges of discrimination, but in spring 1980 Miami was rocked by a tidal wave from Cuba.

On April 1, Havana sentries fired on a bus full of asylum-seekers as it crashed its way into the Peruvian embassy. A guard was killed—apparently by a bullet ricocheting off the vehicle—and Cuban authorities demanded that the fugitives be turned over to them. When the Peruvians refused, Cuba withdrew the embassy police. News of the unguarded compound swept the island, and by the next day a reported fifteen hundred Cubans had massed on the grounds. Shortly thereafter, Cuba's Foreign Ministry told an astonished world that all Cubans, except those who had originally crashed the gate, were free to go to any country that would have them. Within twenty-four hours, an estimated ten thousand Cubans had assembled, many standing virtually toe to toe, taking shelter wherever they could find it—including, for a few, in a huge mango tree—as Cuban patriots outside the compound peppered them with stones.

For two weeks, diplomats dickered. Peru refused to accept all ten thousand. The United States offered to let them apply for visas but said they would have to wait in line behind thirty thousand of their countrymen who had properly applied earlier. As international pressure mounted, the United States agreed to take thirty-five hundred. Meanwhile, Costa Rica offered to temporarily accept all the would-be émigrés until they could find permanent sanctuary. Shortly thereafter, Castro abruptly halted the airlift to Costa Rica and decreed that anyone wishing to go to the United States could leave from Mariel Harbor.

That announcement galvanized the Cuban exile community. Many families plunged into substantial debt to charter boats—at prices as high as fifty thousand dollars a trip—to rescue loved ones. In late April, the first boat reached Mariel. The crew, after loading its human cargo, was told it was free to return for more. Many who went to Cuba in search of their families came back with boatloads of strangers (since Cuban officials insisted that would-be rescuers take anyone loaded into their boats), but the effort continued to pick up steam. Florida's press dubbed the émigrés' fleet a "freedom flotilla" and enthusiastically embraced their cause. With some fifty boats already en route, the *Miami Herald* (despite pointing out that importing exiles constituted a felony) offered a host of helpful hints, advising would-be liberators to take life preservers, avoid overloading of boats, and to contact U.S. Customs before setting sail.

The first Sunday in May, fifty-seven vessels carrying thirty-six hundred Cubans arrived. Thousands flooded into Miami in subsequent days. For many newcomers, the arrival climaxed years of waiting. One former science professor recalled shivering with excitement during the bus trip to Mariel Harbor as he looked down the hill and saw hundreds of lights from the endless string of boats come to take them away. When he got to Florida, he was so relieved that, upon disembarking, he stopped the queue to sing a hymn of thanks for finally having reached freedom.

President Jimmy Carter denounced the boatlift even as he worried over political repercussions for doing so. Locked in a bitter presidential-nomination battle with Edward Kennedy, Carter had no desire to offend liberal Democrats who supported his humanitarian values. Neither—amid rumors that a quarter-million Cubans were waiting to come—did he wish to bring a new torrent of refugees into a region already suffering exhaustion and high unemployment. Seeing no graceful way to stem the tide, the White House abruptly reversed itself, and Carter pledged to welcome the Marielitos with "an open heart and open arms."

For several months, the Congressional Black Caucus had debated how to address the Haitian issue. To embrace the Haitian refugees would be to reject the Haitian government. Some members—Congressman Charles Diggs from Michigan, in particular—were reluctant to criticize a black government's record on human rights, fearing such criticism might open the floodgates for condemnation of a number of black African regimes. Shirley Chisholm, the daughter of immigrants (a Guyanese father and Barbadian mother), had been asked to lead a task force to come up with a Black Caucus strategy. When the Mariel exodus erupted, Brenda Pillors, an aide to Congresswoman Chisholm, took a call from Dale Frederick "Rick" Swartz, an attorney with the Lawyers' Committee for Civil Rights Under Law, who had helped represent Haitians in Miami. "We've just been blown out of the water," cried Swartz. "Mariel is going to kill our issue." Rulx Jean-Bart, a community organizer for the Haitian Refugee Center, thought otherwise. "I was not sure what to expect, but it was clear to us that we could exploit it politically, because we had boat people coming here under the same conditions," he recalled.

On May 14—with more than fifty thousand Marielitos landed in Florida—Carter ordered an end to the flotilla. He also promised that the U.S. government would transport the remaining Cubans—provided a plan could be worked out with Castro for orderly departure and screening of emigrants. The day after Carter's order, more than six thousand Cubans arrived. The next day, another four thousand landed at Key West, and thousands more were en route or waiting at Mariel.

The flotilla was not Miami's only source of stress. In neighboring Tampa, four white policemen were on trial for causing the death of black insurance man Arthur McDuffie. Five months earlier, McDuffie had been captured on a motorcycle after a high-speed chase. While handcuffed, he had been beaten to death. Because of the potential for violence in the racially charged case, the trial had been moved to predominantly white Tampa—which had resulted in an all-white jury. The case had no direct connection to the Mariel migration, but for many Miamians the linkage was inescapable. As Marielitos poured into Miami, numerous black Americans could not help but compare the status of the Cuban exile community with that of their own. "We are third-class citizens in our own country," a community activist lamented. "At least in other cities, blacks are second class. But here, we're not even up to that." "They bring everybody to Miami—Nicaraguans, Cubans, Haitians. And we're still on the bottom," a resident of the predominantly black Liberty City neighborhood complained.

Shortly after the boatlift began, the Reverend Irvin Elligan, Jr., chairman of the Dade County Community Relations Board, had warned, "From every angle, every perspective . . . Dade County is in a state of crisis. . . . The potential for open conflict . . . is a clear and present danger." His concern centered largely on attitudes—and conditions—in Miami's black neighborhoods, which he found in an alarmingly volatile state. For many in those neighborhoods, the trial, in effect, had become a test—a way of judging how seriously black Miamians' grievances and aspirations would be taken in a city preoccupied with absorbing people from somewhere else.

After deliberating two hours and forty-four minutes, the jury found the defendants innocent of all thirteen counts. An ex-policeman who had testified against his former colleagues called the verdict "the most sickening thing I ever saw in my life." The dead man's mother cried out in court, "They're guilty. They're guilty. God will take care of them now."

Many residents of Liberty City were in no mood to wait for God. Following the reading of the verdict, a large crowd smashed the front entrance of the Dade County Metro Public Safety Department. Police scattered the mob, but anger mounted; and as the warm Saturday afternoon turned to evening, rage exploded in random destruction. Two whites were pulled from cars and beaten to death. Two others—one with a lopped-off ear, a slashed tongue, and a bullet hole in his side—were rescued by police. By the time night was over, four persons were dead and more than one hundred had been treated at hospitals. The turmoil continued through Sunday. Several policemen contributed to the anarchy—waking one community shortly before dawn by smashing windshields in a Zayre parking lot where they apparently believed rioters had parked. By Monday, with fifteen persons dead—and nearly four thousand national guardsmen on duty—the violence had all but subsided. Through it all, Castro's castaways kept coming; the weekend of the riot, fourteen died at sea as their boat capsized in five-foot waves.

That a riot would erupt in the midst of the Mariel crisis was, in large measure, no more than a coincidence of fate— though some recognized it as much more. "Members of the black community without jobs saw Cubans coming into the area and obtaining jobs and even political positions that have not been available to black people in three hundred years in this country," observed Detroit mayor Coleman Young. Whether connected or not, the riot and the refugees fused for many Miamians—and for much of the world looking on—into an unsettling portrait of Miami. At the same time the image of the new émigrés—who early on had been hailed as heroes— was changing for the worse.

Two of the refugees, upon arrival, were hit with criminal charges for hijacking a plane to Cuba in the 1960s. Others were said to be transvestites, common criminals, or released residents of mental institutions. For many older and more settled Cubans, the newcomers created substantial discomfort. The old-timers felt compelled to reach out to them and to ease the transition in whatever way they could. Yet they worried also that the new arrivals might undo the progress they had struggled to achieve. The press, initially so supportive, did little to alleviate such concerns. "Miami Beach is filled with stories of refugee criminals, with wild rumors of how hordes of newly arrived Cubans have preyed upon the elderly. But some of the stories are more than empty rumors," reported the *Miami Herald* as it related the tale of four refugees who had stolen a man's car, money, and jewelry.

Without doubt, the new Cubans were different from the old. Though few were actually criminals (under 2 percent were convicted felons), many were from the lower echelons of Cuban society. Roughly 71 percent of the newcomers were blue-collar workers compared to 22 percent of previous arrivals, and 70 percent were male. A large proportion of the Marielitos were also single, and many were black. The new arrivals more closely resembled the racial composition of Cuba—which counted approximately 70 percent of its residents as white— than of the nearly 95 percent white group that had fled shortly after the revolution.

By the end of May (at which point roughly one hundred thousand had arrived), relief workers were having difficulties coming up with sponsors for the exiles—particularly for those who were young, black, male, and unattached. More than eight thousand Marielitos remained at Eglin Air Force Base in Florida. Some nineteen thousand were at Fort Chaffee in Arkansas, and nearly as many languished at Indiantown Gap, Pennsylvania. Hundreds also were still sleeping in cots at the Orange Bowl.

As Miami strained under the weight of its newest flow of immigrants, Port-au-Prince rocked with fireworks of celebration as President Jean-Claude Duvalier took the hand of Michele Bennett in marriage. The ceremony occurred in Notre Dame Basilica, bedecked with thousands of Florida flowers flown down for the occasion. Following a 101-cannon salute, the Duvaliers and four thousand guests retired to the presidential ranch at Crox-di-Bouquet for a lobster feast and dancing. Haiti's several million poor—though not allowed at the wedding— were provided for through a special government grant of $300,000 for parties in the streets. For many Haitian expatriates, the multimillion-dollar extravaganza was an outrage that epitomized the excesses that had driven them from their home—excesses even the U.S. government acknowledged, while insisting that Haitians still did not qualify as refugees.

The U.S. position made many members of the Carter administration uncomfortable. Oliver Cromwell, then a spokesman for the Department of Health and Human Services' Office of Refugee Resettlement, recalls that many of his HHS colleagues felt the Haitians deserved as much compassion as the Cubans; and they objected to Haitians routinely being arrested while others with reasonable claims to refugee status entered the United States without difficulty. Still, with national unemployment at nearly 8 percent (and rising) and with the nation suffering through a recession, the White House was hesitant to embrace the Haitians, particularly when administration plans already called for letting in 230,000 refugees (primarily Indochinese) before the year was out. Adding an additional 115,000 or so Cubans and another 16,000 Haitians—plus expenses for resettlement—would be risking public outrage. And even if the public accepted it, Carter could not assume that Congress would.

Trapped between unpleasant options—and under pressure from Kennedy and the Black Caucus to act—Carter decided, in effect, to change the rules of the game. He paroled the refugees in as "Cuban/Haitian entrants," a newly invented status that placed both groups in a definitional limbo somewhere between refugee and illegal alien. For the Marielitos, it meant fewer benefits than those enjoyed by previous groups of Cubans; and for the Haitian boat people, it meant that they finally would be something other than pariahs. The new designation also allowed the government to pay about one third of the resettlement costs it would have borne under the new Refugee Act. The funds would be sufficient for the Haitians and Cubans to survive, but "not at a level that represents an invitation for future arrivals," said Carter's refugee coordinator.

Many critics saw the policy as an absurdity, and Carter's unwillingness to use the Refugee Act—and to take the political heat for doing so—as an act of moral cowardice. "After two months of not making decisions, the Carter administration has reached a nondecision on the Cubans," said Kennedy, who also castigated Carter for dumping resettlement costs on states, local governments, and voluntary agencies. Elizabeth Holtzman, head of the House Immigration Subcommittee, was even more caustic: "The administration has labored since April and brought forth a mouse."

The Carter approach of cutting back funds for exiles' assimilation while simultaneously granting permission for them to stay struck many local officials as an evasion of federal responsibility—and led an outraged Dade County school board to defy federal rules requiring special acculturation programs for refugee children. "We will do everything we can with the money we have, but we are not going to take anything from the other students," explained school-board member Robert Renick.

Yet Haitian activist Jean-Bart saw the new status as a significant improvement over what had existed previously: "You could get food stamps. You could get health care. . . . It was a very good sign." Moreover, in renouncing its efforts to categorically deport Haitians, the government was finally making a concession Haitian exiles had long sought: recognizing—if only in the most left-handed manner—that maybe their cries of persecution were not altogether self-serving. And even though the new status was odd and unprecedented, it would allow most "entrants" to eventually become permanent resident aliens—and, presumably, American citizens.

Less than a month after the Carter administration's action, U.S. district judge James King handed down a decision that offered protection to many Haitians who had arrived before the Marielitos and who therefore were not covered by the new White House program. The ruling resulted from a suit filed by the Haitian Refugee Center alleging discrimination against Haitians seeking asylum.

The Haitians came to America seeking freedom, noted King, but "what they found was an Immigration Service which sought to send them back without any hearing . . . and a systematic program designed to deport them irrespective of the merits of their asylum claims. . . . They came to a land where both local officials and private groups were compassionate . . . and then their applications for asylum were denied *en masse* by a somewhat less than compassionate INS. . . . Much of the evidence is both shocking and brutal, populated by the ghosts of individual Haitians—including those who have been returned from the United States—who have been beaten, tortured and left to die in Haitian prisons. Much of the evidence is not brutal but simply callous—evidence that INS officials decided to ship all Haitians back to Haiti because their continued presence in the United States had become a problem."

All Haitians seeking political asylum had been initially turned down, observed King, and only a few had been granted asylum upon reconsideration. Yet, he pointed out, prior to the Mariel exodus, all Cubans routinely had been granted asylum. How was that justified, he asked, when Haiti was "the most oppressive regime in the hemisphere"? He ordered that the Haitians not be deported unless they received a fair hearing.

Later that year, Federal District Judge Alcee L. Hastings reversed an Immigration Service decision to revoke work authorization for Haitian refugees until their asylum claims could be resolved. That ruling resulted in work permission not only for the Haitians but also for the growing numbers of Nicaraguans converging on Miami.

Those triumphs were not without cost. They contributed to the feeling—in Miami and in the nation—that the United States was no longer in control of its borders, that escapees from anywhere could simply wash up on Miami Beach and depend on America to take them in. One woman who identified herself as the president of the Northeast Miami Improvement Association wrote to the editors of *The New York Times:* "I urge you and your readers to think about how you would like . . . to bear the burden of 60,000 to 100,000 illegal aliens, most of them unskilled, uneducated, unhealthy, illiterate, non-English-speaking and unacquainted with modern customs, including sanitary practices and traffic laws. Perhaps you would like to offer to take some of these people into your communities and neighborhoods."

Such sentiments sprang in part from the sheer size of the inflow. (By September 26, when the last boats were ordered out of Cuba, a total of 125,000 exiles had left the harbor at Mariel. By late December, all but about six thousand had been resettled—with more than half of the total ending up in the Miami area.) Also, because the migration had come in such a frenzied manner, with thousands of émigrés landing daily, many Floridians had felt under siege.

Few within Anglo Miami saw the Mariel influx as any kind of boon. In a poll of readers conducted that fall, the *Miami Herald* found that 68 percent of non-Hispanic whites and 57 percent of blacks expected the new Cubans to have a detrimental impact on Miami. A poll, however, could hardly capture the emotions many felt at seeing the city—in their view—snatched away by foreigners. "We have been Cubanized to death," one resident fumed. Much of the resentment was channeled into an English-language campaign.

"We'd like to keep Dade County as part of America," explained Emma Shafer, a German immigrant who led the effort to get 26,213 signatures supporting an English-only referendum. The referendum, placed on the November ballot, prohibited spending Dade County's money for "the purpose of utilizing any language other than English or promoting any culture other than that of the United States." It also mandated that all county meetings, hearings, and publications be in English only. The crusade clearly had less to do with English than with the need to register a protest at what Miami was becoming.

Many American blacks—though hardly sanguine about the

coming of the Cubans—saw the English-only referendum as a pernicious response. For it seemed designed not only to harass the newcomers, but to further enshrine white culture as law. "This statement implies that the only culture that should be promoted is that of the dominant group, the North American white group," said a resolution passed by the Greater Miami chapter of the National Association for the Advancement of Colored People. Some whites were equally alarmed. "What is United States culture?" asked Dade County attorney Robert Ginsburg. "After all, Florida was discovered by Ponce de Leon and certainly Spanish was spoken here long before English."

Such reservations notwithstanding, the proposal easily passed—by a ratio of three to two. An estimated 71 percent of non-Latino white voters supported the measure, according to a *Miami Herald* survey. The majority of blacks rejected it. Latinos—while over 40 percent of Dade County's population—then accounted for only 17.2 percent of those registered to vote since less than half were U.S. citizens.

In the aftermath of the Liberty City riot, Florida's legislators talked much about providing money for redevelopment of black areas of the city. Very little was forthcoming. State representative Barry Kutun gave one explanation of why. "No way," he said, "will legislation be passed that will be a reward for rioting." The statement was more than an expression of outrage against rioters. It was also saying that Miami was not one community but at least three—black, Anglo, and Hispanic—and that the riots, having taken place in the black community, were that community's problem. Such tribalism was to become emblematic of Miami's politics as it was for many cities in America. And repeatedly Miami was to explode because of it—with riots after the shooting of blacks by white and Latino policemen, with fisticuffs after the ejection of a Haitian from a Cuban-American store, and in a thousand untallied ways as the citizens of Dade County went about their daily lives.

Shortly after the Mariel influx, *Business Week* ruminated on "the country's failure to come to grips with the mass migration of peoples from Latin America" and the economic and social

strains they would exert on "an already fragile social fabric."
The weekly concluded that Mariel "has focused the attention
of the nation on a problem too long ignored. If a solution is
not found soon, the nation is heading for social and economic
explosions that will make the recent fiery riots in Miami . . .
look like a Boy Scout's campfire."

With an urgency reminiscent of the 1920s, America was
focusing on immigration, on the ostensible flooding of the
borders, and on questions of how to absorb—or keep out—
those who seemed, in some fundamental sense, unassimilable.
In a way that even the most unaware person could understand, Mariel had dramatically illustrated the problems lurk-
ing at the door; and it had provided an incentive—for some,
at least—to fight to keep those problems out.

11

🎇

After the Deluge

The Mariel influx had barely ended when Ronald Reagan accepted the 1980 Republican presidential nomination, invoking a favorite theme: "Can we doubt that only a Divine Providence placed this land, this island of freedom, here as a refuge for all those people in the world who yearn to breathe free? Jews and Christians enduring persecution behind the Iron Curtain; the boat people of Southeast Asia, Cuba and of Haiti; the victims of drought and famine in Africa, the freedom fighters in Afghanistan, and our own countrymen held in savage captivity." Yet America, sweating through the aftermath of Mariel and a continuing stream of Indochinese and Mexican migrants, increasingly wondered—in a world of billions yearning "to breathe free"—where to draw the line.

What impact would so many newcomers have on America's most treasured institutions and ideas? Would they fade inconspicuously into the landscape or create cultural and financial chaos? Would they overwhelm school systems, drive up unemployment, wreck municipal budgets, and make America one huge slum? Or would they, like a sprinkling of precious spice, enhance the best of what America already was? For many of America's most thoughtful, the early 1980s became a time to reflect on what the future might hold if present trends continued.

Colorado governor Richard Lamm argued that in the past immigrants had served the nation well, but in the 1980s, they could only hurt. "America is no longer a nation of empty frontiers in need of settling," suggested Leon Bouvier of Washington's Population Reference Bureau. That those arguments were precisely the same that restrictionists had employed in the 1920s and 1950s did not make them any less timely to the public. With news reports accusing Marielitos of rioting, rape, and murder, and commentators suggesting Mexicans were putting U.S. citizens out of work, many Americans were saying enough is enough. Eighty percent wanted legal immigration slashed, and 91 percent favored action against illegal immigrants.

The Christian Science Monitor warned of mounting ethnic tensions: "Backlash is already felt as a result of economic strains placed on New Jersey, Florida, and other communities. . . . Beyond such temporary strains is also the uneasy and growing feeling that the country's basic social cohesiveness may be threatened by the uncontrolled entry of immigrants, especially of Spanish-speaking migrants, and the inability to assimilate them fast enough to prevent social and political divisiveness." Author Theodore White hinted at grave social consequences for America's major cities as they became beset by "minority cultures so different from the general culture." "Whether these new immigrants can, as did the earlier waves, bridge the gap between their own cultures and the European culture which in the past shaped American life is the great social experiment of our time," wrote White.

Nowhere was the matter given greater thought than in California, where more immigrants were settling than anywhere else, placing great strain on public services. In Los Angeles County, where one seventh of the residents were thought to be illegal immigrants, officials estimated they spent $214 million serving the undocumented population in fiscal 1980–

81. Health-care costs alone were put at $100 million annually. Troubled by the prospect of spiraling medical expenses, the Los Angeles Board of Supervisors voted to bar illegal entrants from a free health-care program intended for the area's poor.

More frightening to many than costs was the prospect of cultural conflict. The *Los Angeles Times,* for instance, warned in 1981 that gangs of poor, desperate inner-city Latino and black youths had taken to preying on middle-class white suburbs. Long Beach prosecutor Arthur Jean described the behavior of the "marauders": "You can be sitting in your home on Christmas Eve, sitting around with a group of people, and there's a knock at the door. You answer the door. A gun comes into your face. You back off with your family and friends. Everyone is robbed—and one of the women is culled out and into the other room to be raped."

Between 1950 and 1980, Latinos in Los Angeles County had grown from just under 7 percent to nearly 30 percent of the population. Non-Hispanic whites made up barely half of the county's residents, with the percentage rapidly declining. The crime wave, argued the *Times,* was attributable to the blacks and Latinos taking their place. The criminals were much alike, noted the *Times,* but "the Latinos have taken a larger leap into robbery, burglary and illegal possession of weapons." In Sacramento residents were less concerned about minority malefactors than about basic cultural incompatibility; there, a group of homeowners, claiming Vietnamese refugees were stealing and eating their pets, asked a grand jury to consider the prospect of setting up internment camps for the Indochinese. In Santa Ana—where more than half of the population was Latino—a referendum to reorganize city government that was expected to result in increased Latino representation was defeated, in part by pamphlets warning of the city turning into a slum. Santa Ana city councilwoman Patricia McGuigan summed up the public's anxieties with: "It's the influx over the border . . . The area's just teeming with them . . . People are threatened. They are mad, they are resentful and they are becoming prejudiced."

Many whites were simply leaving. In the San Gabriel Valley, the proportion of whites dropped from 78 percent in 1970 to less than half that in the 1980s, as the Asian and Latino populations soared. In Orange County, whose minority population was also skyrocketing, a polling expert found widespread worries that property values would drop, the crime rate rise, and higher taxes be needed to accommodate the newcomers. Whites, he asserted, "came out here to get away from this."

Similar frustration was building outside of California. In Arlington, Virginia, the Central American and Southeast Asian populations had shot up so much that nearly forty cents of every public-health dollar was going to refugee needs, calculated the Department of Human Resources. In Arizona an overburdened hospital won a court ruling that the county—not hospitals—had to bear the cost of emergency medical care for illegal entrants. In Washington John Tanton's Federation for American Immigration Reform announced formation of a political-action committee to support those candidates who would work to eliminate uncontrolled immigration.

Despite widespread demands for action against illegal entrants, federal policymakers were not convinced that any feasible response would be adequate. Many were inclined to agree with Dale Cozart, a border-patrol official in El Paso, Texas, who insisted that trying to stop illegal migration would be "like trying to push the ocean back." "We have neither the resources, the capability, nor the motivation to uproot and deport millions of illegal aliens, many of whom have become, in effect, members of the community," admitted Attorney General William French Smith.

Within months of taking office, reacting to outrage over the Mariel/Haitian inundation, Reagan, despite his convention rhetoric, denounced the Haitian boat people as a "serious national problem detrimental to the interests of the United States" and ordered the Coast Guard to intercept and board vessels in international waters and turn back those trafficking in illegal migrants. Yet, the Haitians—according to U.S. Justice Department estimates—accounted for less than 2 percent of illegal immigration. Stopping their boats on the high seas had no effect on the infinitely larger flow across the Mexican border; and Reagan appeared most uncertain of how—or whether—to stop the stampede from the south. In an interview with CBS newsman Walter Cronkite, the president—who enjoyed warm relations with Mexican president José López Portillo—appeared to believe that allowing Mexicans to slip across the border was merely providing a needed safety valve: "We have to remember we have a neighbor and a friendly nation on an almost two thousand–mile border down there. And they have an unemployment rate that is far beyond anything—a safety valve has to be some of that that we're calling 'illegal immigration' right now."

Through the years, Congress had been scarcely less befuddled than the president in trying to sort out immigration priorities. To clear up the confusion, Congress had created a blue-ribbon Select Commission on Immigration and Refugee Policy in 1978. The sixteen-member commission reserved eight seats for members of Congress, equally apportioned between Democrats and Republicans on the House and Senate Judiciary Committees. Four slots went to Cabinet members and four to luminaries not employed by the federal government. Chaired by University of Notre Dame president Theodore M. Hesburgh, the commission concluded its deliberations early in 1981 with the release of a report that said the United States must recognize when to say enough is enough: "If it is a truism to say that the United States is a nation of immigrants, it is also a truism that it is one no longer, nor can it become a land of unlimited immigration. As important as immigration has been and remains to our country, it is no longer possible to say . . . that we should take all of the huddled masses yearning to be free."

In its essence the report was (or at least was looked upon as) less an overall immigration game plan than a blueprint to deal with what official Washington—and much of the American public—saw as the central problem: the large and uncontrolled illegal flow into the United States. "One does not have to be able to quantify in detail all of the impacts of undocumented/illegal aliens in the United States to know that there are some serious adverse effects. Some U.S. citizens and resident aliens who can least afford it are hurt by competition for jobs and housing and a reduction of wages and standards at the workplace. The existence of a fugitive underground class is unhealthy as a whole and may contribute to ethnic tensions," concluded the commission.

Moreover, the spectacle of hordes of foreigners cascading into the United States was deeply disturbing to Americans: "Nothing about immigration—even widespread visa abuse and illegal border crossings—seems to have upset the American people more than the Cuban push-out of 1980. . . . Their presence brought home to most Americans the fact that U.S. immigration policy was out of control. It also brought many letters to the Select Commission calling for restrictions on U.S. immigration." The commission struggled mightily to respond to such concerns, even as it tried to satisfy advocates of increased immigration.

The plan, basically, called for shutting down the border as tightly as possible, legalizing most of the undocumented migrants who had already settled in the United States—and making life virtually intolerable for any who tried to follow. Such a strategy, noted the commission, would require substantially more manpower at the border—which at present was guarded by a maximum of 450 border-patrol agents at any given time. And it would require punishing those employers who persisted in hiring illegal migrants.

Yet once the door was slammed shut, argued the commission, America would gain nothing by keeping the undocumented in an illegal status—and would be wise to legalize them. For one thing, "No longer exploitable at the workplace, these persons no longer will contribute to depressing U.S. labor standards and wages." Encouraging them to step forward would provide information on how people were smuggled into the United States and therefore "will contribute to the targeting of enforcement resources to stop illegal migration in the future." The commission also saw amnesty for illegal entrants as a matter of basic fairness: "Many undocumented/illegal migrants were induced to come to the United States by offers of work from U.S. employers who recruited and hired them under protection of present U.S. law. A significant minority of undocumented/illegal aliens have been part of a chain of family migrants to the United States for at least two generations."

Father Hesburgh spoke of his evenhanded approach as "closing the back door to undocumented/illegal migration" while "opening the front door a little more to accommodate legal migration in the interests of this country." In striving to maintain a political consensus, the commission very consciously avoided some areas considered highly controversial; it did not, for instance, forthrightly recommend striking down laws excluding aliens who were communist or homosexual. (Instead, the committee delicately suggested that the present exclusionary grounds not be retained.) Nor—despite the strong feelings of some commission members—did it recommend the adoption of a national identity card. Because of its balanced tone, the report was embraced by politicians across the political spectrum and became the starting point for a searching—and, as it turned out, divisive and years-long—debate.

The commission's recommendations were formally presented in May 1981 at congressional hearings cochaired by Romano Mazzoli (who headed the House Subcommittee on Immigration, Refugees and International Law) and Alan Simpson (chairman of the Senate Subcommittee on Immigration and Refugee Policy). The fundamental conflict that would define the debate surfaced almost immediately. The American Federation of Labor and Congress of Industrial Organizations and the NAACP endorsed penalties for employers of undocumented immigrants as a way of protecting American workers. The Mexican American Legal Defense and Education Fund sharply disagreed. "For . . . Americans who share the physical characteristics of persons thought to be undocumented, employer sanctions will exacerbate . . . discrimination. Well-meaning employers . . . will shy away from hiring us. Racist . . . employers will simply use the fear of sanctions as an excuse to avoid hiring us," said Vilma Martinez, president and general counsel of MALDEF.

Simpson and Mazzoli dismissed her concerns and introduced identical legislation, on Saint Patrick's Day, 1982, called the Immigration Reform and Control Act. Its centerpiece was employer sanctions. "Illegal aliens come here to work and unless we end that lure, the flow will never stop," explained Mazzoli. In addition to establishing fines and prison terms for those employing illegal entrants, the bill gave the executive branch three years to develop a system to help employers determine who was eligible to work. Despite Reagan administration suggestions that they do so, Simpson and Mazzoli proposed no new "guest-worker" program; nor did they advocate giving Reagan "immigration emergency" powers he had sought—to close down harbors, airports, and roads in the event of a future invasion of undocumented immigrants.

Under the Simpson-Mazzoli bill, undocumented immigrants who arrived before 1980 would be allowed to apply for citizenship within a maximum of seven years. Those who arrived before 1978 could become permanent residents immediately and apply for citizenship in five years; and those who arrived after January 1, 1980, would, in most cases, said Mazzoli, "have to go back home." To its sponsors, the approach seemed both sensible and politically sound. Hispanic opposition, they assumed, would be largely defused by the prospect of lawful sanctuary for millions—mostly Latinos—who lived in constant fear of discovery and deportation and who, through legalization, would finally be allowed to emerge from society's shadows. At the same time, Simpson-Mazzoli's hard line on employers would show that America at long last was serious about taking control of its borders. Events would prove the legislators' assumptions to be gravely flawed, as their foray into immigration politics turned into a years-long ordeal.

Neither politician had handled immigration legislation previously. To Mazzoli's constituents, who lived largely in Louisville, Kentucky, immigration was not an important issue. His only connection to the subject was through Select Commission chairman Theodore Hesburgh, who had risen to the presidency of the University of Notre Dame (in 1952) while Mazzoli was an undergraduate. The two had stayed in touch.

But not until the 1980 elections—when two subcommittee chairs fell vacant—did Mazzoli, first elected to Congress in 1970, think of taking over House stewardship of immigration. Immigration Subcommittee head Elizabeth Holtzman was running—unsuccessfully, as it turned out—for the U.S. Senate, and Father Robert Drinan's chairmanship of the Criminal Justice Subcommittee was ended by Pope Paul II's edict that Catholic priests could not hold elective office. Either chairmanship, Mazzoli was told, was his. Criminal justice, he realized, was the politically sounder choice. As captain of the House's war on crime, he could author a host of tough-sounding bills, generate a torrent of favorable publicity, and swiftly become the congressional equivalent of a crime-busting crusader; but Father Hesburgh urged him to accept immigration, as did Dan Lungren—a Judiciary Committee colleague (and Republican) from Long Beach, California, who had also gone to Notre Dame.

Lungren argued that the subcommittee had long been the province of Easterners with large immigrant constituencies who were constrained by tradition and politics from making tough and proper calls. Mazzoli, however, would be free to vote his conscience and to make a meaningful mark on society. That appealed to Mazzoli, as did the thought of continuing Father Hesburgh's work. That he would also be carrying on the work of Peter Rodino—a former Immigration Subcommittee chairman—was a plus; for Rodino, chief of the Judiciary Committee, would be a key source of support. In fact, Rodino's identification with immigration was so strong that some members of his staff were distressed that Mazzoli, not Rodino, would be championing (and attaching his name to) the most important immigration legislation of the era. Nonetheless, Rodino pledged Mazzoli total cooperation, confident that when, maneuvering over, the bill began in earnest, he—as full committee chairman—would be "in a position to really lead it, direct it, move it."

Simpson, a former state legislator elected to the U.S. Senate in 1978, had been introduced to immigration policy as a member of the Select Commission. Because undocumented workers were not much of an issue in Cody, Wyoming, where he had practiced law, Simpson had been surprised when Senate Minority Leader Howard Baker told him he would be named to one of the eight congressional seats on the commission. When Simpson protested that he knew little about immigration, he was advised that Strom Thurmond—Judiciary's ranking Republican—had already recommended him, and that, as the committee's newest member, he had best acquiesce.

Ronald Reagan's landslide had left Republicans controlling the Senate, and therefore the committee chairmanships. South Carolinian Strom Thurmond had taken over the Judiciary Committee chair—along with responsibility for immigration—from Edward Kennedy, who had dissolved the Immigration Subcommittee as a way of maintaining direct control of immigration legislation. Thurmond did not share Kennedy's passion for immigration and had reconstituted the subcommittee, offering Simpson the chairmanship. "I'm fully aware," Simpson said shortly thereafter, "I'm going to be called a Neanderthal, uncaring, an unloving slob, a racist and just some old cob." But he insisted that his voice was that of America herself: "There is one group of people in the world that is not being heard, and that's the people of the United States of America that are already here. I think their cares and fears and concerns should be addressed on this issue, instead of addressing what we do to the Dominican Republic, what we do to the Caribbean, what we do to Mexico or Canada."

When the Simpson-Mazzoli bill was proposed, *The New York Times* raved that it was "at once tough, fair and humane" and applauded the legislators' masterful act in balancing "the ideas of the Administration and a blue-ribbon immigration commission; of labor, employers and minority groups; of different regions; of other countries." Such admiration was not shared by the Mexican American Legal Defense and Education Fund, the League of United Latin American Citizens, the National Council of La Raza, and the U.S. Chamber of Commerce, all of whom warned that the bill would create new discrimination against "Hispanic-looking" workers. "A law that requires the federal government's permission before a U.S. citizen can accept a job and before an employer can hire that U.S. citizen is both extremely costly and unworkable," contended chamber attorney Christopher Luis.

Simpson's insistence that the bill's prospects were excellent proved to be half right. It passed the Senate by a four-to-one margin that August—but got bogged down in the House after running into opposition from a ragtag coalition of agribusiness, labor, Latinos, and civil libertarians. That such a challenge emerged was an indication of how much Washington (and America) was changing. In 1972, with the backing of the Nixon White House, Congressman Peter Rodino had introduced legislation to fix fines for those who employed undocumented workers. Even without the carrot of legalization, his proposal had passed the House in 1972 and again in 1973. Neither Latino groups nor mainstream liberals had protested. The bill had died primarily because Senate Judiciary Committee chairman James Eastland had ignored it. Since then, numerous human- and civil-rights proponents—already embroiled in America's ongoing refugee crises—had focused on broad immigration-policy issues. At the same time, Hispanic organizations were experiencing a political awakening. Several had fought in the bruising battle (concluded in summer 1982) over extension of the Voting Rights Act, and they had every intention of interjecting themselves into the congressional immigration debate—especially since many had felt excluded from the Select Commission process.

At first Hispanic rights advocates were uncertain how to proceed. The virulent anti-alien campaign of former INS director Leonard Chapman and the emergence of the English Only movement had "put us . . . on the defensive," recalled Raúl Yzaguirre, head of the National Council of La Raza. More so than most Latino organizations, NCLR was searching for a middle ground, for a way of addressing concerns about the legislation's likely discriminatory impact while retaining NCLR's reputation as a team player and a moderate voice. In the aftermath of the bill's overwhelming passage by the Senate, NCLR found its commitment to moderation crumbling. For one thing, growers easily won expansion of the so-called H-2

program, allowing temporary workers into the country and
paving the way for government-sanctioned worker exploitation. For another, said NCLR lobbyist Charles Kamasaki, "We
knew in our bones this [legislation] was going to cause discrimination," but that concern was being ridiculed by many whom
NCLR had thought of as friends. Kamasaki and his allies ultimately saw no solution other than to "carry out really what
amounts to . . . guerrilla warfare" when the Senate-passed bill
moved to the House. Instead of genteelly attending hearings
and offering a few amendments, NCLR and its allies did
"everything and anything necessary and possible to slow down,
discourage, and make painful the movement of this bill."

For others the decision was not nearly so tortuous or trau-
matic. Both the Mexican American Legal Defense and Education Fund and the League of United Latin American Citizens
concluded early on that the Simpson-Mazzoli bill—unless radically restructured—was worse than no bill at all. In a *New York
Times* op-ed piece, MALDEF complained, "The Simpson-Mazzoli H-2 program is really just a replay of the bracero [Mexi-
can labor] program." MALDEF also felt the sanctions program
would lead to an avalanche of discrimination complaints, and
therefore to an immense drain on organizational resources.
Long after the debate was over, MALDEF—an organization
comprised largely of litigators—feared it would be fighting
lawsuits. MALDEF felt it could not give in—whatever the cost.
"I would dance with the devil if I had to, to see this bill not
pass," said Antonia Hernández, a MALDEF lobbyist who was
eventually to head the organization.

Hernández had originally came to Washington to work on
the Senate Judiciary Committee under Kennedy. At the time,
Kennedy—also a member of the Select Commission—was obsessed with his presidential campaign, meaning the commission's strongest liberal voice was often absent from the dialogue
as commissioners drifted in directions that Hernández found
repugnant. She soon became convinced the commission was
an exercise in "confirming and giving credibility to predis-
posed positions." As MALDEF made the decision to stead-
fastly oppose the bill, Hernández realized that the inflexible

position might mean giving up the organization's ability "to be a player." Yet if being a player meant accepting employer sanctions, Hernández felt she had no alternative.

The League of United Latin American Citizens adopted a posture that, while stridently opposed to Simpson-Mazzoli, allowed for backpedaling if compromise became necessary. LULAC executive director Arnoldo Torres also broadened the assault beyond the legislation itself, speaking out against those—including church organizations—who supported provisions he thought detrimental to Hispanics. Some of those organizations responded by edging closer to LULAC's position, reasoning that if Hispanics felt the bill was discriminatory, "then who are we to be second-guessing that concern?" recalled Church World Service Washington representative J. Michael Myers.

The American Civil Liberties Union entered the debate out of fear that Congress would sanction a national identification card—which the ACLU thought would violate Americans' privacy rights. After taking a harder look at the pending legislation, the ACLU ended up siding with Hispanic organizations. "It became obvious this was something in need of a sharper civil liberties debate," said Wade Henderson of the ACLU Washington office. That August, John Shattuck, the ACLU's Washington director, published an op-ed piece criticizing several aspects of the Senate-passed bill, including its disallowance of court appeals for those denied asylum and its likely discriminatory impact on Hispanics. The Senate, he suggested, was more interested in controlling immigration than in providing "equal protection of the laws." Around the same time, the National Immigration Citizenship and Refugee Forum, conceived by immigrant-rights activist Rick Swartz as a coalition to deal with a range of refugee and immigrant issues, was swept into the anti–Simpson-Mazzoli camp.

Much of the press could not understand why the groups were raising such a fuss. "What's all the shouting about?" asked *The New York Times.* "The only practical right the Simpson-Mazzoli bill would curtail is the right to use counterfeit identification." "Save Simpson-Mazzoli," urged *The Washington Post,* arguing that the legislation appeared "to contain something for everyone." By then, however, the bill was in deep trouble. The measure that had sailed so swiftly through the Senate was barely alive in the House.

The main battle was fought in the House primarily because the largely pro–civil-rights, pro-immigration lobby expected little empathy in the Republican-controlled Senate. In addition, the House, being larger and more unwieldy, was infinitely more vulnerable to a guerrilla-style attack that entailed seeking out friendly legislators—Hispanics, blacks, liberals, and anyone else who showed an interest—and having them stall the measure in subcommittees for as long as possible.

By early December, the bill had cleared the subcommittee hurdles and was sent to the Rules Committee to be scheduled for debate on the floor. The legislation, fretted one editorial, had become "as delicately balanced as a clock." The AFL-CIO threatened to oppose the bill if any type of guest-worker program survived. Growers threatened to oppose it if the guest-worker program perished. Conservatives demanded the elimination of legalization. The Congressional Black Caucus urged that the bill not be voted on. And the Congressional Hispanic Caucus was threatening to procedurally tie the House in knots if the bill was brought up for consideration.

Mazzoli complained that the special interests were out to destroy the bill. The assessment was not one opponents would dispute, for the Immigration Reform and Control Act had come to be defined by its most objectionable parts. Like many compromise measures, it evoked not so much support as varying levels of reluctant acceptance. Few backers were prepared to wage war to keep it alive and, in the end, the IRCA legislation was murdered by amendment.

In arguments before the Rules Committee, the Hispanic Caucus had won the right (under a "modified open rule") for legislators to offer as many amendments as they wished—as long as those amendments were submitted in time to be printed in full in the *Congressional Record* several days before the floor debate. Organizations opposing the bill held marathon sessions writing amendments to be inserted in the *Record* by friendly lawmakers.

For Myers and his colleagues at Church World Service, the decision to participate was not easy. "There was always a tension over whether it was appropriate for us to be playing that kind of almost mean political role," said Myers. They were extremely troubled by the thought that, as a church body, they would "go around killing things"—even if the thing, in this instance, was an already-moribund bill. They rationalized the decision by concluding that they were not so much destroying the bill as offering, through their amendments, a vision of what it should be. The rationale adopted by the ACLU was similar. Uncomfortable with the idea of filibustering a bill to death, the ACLU only drafted amendments to correct what it saw as bona fide problems with the legislation. Much of the discomfort stemmed from the realities of doing business in Washington. To burden the bill with amendments would be to perpetrate a violation of House protocol. As one collaborator acknowledged, "You don't ask for an open rule and then come in with three hundred amendments." To pursue the strategy was to guarantee that some relationships—nurtured through quiet cooperation—would be strained or severed.

Many of the groups planned to funnel all their amendments through Congressman Edward Roybal of California, who was the most outspoken champion of the strategy. Others, LULAC in particular, felt that the amendments should be spread around. If a larger group was involved, the stage would be set for a broader resistance if the bill surfaced—as most assumed it would—in the succeeding session of Congress. Also, LULAC lobbyist Arnoldo Torres knew that Roybal was not a favorite of the House leadership. In the future, worried Torres, Roybal might not be able to deliver for LULAC—or perhaps would not be interested in doing so. LULAC offered its amendments to Augustus Hawkins of California, Mickey Leland of Texas, and other members of the Congressional Black Caucus. Several white members of Congress were recruited as well. Ultimately nearly three hundred amendments were presented to the lame-duck session of Congress at a time—just a few days before Christmas—when legislators were anxious to dash off to enjoy the holidays.

Roybal made much of the fact that the bill was being considered so late in an already exhausting session. The legislation, he said, had come before Congress "at the worst possible time." That almost three hundred amendments were offered, he added, was not only a show of great displeasure with the bill but a guarantee that the measure would be totally rewritten at an hour when Congress had more pressing things to do. The legislators knew—even as they went through the motions—that the bill was dead, that in the few hours allotted to debate, no more than a fraction of the amendments could be considered. Their oratory had the hollow quality of speeches not meant to persuade—but spoken for the record. Rodino used his time to recall the occasion ten years earlier when he had first implored his colleagues to take action against undocumented immigration. Mazzoli lauded Rodino as the father of the current bill. Others spoke of the need for America to better police her borders or warned that the problems of illegal immigration would not go away. The real passion in that closing session, however, was in the speeches of the blacks and Latinos.

E. "Kika" de la Garza of Texas fumed with outrage at the idea that Hispanic-looking citizens would have to prove their right to live in America every time they searched for a job. Henry Gonzalez, also of Texas, denounced what he saw as the abiding hypocrisy in U.S. immigration policies "torn between spite and generosity." "Central Americans fleeing from imminent danger are turned back," he thundered, "but Cubans who were simply an inconvenience to Castro were welcomed until we found out that most of them were black. Then all of a sudden that welcome mat was removed. All of a sudden we had a dilemma here and we start saying, well, these are all castoffs that Castro wished on us. Southeast Asians swept up in the tides of war have been welcomed, but not Haitians who live in oppression as grim as any on the face of this Earth." Do Latino congressmen "not know anything about their own problems?" roared John Conyers, calling "this charade that is going on now" an "insult to the Hispanic people of this country."

Finally Henry Hyde of Illinois moved to bring the debate

to a close. No one, he told Mazzoli, could have done a better job of tackling "the single most difficult problem, including social security, facing America." Then he acknowledged what everyone already knew, that Mazzoli's legislation was dead: "The sensitivities involved, the emotions involved, the legal questions involved are prodigious. And the time has not been wasted, even though this bill is not going to pass, because the issues have been ventilated, they are out on the table now, they will be thought about over the next few weeks, and we start the next session well ahead of the game." Hyde's tribute went on, and, as the discourse ended, the chamber erupted in a standing ovation for Mazzoli, who took the applause to mean that he would have another chance to put forth his bill—that the battle would soon be joined again.

12

No Room for
Compromise

"All we needed was time," grumbled a crestfallen
Mazzoli, following the collapse of his bill in 1982.
Later, he admitted that passage had never been in
the cards, that he was fortunate the bill even got to the House
floor. "I think [House speaker Thomas] Tip [O'Neill] was just
sort of doing us a favor," he said. O'Neill acknowledged as
much. When Congress reconvened in 1983, O'Neill remained
lukewarm to the legislation, and Latino groups were still opposed. Once again, the bill zipped through the Senate ("An
impressive win for all Americans," exclaimed *The Christian Science Monitor*) and faltered in the House. *The Washington Post*
implored Congress to complete the task "before the rush to
adjournment and the partisan pressures of an election year."
But as far as Congress was concerned, the presidential competition had already begun.

In 1980, Ronald Reagan had won roughly 30 percent of
the Hispanic vote—more than any other Republican presidential candidate in memory. He hoped to do even better in 1984,
despite polls showing that Latinos were abandoning the party.

Reagan made a point of attending a *Cinco de Mayo* celebration in San Antonio, Texas. At the fiesta in Plaza Nueva—commemorating an 1862 battle where heavily outnumbered Mexican soldiers routed the French—Reagan extolled Hispanic values and reminded his audience that his administration had placed 130 Hispanics in prominent positions.

By August 1983, Reagan was darting about the country addressing a host of Latino organizations: a Hispanic business association in Los Angeles, the United States Hispanic Chamber of Commerce in Tampa, the American GI Forum in El Paso. That same month, he jetted to La Paz, Mexico, to meet with President Miguel de la Madrid Hurtado, and also invited a group of prominent Hispanics to a White House luncheon to discuss the problems of their communities.

In September the courtship grew even more fervid. The White House proclaimed National Hispanic Heritage Week, during which Reagan held a half-dozen meetings with Hispanic groups and trotted out numerous notable Latinos, including Franklin Ramon Chang-Diaz, America's first Hispanic astronaut. At the White House ceremony to launch the week, Reagan introduced Katherine Ortega, his new nominee for U.S. treasurer, as a symbol "of the values the Hispanic community represents." He boasted once more of his Hispanic appointments and added that he soon would be appointing twenty or twenty-five more.

Tirso del Junco, the Republicans' chief Hispanic strategist, saw the overtures as a way of neutralizing hostility from women and blacks. Republicans, he contended, had a better chance of attracting Hispanics than those from communities "where eighty percent of the people are against the death penalty . . . [and] seventy-five percent are in favor of abortion." Elsewhere, the outreach effort was greeted with derision. "Mr. Reagan's idea of a statement to the Hispanic community is to point out he served enchiladas to the Queen [of England]," grumbled LULAC's Arnoldo Torres. Bob Neuman, a Democratic National Committee official, ridiculed Hispanic Heritage Week as "Hispanic Hysteria Week." The Republicans, he added, "don't know what subtlety is."

Nor were Hispanic politicians subtle in flexing their growing political muscle. New Mexico governor Toney Anaya was
heading up a coalition calling itself "Hispanic Force '84," and
a National Hispanic Voter Registration Campaign, launched
in San Antonio, Texas, set a goal of registering a million new
voters before the 1984 elections. Vice President George Bush,
who attended the San Antonio meeting, told participants that
the Reagan administration "shares the Hispanic values of family, neighborhood, church, freedom and opportunity." Edward Kennedy told the same audience that Reagan's was "the
most anti-Hispanic administration in modern history."

Such politicking notwithstanding, relatively few votes were
at stake. Though the most recent census had counted 14.6
million Hispanic residents, registration campaign organizers
estimated that only 5.5 million were American citizens old
enough to vote—of whom about 3.4 million were registered.
Hispanics, however, were disproportionately concentrated in a
few states with many electoral votes—most strikingly California and Texas—and in a close race could possibly determine
the winner.

That fact, as evident to Democrats as to Republicans, gave
the public-interest groups fighting the immigration bill a certain amount of leverage; and Hispanic lobbyists—generally
young, single, and with time to spare—made the greatest possible use of it. At the same time, Latino officials across the
country were stepping up anti–Simpson-Mazzoli rhetoric. At
a Congressional Hispanic Caucus meeting, Congressman Roybal sparked an emotional ovation by speaking out against the
bill. Others, throwing protocol to the winds, were calling supporters of the legislation "racist."

Mazzoli experienced intense frustration as his bill was twisted
by amendments while precious time was wasting. Simpson found
the hostility in the Hispanic community bewildering. At one
point, Simpson, scheduled to give a speech to a Latino organization in California, was astounded by a Secret Service request to cancel the appearance because of death threats. The
animosity was all the more baffling because he had stood up
for amnesty at a time when most conservatives abhorred the

idea of legalizing millions of undocumented Latin Americans. Infuriated by the displays of ill will, Simpson cornered Hispanic lobbyists and demanded, "How can you guys screw me?— a bald, Anglo guy from Wyoming who is going to lead two or three million of your people out of the darkness. . . . You're sticking it in my rear end. . . . I'm tired of it, but I don't have to take that crap from you. And when I go to give a speech in Denver or Detroit and there are your people wandering around in there with placards giving me the business, I'm just going to stop them right in mid-protest and say, 'Who is it that speaks for the Hispanics of this country. It sure as hell isn't your leader standing over there in that goofy-looking suit. Because if you kill my bill, there will be no amnesty. There will be nothing for you at all.' "

Blazing with such righteous indignation, Simpson recalled, "Mazzoli and I would go to their conventions and stand like a couple of two-gunners at the Old West corral and listen to them rail and rant." But if the ranting did not deter Simpson, it greatly discomfited O'Neill, who had little appetite for pushing a bill so many Latinos bitterly opposed. To make matters worse, the White House had hinted that Reagan might not sign the Simpson-Mazzoli legislation because of amendments attached by House subcommittees. One of those amendments would provide Medicaid benefits for newly legalized pregnant women and young children; another would grant certain civil-rights protections to permanent resident aliens. Attorney General William French Smith had complained to Judiciary chairman Peter Rodino that such provisions made the House bill unacceptable.

During the congressional recess, the restrictionist-minded Federation for American Immigration Reform released a poll purporting to show that blacks and Hispanics favored the Simpson-Mazzoli legislation as much as other Americans did. The survey reported that 66 percent of Hispanics who were American citizens backed employer sanctions, and that 53 percent of those who were not citizens favored sanctions. FAIR also claimed that 60 percent of blacks and 57 percent of Hispanics opposed making illegal immigrants eligible for welfare.

A majority of both groups thought "illegal immigrants hurt the job situation for American workers by taking away jobs." Minority congressional members were "totally out of step" with their constituencies in their opposition to Simpson-Mazzoli, concluded FAIR president Charles R. Stoffel. "All Americans seem to agree on this issue."

The poll was an important weapon in FAIR's public-relations war. In a fund-raising solicitation, executive director Roger Conner touted the results as a way of fighting the special-interest groups opposed to stricter immigration rules. "We can now destroy their last line of defense," wrote Conner. "We can now discredit their effort of bullying the American people and many of our congressmen." In fact, Stoffel overstated his survey findings. Not having surveyed groups other than blacks and Hispanics, he could not compare their responses to those of "all Americans." And intriguingly the FAIR poll differed radically from a statewide survey done for the *Los Angeles Times* that showed that—at least in California—Latinos' attitudes on immigration differed sharply from those of whites and blacks. Only 34 percent of Latinos in the *Los Angeles Times* survey agreed that employers "should be punished when they hire workers who come to the U.S. without proper papers." By contrast, 70 percent of whites and 85 percent of blacks agreed that they should. While 75 percent of Latinos favored amnesty for illegal immigrants, only 39 percent of Anglos and 30 percent of blacks supported the concept. Ten percent of those Latinos responding to the *Times* survey admitted they did not have immigration documents. As to be expected, the undocumented were overwhelmingly opposed to employer sanctions.

Even so, editorialists seized on FAIR's poll as evidence that Hispanic groups were misrepresenting their constituencies. "Though leaders of Hispanic organizations oppose the bill, a national survey last summer showed that a substantial majority of Hispanics favor its two major themes," declared *The New York Times*. Latino organization lobbyists were in no mood to hear their commitment to their own constituency questioned—either by anonymous editorialists or by Simpson and Mazzoli. "Who the hell were they to tell us what our interests were?" asked Kamasaki. "We made a very difficult judgment call. . . . It was pretty paternalistic and condescending on their part to tell us that we had made the wrong judgment." LULAC's Torres grumbled that the press never assailed black or Jewish leadership in such a disrespectful way.

Rumors snowballed that the House leadership would quash the bill. "Are reports true that top Democratic leaders in the U.S. House of Representatives are deliberately attempting to bury the Simpson-Mazzoli immigration reform bill this year?" asked *The Christian Science Monitor*. "If the reports are true, the action . . . would have to be considered a cynical effort to frustrate an overriding objective of the American people: namely, restoring order on the nation's borders." "Perhaps a partisan case could be made for denying the President a victory he might celebrate in the coming campaign," said *The New York Times*. "What a tragedy that would be for a reform that so many . . . have worked so long to achieve."

In early October, O'Neill put the rumors to rest by telling a group of Capitol Hill reporters that the legislation would not reach the floor in 1983, and perhaps not even in 1984—unless it could be rendered acceptable to Hispanic members of Congress. He had heard, said O'Neill, that President Reagan planned to allow the bill to pass and then veto it to curry favor with Latinos. O'Neill had no intention of allowing that to happen. "Do I think the president is political enough to veto a bill to gain votes for his party?" asked O'Neill rhetorically. "The answer is yes. He's the most political man I've ever seen over there." The speaker also made clear his own feelings about Simpson-Mazzoli's identification provisions, comparing them to policies practiced by Nazi Germany. "Hitler did this to the Jews, you know. He made them wear a dog tag."

For many legislators, O'Neill's action elicited a sigh of relief. "There's nobody in the House who really wants to vote on this," said Congressman Tony Coelho of California. Hispanic congressmen, in particular, were delighted. Roybal praised O'Neill for showing political courage. Robert Garcia, chairman of the Hispanic Congressional Caucus, said the speaker "put his neck on the line, and I applaud his efforts." Newspapers,

however, denounced O'Neill's act as political cowardice. And
Simpson vowed to try to change O'Neill's mind—even "if I
have to go up and sit on his front porch in Boston." Meanwhile, the White House issued a statement rejecting O'Neill's
theory of a political double cross and expressing hope that he
would reconsider "and allow the House to vote on a bill that
is essential to the future well-being of this nation." Administration officials had testified before Congress twenty-eight times
in support of the bill, said a presidential spokesman, adding,
"The President sent the original immigration reform legislation to the Congress more than two years ago. He supported
it then. He supports it today."

At a press conference several days later, Reagan said he
had worked hard for passage of the Senate bill, and that though
he had problems with the House legislation, he expected
everything could be ironed out in Senate-House conference.
"I want to sign, as quickly as possible, immigration legislation,"
he said. Around the same time, a group of twenty-one prominent Americans—including Jimmy Carter, Gerald Ford, and
Theodore Hesburgh—telegrammed O'Neill to express support for the bill.

In late October, Simpson stopped by O'Neill's office steeled
for a confrontation. "You don't even know me," railed Simpson. "Why the hell are you sticking it in me? What have I ever
done to you?" In response O'Neill told of prior occasions when
he had been blindsided by the White House. To prevent another such occurrence, Simpson promised to get presidential
approval of the bill before the House took a final vote. In return O'Neill pledged to bring the measure up for consideration before Congress adjourned in 1984, but added, "If you
say a single word about this, you'll never see your bill again."

"I didn't even tell my wife," said Simpson.

Several weeks later, O'Neill's staff announced that the
speaker would send the bill forward shortly after Congress reconvened in 1984. O'Neill was "satisfied that the political risks
have been diminished," announced aide S. Ariel Weiss, who
privately told Hispanic lobbyists that the bill was no longer
stoppable, but that the speaker would try to address their

principal concerns. Meanwhile, the bill's opponents sought to get presidential candidates to sound off against it. Democratic candidates were quite willing to play the game. Gary Hart said that U.S. immigration problems were so interrelated with Mexico's economy that no legislation could solve them and pledged to reject the Simpson-Mazzoli approach. Walter Mondale and Jesse Jackson also spoke against the bill. "We cannot have one policy for nonwhite people from the Caribbean, South and Central America and another for people from Canada and Europe," said Jackson.

LULAC executive director Torres hoped that, in addition to providing statements of opposition, the candidates—especially front-runner Mondale—would help kill the bill. In early 1984, he asked a Mondale aide to have his boss send a letter to O'Neill seeking the shelving of Simpson-Mazzoli "until the House has given full consideration to the alternative immigration legislation introduced by Congressman Edward Roybal, or any other alternative legislation which may be introduced." Eventually Mondale made the call, not only in response to LULAC's request but because the June 5 California primary was approaching, and the campaign feared the loss of Hispanic votes. During the conversation, O'Neill promised to keep the bill from being debated until the polls closed in California. By then, LULAC's demands had escalated. The organization wanted Mondale not only to maintain pressure on the Democratic leadership but to lean on the AFL-CIO.

From the perspective of many Hispanic activists, the labor federation was shaping up as a major problem. AFL-CIO president Lane Kirkland had gone on record endorsing employer sanctions as the "single most important deterrent to illegal immigration." The unionists sided with Hispanics, however, in objecting to the foreign agricultural-workers program added to the House version of the bill. "There have been no documented studies to show that American workers won't take these jobs," AFL-CIO secretary-treasurer Thomas Donahue told a House subcommittee at one point. "Dishes were washed in this country and vegetables were picked long before we had an illegal immigrant problem." Many Hispanic leaders feared the Democratic party could be placed in a position of having to choose between them or Kirkland. Former MALDEF president Vilma Martinez put the matter starkly: "For the party, it comes down to the question: Whom do you love more?" Mondale, many of them hoped, could avoid such a distressing situation by engineering a rapprochement with Kirkland.

The demands took Mondale by surprise. He had been extremely confident of his civil-rights records and of his status in the Hispanic community—"more confident than he should have been," observed deputy campaign manager George Dalley. Mondale had anticipated no particular need to cater to Hispanics. "In reality," said Dalley, "there were . . . danger signs." Despite Mondale's liberal politics and pride in his record, he had few deep ties in minority communities. As a senator, recalled Dalley, who had once worked on the Hill, "Mondale . . . would have no more than one black at a time, and generally no Hispanic [on his staff]." Mondale had followed much the same practice when selecting his campaign team.

As deputy campaign manager for "constituencies," Dalley had originally been expected to act as liaison to women and all ethnic minorities. "It became clear in the first six months," said Dalley, "that the women were not going to tolerate me being head of women's affairs." Later, Hispanics would express disappointment that Mondale had no senior Hispanic staff person but instead had designated Dalley, an African-American, to represent them. That Mondale—and the Democratic party—took Hispanics for granted was a big part of the reason the demands became as insistent, and as emotional, as they eventually did.

Putting heavy pressure on the AFL-CIO was not something Mondale was prepared to do. The AFL-CIO had been an essential element of Mondale's campaign since October 1983, when nine hundred impassioned delegates, chanting "We want Fritz!," awarded him the AFL-CIO's endorsement at the federation's annual meeting in Hollywood, Florida. That endorsement—the first ever given by the AFL-CIO prior to the major-party conventions—meant access to the AFL-CIO's nearly 14 million members, as well as to union telephone banks, newsletters, and mass-mailing services. Forced to choose between Kirkland and the Hispanic groups, Mondale would have no alternative but to choose the unions. "Bottom line, Mondale . . . did not want to risk what he had seen as the cornerstone of his strategy," said Dalley. Besides, having been called the candidate of special interests, Mondale had no desire to confirm that label by appearing to cave in to Latino demands.

In June of 1984, with the Democratic Convention a month away, O'Neill kept his promise to Simpson. To the great consternation of the Mondale campaign, Mazzoli's bill finally landed on the House floor.

The debate lasted a week. Sixty-nine amendments were offered. The most explosive, authored by Bill McCollum of Florida, would have retained employer sanctions but stripped legalization from the bill. "It is a great slap in the face and a cruel hoax that we perpetrate . . . by giving legalization to those millions who are here already illegally," declared McCollum. Don Edwards, of California, shot back in response: "We really have only three choices: we can engage in mass deportation of millions of people; we can allow them to stay here and condone their continued exploitation; or we can recognize the reality of the situation and bring them under the protection of our laws. The undocumented are here. They came illegally. There is no attempt to deny that. This outrages the American sense of justice. But the majority came out of desperation, out of hunger, out of fear. And . . . I have not heard anybody say that Americans have the heart for mass deportation, and I do not believe that we do."

Following the amendment's defeat (235 to 195), the bill finally came to a vote. For Mazzoli, who worked the House floor along with Republican counterpart Dan Lungren, seeing his handiwork at long last come before his colleagues was so important an occasion that he had his wife and daughter watch the count from the gallery.

The actual vote took roughly fifteen minutes, with cumulative totals showing on the electronic tote board. For most of that period, "no" votes were ahead of "ayes," and Mazzoli was on the edge of panic. "I looked at that score; and son of a gun, we were down. And I'm on the floor and I'm trying to talk to every member; and I don't have this thing organized as well as I . . . probably should."

He acutely felt the lack of party support. No whip apparatus was cracking, telling him who was defecting and projecting the result. Instead, Mazzoli was trying to keep track of everything himself. If he sensed an ambivalence in a colleague, he would beg for the vote. If he sensed opposition, he would plead for delay—until others, in his corner, could get the steamroller going. In at least two cases, his desperate tactics worked; he shifted two northeastern congressmen previously tilting against him into the "yes" column.

The final vote was 216 for passage and 211 against, with the majority of Mazzoli's own party members opposing him (138 to 125). "Nothing in my life," said Mazzoli, "including the birth of our children . . . left such an indelible mark on my brain as that few minutes on the floor going to final passage."

Still ahead was the House-Senate conference, during which negotiators would try to reconcile the widely disparate House and Senate versions of the bill. That would have to wait until after the Democratic and Republican conventions. For the moment, Mazzoli could savor his hard-won victory, along with the rush of media attention that it merited. "For a while," he recalled, "Al [Simpson] and I were the lions of the scene around here."

At LULAC's annual meeting, which convened shortly after the House vote, anger over passage of the bill was so great that LULAC president Mario Obledo pushed through a resolution urging Hispanic delegates to the Democratic National Convention to withhold their votes during the first ballot. Later, in a letter to the 291 Hispanic delegates, Obledo explained: "As Hispanics become more and more politically aware and active, so too do our desires to be treated fairly and with dignity. We should not accept what is offered simply because the other political party is offering so much less . . . We must break away from 'politics as usual' in an attempt to establish our own power base."

Jesse Jackson, the only presidential candidate to come to the LULAC convention, heaped abuse on the other candidates for not showing up, and in a twist on the Torres-Obledo theme, he said that black, Hispanic, and female delegates should make the first ballot one of "conscience and conviction," by which he apparently meant that they should vote for him.

Less than a month later, on the eve of the Democratic Convention, a bipartisan group of Hispanic notables—including San Antonio Mayor Henry Cisneros and Mexican-American Republican Council chairman Fernando Oaxaca—met in Los Angeles and released a statement calling the Simpson-Mazzoli legislation a "sham and an attack on our community." The group asked Cisneros to act as an emissary to Democratic party and labor officials to secure their opposition to the bill. "Already we have seen alarming instances of confused employers firing workers they believe to be here illegally," claimed former INS commissioner Leonel Castillo during the meeting.

Meanwhile, LULAC president Mario Obledo circulated a memo to Hispanic officials outlining current LULAC strategy. "It is imperative that Mondale, O'Neill, [House majority leader] Jim Wright, labor leaders and others make clear and unequivocal *public statements* during the Convention of their intent to defeat the [House-Senate conference committee version of the] Simpson-Mazzoli bill," he wrote. Obledo also considered it important that Mondale and O'Neill, "facilitate a meeting of [Lane] Kirkland and Hispanic leaders to insure that labor stick to its original position of opposition to Simpson-Mazzoli unless Hawkins-Miller [antidiscrimination] amendments are approved."

LULAC's leadership arrived at the Democratic Convention in San Francisco intent on promoting its boycott strategy unless Mondale and other party leaders agreed to vigorously fight Simpson-Mazzoli. "We recognize the boldness and courage it will take . . . but we firmly believe that this type of act is necessary in order to bring about the full integration of Hispanic political concerns within the Democratic Party," wrote Obledo in his memo to Hispanic delegates.

The threat set Democratic party bosses on edge and led to a flurry of harried meetings. Lane Kirkland promised a delegation of Hispanics to oppose Simpson-Mazzoli as presently constituted but made no guarantees concerning the eventual AFL-CIO position.

Some of those involved in the intense negotiations with Democratic party chieftains would later see that period as a benchmark for Latinos, a period during which Hispanic activism reached a new and more sophisticated level. Simpson-Mazzoli had created a cause around which Hispanics (and their allies) from every party of the country and of every political and ethnic stripe—from Cuban-American conservatives to Chicano liberals—could willingly rally. "It was the most exciting time in the history of our political presence in Washington," said Torres. "We grew up. . . . We earned our teeth."

Despite the initial show of Hispanic unity, the Democratic Convention proved an extremely frustrating affair. During the second day of the convention, Mondale met with several Hispanic luminaries—including Mayor Cisneros and Congressman Garcia—but pointedly excluded LULAC's leadership. Afterward, Mondale released a statement calling Simpson-Mazzoli a "harmful" bill that would "cause human suffering." And he pledged to communicate his opposition to the congressional leadership. Roybal declared that the statement was "good enough for the delegates and good enough for the convention."

Others attending the convention were not so easily satisfied. At a Hispanic caucus session following the Mondale meeting, Mondale's son was booed when he asked support for his father. Cisneros was also booed when he argued that abstaining would only harm Mondale, "who has already said he is against Simpson-Mazzoli," and help Ronald Reagan, "who has already said he is for it." When Roybal asserted "a more positive position [than Mondale's] could not possibly be taken by anyone in Congress," he was interrupted by shouts of "Yes, it can!" At the tumultuous meeting a motion to proceed with the boycott—prompted by delegates committed to Gary Hart and Jesse Jackson—was barely defeated by a tie vote. Obledo said a boycott remained a possibility unless the party's leadership mobilized to kill the bill.

The next day, Mondale's supporters within the caucus were better organized. They decisively defeated an attempt to resurrect the boycott. Subsequently Mondale, along with running mate Geraldine Ferraro, appeared before the caucus and pledged that Simpson-Mazzoli would die: "We're going to fight it. We're going to beat it." Mondale also offered an emotional thanks for the Hispanic support he had received throughout the election season, especially during the Texas caucuses—which Mondale had won at a critical point in the campaign. "I said then, 'If you remember me, I'll remember you,' and I will," said Mondale. Many in the room were unpersuaded; and despite the defeat of the LULAC initiative, some delegates abstained on the first ballot. The largest block—twenty-three Hispanics and four Asian-Americans—was from California. Apparently none was committed to Mondale, who easily won the nomination.

Still unsatisfied, Torres went to the Republican Convention in Dallas the following month and got José Martinez, a staff assistant to Texas senator John Tower, to arrange a meeting with his boss. Tower, who had already gone on record opposing employer sanctions, had been honored at the LULAC convention in June for his "long record of concern for Hispanics." At the meeting in Dallas, Torres secured what he interpreted as a commitment that Tower would filibuster the Simpson-Mazzoli legislation if it came up for final passage following the House-Senate conference.

When the Conference Committee convened in early September, compromise seemed a most uncertain possibility—especially given the committee's unwieldy composition. On one side were seven senators, led by Simpson, while on the other were twenty-nine congressmen representing the several committees that had claimed jurisdiction in the House, with House Judiciary chief Peter Rodino serving as chairman.

Paragraph by paragraph, the members worked their way

through the bill, with prospects for agreement shifting daily. Early on, negotiations threatened to crumple when conferees deadlocked on a House-added antidiscrimination provision, but eventually New York congressman Charles Schumer won acceptance of a compromise that retained most of the amendment's protections—though only for those legally present who had explicitly declared their intention to become citizens. Collapse was similarly averted when House members agreed to drop the foreign agricultural-workers proposal in exchange for expansion of the already-extant "H-2" program. But though the compromises brought negotiators closer to agreement, they also undermined constituent support. The agribusiness lobby, in particular, was unhappy with loss of the temporary-workers program. Conversely AFL-CIO lobbyists thought H-2 expansion a catastrophe.

Negotiations finally collapsed over disagreement on a $1-billion cap on federal payments toward health care and social services for newly legalized immigrants. The White House threatened to veto the bill unless the number was written into law. House brokers were reluctant to do that. With conferees unable to reach a compromise as Congress prepared to adjourn, Simpson dissolved the conference.

"I just decided, 'I don't have to sit here,' " said Simpson. "I had tried everything. I had been accommodating, continually, and then guys would wander into the room from other committees" who "didn't really have any sense of what the hell was going on . . . but they had to deal with [immigration]. . . . I just thought, 'This old cowboy doesn't have to take that. I'm doing one here which doesn't give me one nickel of any kind of political power, fame, fortune, what in the hell. I came here to work and these guys came here to screw around. I haven't even seen these bastards [previously].' " Simpson believed many had showed up just because television cameras were rolling, and he resented that as much as he did their uninformed comments and contributions.

The inability of conferees to agree on federal payments was widely conceded to be a face-saving stratagem to dissolve an agreement that never could have held up in the face of intense agricultural-industry opposition. "You could see that the cap was being used when you saw three legislators vote against the cap who would ordinarily have supported it because the growers in their district got to [them] and said, 'Here's a way to kill the bill,'" grumbled Simpson. Mazzoli also saw the federal funding issue as a camouflage. "In my judgment, a bill like that is not going to go down over money. . . . It went down for other reasons. There were sub-rosa signals being given out by different groups. . . . People who allegedly supported it were killing it with kindness [by getting] . . . caught up in some detail."

Harris Miller, who then worked for Mazzoli, detected the handiwork of certain Rodino staff members in the legislation's demise. "A couple of people on Rodino's staff . . . were actively trying to undermine the bill for all kinds of reasons I never quite understood. . . . [They were] making it difficult to reach compromises because one of the staff people was misleading some of the groups and some of the members as to what was in the bill and what was going on [and] actively trying to dissuade Rodino from intervening when he should have intervened."

Kamasaki picked up similar vibrations. "The last vote of the conference was weird. . . . It almost seemed like Rodino had it wired to kill the bill." The ACLU's Henderson saw things in much the same light: "Ultimately it was Rodino who helped to kill the bill by not helping to pass it." Rodino's staff director, Garner J. Cline, conceded as much. Mazzoli, he observed, needed Rodino to push the bill—"and he wasn't pushing because so many facets were so poorly put together at that time." Cline also acknowledged that throughout the process he "tried to my best ability" to stop the bill because he thought it made little sense: "People did not know what they were doing. We weren't prepared to undertake such a large reactionary bill. More research should have been done."

After the conference breakdown, Rodino concluded the bill could only move forward with strong and visible presidential backing. "I stated I would move the bill myself if we could get the president's support," said Rodino.

* * *

The message, sent from myriad sources and in countless different ways, was sometimes subtle, sometime direct, but always jarringly clear. Mazzoli had to go—or his bill would not survive. Too many factions had been offended; too many calls had been ignored; and too many egos—including Judiciary chairman Peter Rodino's—had been inadequately massaged. Four years from retirement, Rodino had been involved in every immigration debate since 1952. He had accrued standing, relationships, and congressional vouchers that Mazzoli sorely lacked. Propriety alone virtually dictated he manage what Simpson called the "one real item left on the table." Mazzoli realized, only in retrospect, that Rodino had never planned it to be Mazzoli's bill alone; he had meant to be always looming in the background, amiably holding the reins. "I could have easily [succeeded] if Mr. Rodino would ever have said, 'Okay it's yours, and it's not mine,'" conjectured Mazzoli. "But that just wasn't to be."

The Rodino-Mazzoli relationship was likely doomed from the start. Rodino represented the very thing—domination by big-city, East Coast "ethnic conclaves"—that Mazzoli blamed for the immigration laws being such a horrendous mess. Mazzoli never truly could have deferred to him without compromising his own sense of integrity. Nor did Mazzoli enjoy the support of Rodino's staff. Despite repeated offers of assistance, they always seemed to get in his way. Not content with undermining Mazzoli, they turned to his assistant, Harris Miller, and treated him, in Mazzoli's view, like a human soccer ball. "He took body blows that would have knocked Mike Tyson off."

While Simpson could barter for the Republican leadership and the White House, Mazzoli could barter only for himself. And an agreement made without Rodino's proxy, he learned, was not much of an agreement at all. Also, Mazzoli had stirred up a great deal of bile—especially among Democrats who resented his siding with Republicans in voting for a special election following a contested House race in Indiana. Even though the Democrats prevailed in the special-election vote, some hinted they might have problems backing legislation carrying his name. When Simpson finally told Mazzoli, "Ron, you're going to have to bring Rodino into this," Mazzoli simply responded, "I know."

Rodino's entry totally changed the game. The liberals and Hispanics who had harassed Mazzoli became much more agreeable. To Michael Myers of Church World Service, Rodino's sponsorship meant that "good elements [of the legislation] would be protected." For NCLR's leaders, who respected Rodino's civil-rights record, it meant having someone on point whom they could trust. And for several members of the Congressional Hispanic Caucus, who had deep respect for Rodino, it meant the end of the politics of obstruction.

In addition, opposition troops were no longer so willing to travel to Washington to demonstrate or testify. "You can only sustain that kind of anger for so long," conceded Rick Swartz, of the National Immigration, Refugee and Citizenship Forum. And with no presidential election in the offing, legislators, weary of the Latino chorus of complaint, saw little reason to listen. In the end, reflected Kennedy aide Jerry Tinker, "What the Hispanics thought became increasingly irrelevant."

Simpson's scorn for the Hispanic lobby was evident in the bill he introduced in May 1985. Unlike previous versions that presented legalization and sanctions as a package, Simpson's new version held legalization hostage—until after a commission certified that sanctions were working. In explaining his new hard line to colleagues, Simpson cited a Gallup Poll showing only 35 percent of Americans supported amnesty for undocumented entrants. The tough new bill angered and alarmed many Hispanic activists who saw in its harsh and legalistic language the worst of all possible worlds—where employer sanc-' tions were embraced but amnesty indefinitely suspended. Heartsick at the prospect of being squeezed out entirely, some let it be known that they were willing to talk.

Of all the major Latino organizations, MALDEF was most adverse to compromise. Antonia Hernández, who had shaped MALDEF's Washington strategy and became its president in summer 1985, resolved she would "go down in flames" rather than make agreements that would be disastrous for her constituents. As a result, MALDEF would be excluded from meeting, and Hernández would hear from people on the Hill and elsewhere that MALDEF was regarded as an unpredictable kamikaze—liable to sabotage those negotiations it was no longer asked to join.

For those organizations—the Forum, NCLR, LULAC, the American Immigration Lawyers Association, and others—who were playing the insiders' game, legislative relations became a delicate minuet. On one hand, they feared that pure opposition would negate their ability to influence the legislation; on the other, they worried that cooperation would virtually ensure the bill's passage. They tried, in effect, to collaborate and revolt simultaneously: to work at improving the legislation without actually endorsing it—while hoping their cooperation would make the bill so liberal that conservatives would kill it themselves.

The antisanctions lobby never expected much success in the Senate—where one of the few concessions made to Hispanic sentiment was acceptance of an amendment making legalization available if Simpson's commission failed to act within three years. The Senate also added a guest-workers program—despite Hispanic organizations' vigorous opposition, and despite Rodino's pledge to reject legislation that contained any such proposal. Temporary workers, thought Rodino, were just as vulnerable to exploitation and just as likely to displace Americans as the undocumented immigrants Congress was seeking to eliminate. Kennedy ridiculed the hypocrisy of creating a foreign labor pool in legislation intended to decrease immigration, but Simpson accepted the amendment philosophically—claiming the change would please Ronald Reagan's California agribusiness constituents. The bill sailed through the Senate by a vote of sixty-nine to thirty.

Rodino produced a bill more attentive to Latino concerns. It did not, for instance, link legalization to commission certification that America had regained control of her borders. Its centerpiece, nonetheless, remained employer sanctions—even though the bill mandated creation of a special prosecutor to investigate bias complaints resulting from the law.

As usual, House action was slow. One reason was that Rodino—wary of a White House double cross—refused to push the bill until the president gave his personal assurance of support. Rodino waited weeks for the president to call, and Simpson finally arranged a meeting in March 1986. Simpson and Mazzoli accompanied Rodino to the parley, along with Hamilton Fish and Dan Lungren—both Republicans on the Judiciary Committee who supported the bill. With Reagan were Attorney General Edwin Meese, budget director James Miller, and chief of staff Donald Regan.

Reagan seemed only vaguely aware of what the legislation was about or why it had been delayed. When the president said something along the lines of, "This immigration, we've got to do something about it," Rodino had to repress the temptation to snap, "Just what do you think we've been trying to do the past several years?" Instead, he asked Reagan whether he would support it and whether there would be money to fund it. Reagan looked for guidance to budget director Miller, who assured him the money for social services necessitated by legalization—$1 billion a year for several years—would be found.

Even after Reagan signed on, the bill did not pick up much steam. Legislators, deadlocked over treatment of temporary farm workers, required several months to reach a compromise acceptable to Rodino, Simpson, and conservative House members. That agreement replaced the guest-workers program of the Senate legislation with one that would allow migrant farm workers to eventually become U.S. citizens.

Independence Day became an occasion for some to speak out against the legislation—and the racism they believed underlay it. In southern California, the National Task Force for Immigrant and Refugee Rights held a march and demonstration protesting what the organization saw as America's mistreatment of non-European refugees. "There is a reason the Statue of Liberty faces Europe and has its back to Asia and South America. We were never welcomed here," declared task-force chairman William Tamayo. The Simpson-Rodino bill, he said, would not stop immigration but only allow the undocumented "to be exploited until they are . . . deported."

Such animosity toward the legislation notwithstanding, a national *New York Times*/CBS poll conducted just before the Fourth of July weekend found substantial support for key elements of the bill—as well as widespread ambivalence and confusion about immigration in general. While 49 percent of those responding said immigration should be reduced, 42 percent said it should be increased. (When the Gallup Poll had asked the same question in 1965—the year of the Kennedy-Johnson immigration reforms—only 33 percent had favored cutting back.) And even most who opposed increased immigration claimed immigrants would be welcome in their own neighborhoods—despite the professed (and erroneous) belief of 47 percent that immigrants usually ended up on welfare.

Most interviewees favored the two principal elements of the Simpson-Rodino legislation: 69 percent approved of employer sanctions and 58 percent endorsed legalization for undocumented immigrants who had settled in America and—aside from their illegal status—not violated U.S. laws. Fifty-eight percent, however, opposed foreign farm-workers programs. The survey also found—as had the earlier *Los Angeles Times* poll—that whites and minorities viewed immigration differently. In general, minorities were much more kindly disposed toward immigrants and significantly less likely to support restrictions against them. Fifty-two percent of whites said immigration should be decreased; only 39 percent of blacks—and 31 percent of Hispanics—agreed. While 73 percent of whites supported employer sanctions, only 59 percent of blacks and 34 percent of Latinos approved of them. Amnesty was endorsed by 55 percent of whites, but was favored by 79 percent of Hispanics and 65 percent of blacks.

For Rodino, the survey was good news; his views on sanctions, amnesty, and temporary farm workers were solidly supported. The retirement of Judiciary Committee staff director Garner J. Cline—who had quietly undermined previous efforts to pass such legislation—gave some legislators hope that the process might thenceforth proceed smoothly. It did, until late September. With the measure finally set to go before the full House, conservatives, revolting over a rule that would have restrained them from amending the legislation on the floor, refused to allow the bill to come to a vote. Many observers equated the action with killing the bill. "The opportunity to make all this right is not likely to come soon again," mourned *The Washington Post.* Instead of giving up, however, legislators continued to talk. Within days the bill once more headed for the floor. Bitterly disappointed at its revival, Congressman Robert Garcia grumbled, "This is like Rasputin. Immigration reform refuses to die."

When House debate began, Bill McCollum again offered his amendment to purge the bill of amnesty. Citing no source other than his own calculations, McCollum claimed that within ten years—as legalized aliens brought in family members from afar—amnesty would result in 90 million newcomers. "We can take in fifty thousand," he said. "Maybe we can take in a million a year, but we cannot take in ninety million." McCollum's amendment was defeated by only seven votes, with the majority of Republicans supporting it. Shortly thereafter, the House passed the bill—230 to 166.

For Mazzoli, the legislation's ratification evoked none of the magic of 1984. "I still claim part [authorship of the legislation], because it still had the basic elements of the Simpson-Mazzoli bill, but . . . I didn't feel like I was a father to a newborn baby." In the bill's long march toward passage, it had long ago lost its original purity, absorbing the personalities of a multitude of lawmakers who—with amendments covering everything from Central American refugees to free trade with Mexico—had made it the vehicle for their own pet concerns. One such measure, discarded shortly after the Senate-House conference convened, would have prohibited deportation of Salvadorans and Nicaraguans. Another would have ended employer sanctions after a period of six and a half years. Negotiators did accept an amendment—inserted in the Senate bill by Kennedy—requiring the U.S. General Accounting Office to assess whether the law produced widespread discrimination. They also let stand provisions for a special counsel to investigate and prosecute individual claims of employment discrimination. And they went along with the compromise for seasonal farm laborers that Simpson had approved during the previous House negotiations.

At one point during the House-Senate conference, word leaked out that the bill would have a 1981 legalization eligibility date instead of the House date of 1982. Dismayed, Esteban Torres—who was not a member of the negotiating team—confronted conferees and snapped, "You may still get a bill, but you will lose us [Hispanics] forever." Subsequently Rodino fought for the later House date, which Simpson accepted. Even after getting the House amnesty date, minority congressmen were hardly eager to embrace the Simpson-Rodino compromise. When it reached the House floor for final passage almost immediately following the conference, Henry Gonzales opposed it. "Let there be no mistake about it," he said. "This bill . . . solves the problem of the exploiters, and that is about it."

California congressman Norman Mineta—who as a child had experienced life in a Japanese-American internment camp—was no happier with the bill. "Most members of this House will never be asked to affirm, let alone prove their citizenship or residency," he said. "Looking and sounding American, they will never see these sanctions as an important factor in their lives." Nevertheless, added Mineta, the bill "takes us down the road toward an insidious racial discrimination."

Former Hispanic Caucus chairman Bill Richardson endorsed the legislation, but not without making evident his inner turmoil. "Millions of people who have no lobbyists . . . deserve . . . to come out of serfdom," Richardson declared. "I do not want my legacy to be that, as a Hispanic, I obstructed immigration reform."

Although the conference agreement passed 238 to 173, with most Republicans and Hispanic Caucus members voting against it, the threat of a veto hung over the package because of White House fears that its antidiscrimination provisions might spawn a raft of lawsuits. So the day after the House vote—and the day before Senate action—Simpson met with Reagan and other administration officials and was assured that the president would sign the bill.

During the Senate debate, Simpson addressed some of his bluntest language to those who opposed legislation: "Because it is called legalization, or amnesty, it seems to stick in the craw of Americans. . . . But . . . the alternative to legalization is to go hunt for them. If you couldn't find them coming in, how do you find them to get them out? . . . Are you going to be part of the group that goes to a Mexican-American in Brownsville and taps on the door and says, 'Are you deportable?' " The Senate passed the conference report sixty-three to twenty-four—after fending off a threatened filibuster—with a majority of members of both parties supporting the bill, and with Congress due to adjourn the following day.

As finally enacted, the Immigration Reform and Control Act of 1986 established two separate legalization programs instead of one. The first made eligible for eventual U.S. citizenship anyone who had continuously lived in the country since before January 1, 1982. The second program was considerably more liberal, allowing anyone who had worked in "perishable agriculture" for ninety days prior to May 1986 to qualify for legalization. It also authorized so-called replenishment workers, who would enter the United States at a later date, to sign up for amnesty.

The law required firms with at least four employees to check job seekers' documentation and verify that they were legally in the United States, and it prescribed criminal and civil penalties for those who knowingly hired those who were not. The minimum fine for a first violation was set at $250, going up to $10,000 and a six-month jail term for the most serious offenses. In addition, IRCA authorized up to five thousand supplemental visas annually for two years to be distributed among those countries from which immigration had dropped since 1965.

At a White House signing ceremony that November (two days after elections restoring Democratic control of the Senate), Reagan praised the work of Simpson, Rodino, and Mazzoli and predicted that future generations would be thankful for their efforts to control the borders.

After so many years of pushing, few exulted in the passage of the act; exhaustion, not euphoria, was the prevailing mood.

Even those who had fought the bill hardest, however, generally concluded it was, in the words of NCLR's Raúl Yzaguirre, "probably the best immigration legislation possible under current political conditions." Whether the law would do what it was supposed to do was an entirely different matter. In crafting the legislation, Congress had been driven more by political necessity than by knowledge. Prodded by the press to control traffic across the borders, legislators had made two key assumptions. (1) Most immigrants were only coming to take American jobs and would stay home if employers were punished for hiring them. (2) Employers, asked to refrain from hiring undocumented immigrants, would treat Latinos, Asians, blacks, and whites alike.

Even before the legislation passed, many skeptics questioned one or both of those assumptions. In 1984, when Congress seemed on the verge of passing Simpson-Mazzoli, *The New York Times* had run an article datelined from Tijuana, Mexico, that focused on the law's likely targets. A thirty-three-year-old carpenter waiting for darkness before crossing the border had contemptuously dismissed the threat of new legislation. The U.S. Congress was simply trying "to mess with us," he said, adding, "There will still be work; and as long as there's work there will still be 'mojados' [wetbacks]."

In the push to passage, such stories were not given much credence; nor were there very many of them. But a few years after the sanctions were in place, newspapers carried frequent (and often melodramatic) dispatches from a world teeming with fraudulent identification cards where border agents were considered nothing more than an annoyance and where huge numbers of illegal immigrants (many of them unaccompanied children) crossed the border with impunity. They came in cars, trucks, buses, airplanes, and on foot—often with the help of internationally connected organizations that reportedly made millions trafficking in human cargo.

Many who came—particularly from Central America—spoke not of seeking jobs or the American good life but of fleeing the brutalities of war. Even for those whose countries were at peace, employer sanctions seemed no more a barrier than countless others they routinely surmounted. After conducting extensive research in three rural Mexican communities, one scholar found little change as a result of the 1986 law. "There has been no significant return flow of illegals who suddenly found themselves jobless in the United States," concluded the director of the Center for U.S.-Mexican Studies at the University of California. Nor could he find evidence the law was shutting off the flow of new immigrants. Studies conducted by the Urban Institute and the Rand Corporation found any sanctions-related decrease in illegal immigration to be small, perhaps in the neighborhood of 20 percent.

Virtually alone among those doing research, the INS insisted that sanctions were working well. In 1989, it released a report claiming, "Almost immediately after the law was enacted, border apprehensions began to decline." INS statistics did show a sharp drop in apprehensions, from a peak of more than 1.7 million in 1986 to slightly under one million in 1989. The 1986 figure, however, was the highest the INS had ever recorded and may well have been an aberration. In fact, fewer deportable aliens were apprehended in 1980, six years before passage of the law, than in the two years following its enactment. Since apprehension statistics say at least as much about law-enforcement efforts as about illegal border crossings, just what the numbers meant was unclear—especially following implementation of a huge program that presumably legalized many of those who otherwise would be among those arrested and deported. At the very least, however, they indicated that employer sanctions were having a considerably less dramatic impact than predicted.

Legalization expectations were equally off target. Although legislators had originally thought a few hundred thousand persons would sign up for the farm-workers amnesty program, nearly 1.3 million applied. A substantial number of the applications were apparently fraudulent, for the program required little documentation (since agricultural workers are normally paid in cash) and was open to those who had spent as little as ninety days working in the United States. "Thousands of people who have never in their lives picked up a hoe or planted a seed are now claiming to be farmers," wrote one reporter, who described "women with long lacquered nails and men who, when questioned about their background, smile and proudly display hands with no calluses." On the other hand, only 1.8 million applied for the general amnesty program, despite widespread—and often hysterical—warnings that 3–12 million longtime resident illegals were waiting to rush in out of the shadows.

Some experts considered the legalization exercise worthwhile simply because so many formerly living outside the law were finally brought within it. Using such a standard, a report by the Carnegie Endowment for International Peace proclaimed legalization "a success by almost every measure." Such could hardly be claimed for the law's antidiscrimination provisions. In its final report, issued in March of 1990, the U.S. General Accounting Office concluded that "widespread discrimination" had been caused by the legislation. Nineteen percent of employers responding to a massive GAO survey said they had begun discriminating because of the law—either on the basis of appearance, accent, or citizenship status. In areas with large Latino and Asian populations, the numbers reporting discrimination were higher.

The GAO also saw signs of bias when it sent out comparably credentialed Anglo and Hispanic "testers" to apply for jobs. Hispanics were three times as liable to encounter "unfavorable treatment." Anglos were much more likely to be interviewed, and, once interviewed, more likely to be hired. Even after a hiring decision was made, discrimination apparently persisted: "For example, although both testers may have initially been offered the same job, the employer sometimes suggested to the Anglo . . . that he might be able to advance to another job that paid more money or had greater status."

The report predictably produced demands from Asian-American and Hispanic organizations for the repeal of employer sanctions. Bills to accomplish that were introduced by Kennedy and Orrin Hatch in the Senate and Roybal in the House. The effort went nowhere. Having put so much energy into getting the law passed, few felt up to revisiting the issue so soon; and many lawmakers either felt the legislation deserved more time to work or questioned the GAO research. Even if the GAO found discrimination, they reasoned, how could the agency definitely determine that it was caused by the law? Could not society have produced the discrimination on its own? "We want to make sure we're measuring new discrimination," said Senate Immigration Subcommittee minority counsel Richard Day. For Hispanic and Asian-American organizations, such responses were dispiriting. "Our fear," said Raúl Yzaguirre, "is even when the evidence is very clear, our friends will let us down."

In the end, one of the more important effects of the IRCA legislation may have been psychological. It allowed Congress to believe, for a while, that the problem of illegal immigration was solved. Instead of fixating on hordes swarming across the border and how to keep them out, legislators could ponder the more interesting question of how to choose who should get in.

In February 1989, Mazzoli's colleagues consummated a brutal and humiliating coup—stripping him of his Immigration Subcommittee chairmanship and installing Bruce Morrison, a Connecticut liberal considered more likely to act like a Democrat, and more inclined to return phone calls. "I didn't see it coming until the night before," Mazzoli admitted, "which is to say I didn't see it coming at all."

Democrats were angry with Mazzoli for not acting promptly to convene hearings over extension of the legalization program, but the basic animosity stretched back to those days when he had ruffled too many feathers trying to push his immigration bill through the House. Mazzoli acknowledged feeling regret at times at not having taken the Crime Subcommittee, where he could have "passed a couple of little bills and . . . been lionized." But, on balance, he insisted he had done the right thing: "In my own way, when I wrap this thing up, I'll say that I played a role in something that had to be done . . . and I think I came away better for it."

13

A Movement for the Eighties

Early in the battle over passage of the Immigration Reform and Control Act, Alan Eliason, border-patrol chief in El Paso, Texas, acknowledged that a shift had taken place in the attitude of many Americans. "We're never going to see again in this country what we saw in 1954 with Operation Wetback. . . . People won't stand for it," he said. "It's not going to happen." In earlier eras, few Americans would have assumed that undocumented aliens had any special rights—other perhaps than the right to humane treatment during deportation. Talk of a right to legalization or to an American education would generally have been dismissed out of hand. Yet in 1982, the U.S. Supreme Court effectively ruled that undocumented immigrant children had a right to go to school, invalidating the 1975 Texas law withholding educational funds for children not "legally admitted" into the country.

After passage of the law, several Texas school districts had started charging undocumented entrants tuition. Houston set fees of $162 a month. Tyler asked for one thousand dollars a year. Dallas refused to admit the children at all. The Mexican

American Legal Defense and Education Fund and Legal Aid lawyers filed separate suits to nullify the law. Texas maintained that without the law, tens of thousands of illegal aliens would overwhelm the school system. The state also argued that undocumented migrants were not legally under Texas's jurisdiction and that they therefore were not entitled to the constitutional right of equal protection. Children's advocates said Texas was wrong to abrogate the rights of defenseless youngsters who—through no fault of their own—happened to be on U.S. soil.

In an opinion written by Justice William Brennan, the Court held that the equal-protection clause of the Fourteenth Amendment applied to all, regardless of citizenship status, and that Texas required a compelling reason to deny. the children an education. Though public education is not a constitutional right, noted Brennan, "neither is it merely some governmental 'benefit' indistinguishable from other forms of social welfare legislation." Education has "a fundamental role in maintaining the fabric of our society" and in "sustaining our political and cultural heritage"—and its deprivation could result in permanent injury to the child. "It is difficult to understand precisely what the State hopes to achieve by promoting the creation and perpetuation of a subclass of illiterates within our boundaries, surely adding to the problems and costs of unemployment, welfare, and crime. . . . [W]hatever savings might be achieved by denying these children an education, they are wholly insubstantial in light of the costs involved to these children, the State, and the Nation."

As the Supreme Court spoke on the right to education, the sanctuary movement was raising the issue of an alien right to refuge. In 1982 John Fife, pastor of Southside Presbyterian Church in Tucson, Arizona, had unveiled a previously underground movement to smuggle Salvadorans into the United States. Shortly thereafter, other churches began offering asylum to refugees from war-torn Central America, evoking many comparisons to the underground railroad that slaves had used to escape the South. By 1985, the sanctuary movement claimed more than two hundred parishes of virtually all denominations. Around that same time, Berkeley (California), St. Paul (Minnesota), Los Angeles, San Francisco, Chicago, numerous other cities, and even the state of New Mexico declared themselves havens for Central American escapees. Several leaders of that movement were put on trial in 1985 and accused of being part of an "alien smuggling conspiracy." The accused, including two Roman Catholic priests and a Presbyterian minister, contended they were simply Christians following the dictates of conscience and observing the biblical injunction to treat well the stranger who "sojourns with you in your land." In May 1986, when eight of the eleven defendants were convicted on eighteen of forty possible counts connected with transporting and harboring illegal immigrants, they left the courthouse singing "We Shall Overcome." Four years later, the sanctuary leadership was effectively vindicated when the U.S. government (in settling a lawsuit filed by a coalition of religious and refugee organizations) agreed to reconsider the cases of tens of thousands of Central Americans previously rejected for political asylum.

For many supporters of the sanctuary movement, the plight of Central American refugees—like that of Haitian boat people—raised issues not only of asylum rights but of possible discrimination. From 1981 through 1986, the federal government deported nearly eighteen thousand Salvadoran escapees while granting permanent-resident status to only 598. Critics questioned whether Europeans, in similar circumstances, would have been similarly treated. Many of those raising such questions were attorneys and community organizers who were also active in civil rights, such as ACLU Foundation attorney Mark Rosenbaum, who spoke of protection of immigrant rights as the civil-rights issue of the 1980s.

The increasing linkage of civil rights and immigration pulled numerous organizations into the immigration debate who had not previously considered it part of their portfolio. The Congressional Black Caucus and the National Urban League spoke out for Haitian refugees after concluding the Haitians were victims of racial discrimination. Several civil-rights groups became involved in the IRCA battle after becoming convinced the legislation would result in discrimination against Asian-Americans and Latinos. In 1987, after reports surfaced that western regional INS commissioner Harold Ezell had suggested that some illegal immigrants should be "skinned and fried" and deported, a host of organizations—including the Latino Issues Forum, the League of United Latin American Citizens, the American GI Forum, Chinese for Affirmative Action, and the Filipino American Political Association—demanded his firing on the grounds that the comments were racist.

Similarly a rash of assaults against Asian-Americans drew together groups with little in common except a revulsion to racism. The most notorious attack took place in Highland Park, Michigan, in 1982 and grew out of a confrontation that began in a topless bar where Vincent Jen Chin had gone with friends. At that bar, they encountered Ronald Ebens, a Chrysler superintendent, and his stepson, Michael Nitz. In the course of the evening, witnesses said, Ebens turned to Chin (a Chinese-American) and said, "It's because of you little motherfuckers that we're out of work." The exchange led to a scuffle in the bar and, ultimately, to Chin being beaten to death with a baseball bat. Ebens pleaded Guilty and Nitz pleaded No Contest to manslaughter charges, and both were placed on probation for three years and assessed fines of $3,780 apiece. The sentence provoked widespread outrage from Asian-American activists and others who pointed to a string of violent anti-Asian incidents: the burning of Vietnamese fishing boats in Moss Landing, California, the repeated harassment of Indochinese teenagers in Boston, attacks on Korean merchants in various parts of the country. As a result of the uproar, Ebens and Nitz were indicted on two counts of violating Chin's civil rights. Nitz was acquitted, but the jury found Ebens guilty of violating Chin's civil rights—though the verdict was overturned on appeal.

For many, Chin came to represent all Asian-Americans and Asian immigrants who might be vulnerable to similar attacks, who might be blamed, in the words of one Asian-American religious leader, for taking jobs from "real Americans." The message they read into that was that immigration issues could not be viewed apart from the larger question of how America treats racial minorities. Some read the same message into a 1986 memo written by John Tanton, founder of U.S. English and of the Federation for American Immigration Reform.

In the memo, Tanton ruminated on California's fate. Would whites, swamped by more fertile minorities, he asked, "peaceably hand over . . . political power?" Or was apartheid in California's future? How, he wondered, would white and Asian owners communicate with their Hispanic field hands? And how would whites respond to becoming a minority: "Will they simply go quietly into the night? Or will there by an explosion?" Addressing the fertility of California's immigrants, Tanton wrote, "Perhaps this is the first instance in which those with their pants up are going to be caught by those with their pants down." When Tanton's memo was leaked to the press in 1988, Linda Chavez, a onetime Ronald Reagan aide, resigned as president of U.S. English, saying the memo revealed "an anti-Catholic, anti-Hispanic bias." Others went further, claiming it symbolized the racism central to the anti-immigration coalition. "To ignore them would be wrong. . . . They're dangerous," said Melinda Yee, executive director of the Organization of Chinese Americans.

Frank Sharry, who became executive director of the National Immigration, Refugee and Citizenship Forum in early 1990, observed, "It's sort of like after three hundred years of affirmative action for whites, you have twenty years of affirmative action for people of color and [critics say,] 'That's enough. . . . It's gotten out of control.' " His aspiration, said Sharry, was to help build the pro-immigration lobby into "a civil rights movement for newcomers that would turn this backlash into something progressive."

While race had long been an important element of American immigration politics, a strong civil rights–based pro-immigrant coalition had not. The emergence of one was a large part of the reason why the immigration debates of the 1980s and 1990s had as much to do with rights and responsibilities as with restrictions.

14

A Better Class of Immigrant

Alan Simpson had always regarded the Immigration Reform and Control Act as only half a loaf, since it dealt primarily with illegal immigration. His original 1982 proposals had also included provisions aimed at limiting the legal immigration flow. Peter Rodino, however, had insisted that the language be dropped from the bill. Better, he had advised, to keep things simple and to take up legal immigration at a later date. By the time IRCA had passed, Republicans had lost control of the Senate, and chairmanship of the Immigration Subcommittee had reverted to Kennedy. Simpson could no longer ram through a bill on his own. Nor would his approach be the only one seriously considered.

Despite IRCA's focus on undocumented entrants, a little-noted provision authored by Boston congressman Brian Donnelly had placed legal immigration squarely on the table. That amendment, accepted during the House-Senate conference in 1986, set aside ten thousand visas for "adversely affected" countries. Donnelly had also exacted a promise, written into the conference report, that Congress would presently return to "the issues addressed by this particular provision." The "issues" basically boiled down to one: how to reverse the drop in European immigration.

Donnelly's motivation lay in the makeup of his district, considered the most heavily Irish in the nation. It housed (by Donnelly's estimate) roughly ten thousand undocumented Irish. He believed their illegitimate status stemmed from the fact that the United States allocated so few visas to Ireland. At the peak of Irish immigration, between 1840 and 1860, Irish expatriates made up 39 percent of the 4.3 million who came to America to start life anew. In 1986, when more than six hundred thousand newcomers migrated to America, fewer than two thousand of those (with documentation, at least) were Irish.

In arguing for his amendment, Donnelly had noted that the great immigration reform of 1965 had been driven by desire to open America to larger numbers of Southern and Eastern Europeans. Unexpectedly the law had resulted in a flood of Asians—whose "large numbers are squeezing European immigrants out of the mix," putting the United States in the disconcerting position of discriminating "against many of the peoples that built our nation." In searching for a way to rebuild the European-American connection, Donnelly had hit on the concept of "adversely affected" countries. He knew that Congress, operating in the shadow of the "national origins" quota system, would be reluctant to pass immigration legislation singling out Europe for special treatment. By couching his proposal in terms of negatively impacted nations, it became something other than a simple ethnic-preference measure—even if the result was much the same.

As a result of Donnelly's initiative, citizens of thirty-six countries were invited to take part in a visa lottery run by the U.S. government—with permanent U.S. residency as the prize. Those applications arriving either too early or too late were to be discarded without so much as a glance. With only ten thousand visas to go around—and with slots awarded in order of arrival of application—timing the delivery of the petition to the right post office at precisely the right time (after the third Tuesday and before the fourth Wednesday of January 1987) became critically important.

The scheme touched off madness in Washington, where an international array of hopefuls, determined to get their applications in on schedule, stood outside the main post office on January 20 waiting for midnight to arrive. As the hour approached, they shouted out a countdown and, at the stroke of twelve, rushed the postal bin. Others, unable to make the trip themselves, sent couriers from abroad.

In Ireland, just before the deadline, postal officials reported mail to America running at more than one hundred times the normal level. Several post offices ran out of stamps. All told, some 1.4 million on-time applications were received. Several hundred thousand others were thrown away for arriving early or late.

The intense interest in Ireland reflected both the effects of publicity from Irish-American organizations and the state of the Irish economy—which was suffering a protracted slump. Exports and industrial output were falling. Factories were closing. Unemployment—19 percent at the end of 1986— showed no sign of decreasing. And many of Ireland's young, facing an unremittingly bleak future, were seeking to leave the country. For a few, Donnelly's amendment was a godsend. Irish nationals obtained nearly one third of the program's precious visas. Canada and Great Britain also did extremely well—with the three countries together taking more than half of the available slots.

Uncounted thousands of others, unwilling to trust their fate to a sweepstakes, simply entered the United States on tourist visas and vanished into the population. Since many Irish arrived after the general amnesty eligibility date, they were unable to legalize their status under the IRCA statute. Unlike Latin American illegals (or Irish immigrants of the nineteenth century), who were widely seen as peasants likely to drag America down, the undocumented Irish were usually viewed in an extremely favorable light. "At the end of the day, you want to give something to this country, but you can't, because you can't pay taxes. We're here quite willing to work hard, and not able to get work," lamented an undocumented Irish office worker. One reporter described the wave of Irish undocumented as "the cream of another . . . Irish generation." The

United States "needs their skills," editorialized the *Boston Globe.*

Employer sanctions had not been enacted with such people in mind, and politicians reached out to assist them. Boston mayor Raymond Flynn, noting the city's "special relationship to Ireland," encouraged creation of an agency to provide legal aid and medical help for newcomers—leading the head of a center for Haitians to grouse that the city's targeting of the Irish was "not helpful across the board." When Congressman Joseph Kennedy proposed a bill to extend amnesty to Irish immigrants who arrived before September 1987, his idea was promptly dubbed "tribalist" by the *New Republic* and quietly died for lack of support.

Nevertheless, the idea that Europeans were being wronged and needed special treatment continued to surface. Boston mayor Flynn complained, "Many of those who endure the worst burdens imposed by the current law are from nations who have been contributing to the life of this nation since its very founding." Edward Kennedy deplored "discrimination . . . against Irish and other European immigrants" who constituted "the 'old seed' sources of our heritage." Other legislators defined the problem in extremely personal terms. "If our current immigration laws were in place fifty or sixty years ago, my father, a poor immigrant from Italy, would not have been able to come through Ellis Island," stated Congressman Joseph DioGuardi of New York. And Senator Daniel Moynihan complained, "The countries which sent our grandparents and great-grandparents to America are penalized because citizens of those countries . . . do not have close enough relatives here to qualify."

Ironically the system supposedly discriminating against Europeans had been established, at least in part, as a means of discriminating for them. In making family reunification the centerpiece of America's system of immigration preferences, Congress had assumed most reuniting families would be European, not Asian and Latin American. Europeans, however, had shown diminishing interest in coming to America. At the same time, war, revolution, and economic disaster had spurred immigration from the East and South. As legislators proposed to change that by enacting a new quota system, they failed to realize that Americans not particularly interested in recruiting Europeans might see such a scheme as fundamentally racist.

In 1987, when Donnelly (in the House) and Kennedy and Moynihan (in the Senate) introduced their plan to revise immigration law, they saw little reason to cloak their intention in cloudy legalistic language. Their bill was to create fifty thousand new visas a year earmarked, in Kennedy's words, "for older sources of immigration—especially the traditional ethnic flows from Ireland, Italy, other nations of Western Europe, Canada, and other countries." "The goal," explained Donnelly, "is to open our country to a number of immigrants, groups who were shortchanged by the 1965 law." The point system under which the new visas were to be distributed was heavily weighted toward those who were young, English-speaking, well educated, and came from one of the thirty-six "adversely affected countries."

Despite Kennedy's assurances that the bill was fair to all, it struck Simpson as a bit skewed. Kennedy "had set this whole thing up designed for the Irish college graduate," recalled Simpson's chief aide; and Simpson was less interested in admitting Irishmen than in advancing what he saw as the national interest. Under the Kennedy-Donnelly point system, for instance, virtually any English-speaking college graduate from an "adversely affected" nation could easily qualify—regardless of whether that person possessed skills needed in the United States. Hordes of "adversely affected" high school graduates could also make the cut, provided that they knew a trade. Simpson believed that America should be more selective.

As Simpson nitpicked Kennedy's proposal, the notion was taking root in political Washington that America faced a labor crisis. Widely heralded research done for the U.S. Labor Department had concluded that, though the need for skilled labor was escalating, the United States's work force was growing at a slower pace than at any time since the 1930s, and that indigenous white males, previously the backbone of American industry, would not be available to take many of the new jobs. The study's executive summary stated erroneously that only 15 percent of entrants into the labor market in the next thirteen years would be native white males. (The actual statistic, roughly twice that reported, was not generally acknowledged until 1990—three years after the study was issued.) Meanwhile, the assistant labor secretary who commissioned the report was warning that the United States could move "permanently to the status of a diminished economic force in the world" because of the impending labor shortage.

No American politician wished to see such a calamity. To Simpson, the impending labor crisis offered an opportunity for creative lawmaking. About one fourth of visas allocated under the preference system went to brothers and sisters of U.S. residents, many of whom were married and had families of their own. That category was heavily used by Asians, who, in 1987, received 56 percent of all visas apportioned under it. Latinos and citizens of Caribbean countries were also heavy users of such visas. Simpson believed those numbers could be put to better use.

In early 1988, Simpson introduced legislation aimed at meeting the nation's purported labor needs. While limiting normal immigration to 510,000 persons a year, the bill more than tripled the number of visas (to about 180,000 annually) going to those with vital skills. The numbers were subtracted from those formerly allotted to various family members—primarily brothers and sisters. The bill was partly a bargaining device—a way of telling Kennedy the direction in which he would have to move to win Simpson's support. For even though Republicans had lost control of the Senate, Simpson (the only Republican member of the Senate Immigration Subcommittee) retained enough clout that Kennedy would find selling immigration reform difficult with Simpson in opposition. At the same time, Simpson knew he could not win passage of his own bill without Democratic help. Consequently the two opted for compromise: Simpson would accept higher immigration numbers if Kennedy would go along with admission requirements based more on job skills.

Having struck a deal, the two set their separate bills aside and cosponsored legislation shortly thereafter that breezed through the Senate. The bill set maximum annual immigration at 590,000: roughly the current level. The big change was in how those immigrants were chosen. One hundred twenty thousand of them would be "independent" immigrants, many picked by a State Department drawing after qualifying through points awarded on the basis of skills and training presumed to correlate with employability. After three years, the independent category would rise to 150,000. The new visa numbers would largely come from those previously set aside for family members. The legislation also earmarked nearly five thousand slots annually for wealthy foreigners willing to invest a minimum of $1 million in businesses that would create at least ten new jobs apiece.

The rapidity of the Senate action preempted the possibility of significant opposition developing; but the House, as usual, proceeded much more slowly. No bill even reached the floor in 1988, and the entire process had to begin anew. By the time the bill was again before Congress, a number of people were raising serious questions about the Kennedy-Simpson compromise. Many of the questions had to do with race, and were raised by representatives of Hispanic and Asian-American organizations. Why, they asked in essence, was a bill before Congress that would cut back their family members in order to attract skilled Europeans? For Paul Igasaki, of the Japanese American Citizens League, the "fears of being . . . swamped by new immigrants that will dilute America's greatness" were uncomfortably reminiscent of earlier fears that had fed public hysteria over the "yellow peril."

Even many not representing racial minorities were uneasy about the drive to increase "old seed" immigration. The American Jewish Committee warned that by favoring Europeans over Asians and Hispanics, the bill "could produce unnecessary ethnic strife." Senator Paul Simon cautioned against undoing "the tremendous progress of the 1965 act," which had opened doors "shamefully . . . closed." Rick Swartz, who believed skilled-labor issues to be legitimate, was troubled by the "undercurrent . . . that Kennedy-Simpson was designed to increase white migration and limit nonwhite migration."

At times that undercurrent was very near the surface. At

one congressional hearing, Texas congressman John Bryant blurted out, "I am asked over and over . . . , 'Where . . . have all these people come from? Who are these people? What system did they [use to] get here?' They are not only Asians. You can say they are a result of our Vietnam war experience. They are from Africa. They are from parts of Asia that perhaps sent them here [for] . . . some reason not related to the Vietnam war. They are from all over the world."

Some observed that the fairness argument cut more ways than one. If Europeans were excluded, so were others. "The same people who frame things in ethnic terms never talk about bringing in more immigrants from Africa," noted Charles Kamasaki. Some argued that even if current immigrants were disproportionately Asian, that was only fitting given that Asians had been barred in the past. "It's only fair that the doors be somewhat opened up to our communities," said Melinda Yee of the Organization of Chinese Americans. "The irony of the situation is that persons of Asian descent are fifty percent of the world's population, yet we're less than three percent of the United States population, and they're now telling us that we're too much," said William Tamayo of the Asian Law Caucus. Others were offended by the preference proposed for wealthy investors. "Citizenship is something that we can give, but when we try to sell it, we cheapen it," said Milton Morris, research director with the Joint Center for Political and Economic Studies.

Analyses of the bill by government experts added to the controversy over its potential consequences. After projecting the legislation forward several years, researchers from the U.S. General Accounting Office concluded that its ultimate effect would be to eliminate *all* family-based immigration, except that by immediate relatives not subject to limitation. The Senate responded to that concern by amending the bill to guarantee at least 216,000 slots for family members covered by quota.

Other problems were not so easily fixed. The GAO, for instance, refused to vouch that the bill would be of any significant help to employers. An engineer brought in because of job shortages in Los Angeles might well decide to move to

Florida. A Labor Department–certified need for computer scientists might no longer exist by the time computer scientists arrived. "Some would argue that our knowledge of labor markets is so limited, that any current survey or projections of labor force demands or needs would invariably be wrong," said the GAO.

Janet Norwood, commissioner of the Bureau of Labor Statistics, seconded that opinion, testifying that in order to predict how long a labor shortage would last, she would have to know how workers and employers would respond. "Determinations and analysis of this type," she said, "go beyond the expertise of a statistical agency." Such data as could be collected, she added, would be of debatable quality and, in some cases, "prohibitively expensive." Private economist Richard Belous reiterated the warnings about cost, adding that some of the labor-market concepts with which the legislators were tinkering were "quite simplistic" and of dubious utility. Immigration expert Doris Meissner cautioned that expanding immigration "in the name of addressing labor shortages" might "undermine the readjustment required to refit the American workforce."

The GAO suggested that the bill might not even succeed in spurring a large increase in European immigration. Though the point system was set up to increase visas going to "virtually excluded" countries, "other scenarios are possible." In other words, Nigerians, East Indians, and God-knows-who-else might just as well qualify under the Kennedy-Simpson point system as citizens of Ireland and Iceland.

The points awarded by the bill for English language ability hit an especially sensitive nerve among many who fretted that such rules might have kept their ancestors out of America. Much to Simpson's annoyance, even Kennedy backed away from the language points, saying the provision had become so loaded with symbolic significance that it "distorted the whole thrust of this legislation." Under prodding from Senator Paul Simon, the Judiciary Committee removed the English advantage, but Simpson tried to reinsert it when the bill reached the Senate floor in summer 1989.

Simpson recalled that a few years earlier, during the debate over employer sanctions, the Senate had passed a measure approving English as America's official language. Just the
previous year, he pointed out, the Senate had overwhelmingly
voted to go along with his English points. Though it might be
true that various ancestors had not spoken English, suggested
Simpson, America's needs had changed. The nation already
gave preference to those of "exceptional ability in the sciences
and the arts." His bill simply took the concept a bit further.
As to allegations that racism had anything to do with the point
system, said Simpson, "I do not care one whit if the English
skill immigrant is from Nigeria, Jamaica, India, the Philippines or Belize."

During an equally impassioned response, Paul Simon bran-
dished a newspaper article about valedictorians in Boston and
noted that most were foreign-born and had arrived speaking
little or no English. He also listed senators whose forebears
had arrived unable to use the language, and urged that Congress not set a precedent by excluding, for the first time in
history, those not fluent in English. As for the Senate previously passing the bill, he remarked, "My guess is, you did not
have ten people in this body . . . who knew there was such a
provision [in the bill]." The English points were rejected, as
was Simpson's attempt to place strict limits on total immigration, and the bill passed eighty-one to seventeen, bearing only
scant resemblance to the one originally proposed.

The focus for House action became a bill sponsored by
Immigration Subcommittee head Bruce Morrison. Morrison's
bill, pointedly titled the "Family Unity and Employment Opportunity Immigration Act," was more generous in several re-
spects than the Senate legislation. It not only sanctioned higher
overall immigration levels than the Senate bill, but provided
new visas for Africans and for refugees from Eastern Europe.
It also granted three-year stays of deportation for refugees
from El Salvador, Liberia, Kuwait, and Lebanon. And it created a fund—to be supported by employers of foreigners—
that would be used for the education and retraining of American workers. Many attributed Morrison's generosity partly to
the fact that he was running (ultimately unsuccessfully) for

governor of Connecticut and wished, within his immigration bill, to accommodate as wide a range of constituencies as possible.

Unwilling to cooperate with Morrison's something-for-everybody strategy, several House Judiciary Committee members denounced the bill as the servant of special interests. Morever, griped the dissident congressmen, Americans had requested no such bill: "Every poll taken in the past decade has shown that the majority of Americans do not want an increase in legal immigration." Lamar Smith of Texas voiced his primary objection bluntly: "We can either import large numbers of low-skilled workers or we can reach down and train our own underclass. . . . No other nation in the world has the delusion that it can ignore its own poor while importing a whole generation of poor people every year."

Tom Lewis of Florida noted that the law would likely result in the settlement of some 1.6 million immigrants, refugees, and asylees during its first year alone, most of whom would end up in a handful of states. Florida, California, and Texas, he complained, "can no longer afford to bear the burden of this immigration policy."

John Bryant of Texas confessed confusion over the bill's "diversity" provisions. "The authors of this bill . . . [argue] that we need to increase diversity in this country. Yet, the provisions . . . make special allocations of additional visas for people from Europe, when in fact, Anglo-Europeans are the majority group in this country already."

Despite the sniping, the measure passed the House easily, by a vote of 231 to 192. Watching the House's generous giveaways, however, had set Simpson on edge. And rising numbers of arrests along the Mexican border had magnified his misgivings. In late September 1990, shortly before the House vote on the bill, Simpson proposed legislation to force the INS to better secure the Mexican border—and linked passage to the immigration bill. "If this legislation is not approved," said Simpson, "then I just do not believe it would presently be in the national interest to approve of the increases in legal immigration."

Simpson's gambit was widely viewed as a threat to scuttle a

bill whose direction he no longer liked. Following House passage, the threat became even more explicit, as Simpson refused to enter formal conference negotiations because of the high numbers the House bill would admit. Accused by *The Wall Street Journal* of stonewalling, an angry Simpson responded on the Senate floor that he had made his "best honest effort . . . to get a bill."

Finally, with Congress a week from adjourning, Simpson consented to bargain. During the House-Senate conference, he won agreement to a provision for a pilot program for a national identification card that would guard against hiring undocumented immigrants. When news of the deal spread, however, numerous organizations coalesced in violent opposition, with Hispanic groups and the ACLU leading the charge.

In the House, Congressman Esteban Torres likened the proposed identification cards to South African passbooks and U.S. slave certificates. He recalled a period when he had lived in France, and his son, because of "his long curly hair and olive skin," was constantly stopped by police and forced to produce identification. Once the son was thrown in jail after leaving home without his card. "When I went down to the station to secure his release," said Torres, "I vowed to myself and to my children that, if I had it in my power, I would never let such a system take foothold in the United States."

Despite warnings that voting down the conference report would kill the bill, the Hispanic-led insurrection resulted in its defeat, but in eleventh-hour negotiations, Simpson agreed to remove the provision, and the bill came up again for a final vote. House Rules Committee chairman Joe Moakley implored his colleagues to pass it, saying, "This immigration bill helps literally thousands upon thousands of people. It helps the Irish; it helps the Polish . . . and it helps thousands of refugees fleeing war whose lives are literally in the balance. This is a good bill. It is the best we can get." Conversely Congressman Bryant, sensing a final opportunity to stop the legislation, condemned the investors' provision and argued that a sharp increase in immigration was not needed "at a time in which we are unable to meet the basic needs of our own citizens."

In the end, the legislation passed by huge margins in both the Senate and the House; and at a signing ceremony at the end of November, President George Bush called it "the most comprehensive reform of our immigration laws in sixty-six years." Even with many of the House provisions eliminated, the law approved immigration levels that would have seemed astronomical a few years earlier. The legislation essentially said the United States would accept at least seven hundred thousand immigrants a year. After three years, the number would drop to 675,000. (The larger initial number was to provide for the admittance of the children and spouses of persons legalized under the IRCA legislation.)

In reality, the numbers taken in would rise far above the seven hundred thousand figure; for the total did not include those admitted as refugees or those legalized under IRCA. And though the law contained a complex formulation to restrain family-based immigration, it still allowed the entry of immediate family members without restriction. Many believed that under the new law the United States would ultimately end up admitting 30 to 40 percent more immigrants than previously had been the norm.

The act divided visas into three main categories—those intended for family, for employment, and for "diversity." The vast majority would continue to go for family reunification, but 140,000 were set aside for employment-related groupings, with 10,000 of those to go to those controversial investors who put up at least $1 million (or, in some cases, $500,000) and created a minimum of ten jobs. Another forty thousand visas annually were allocated for "diversity immigrants," with at least sixteen thousand of those initially restricted to the Irish. (Needless to say, the abstruse language of legislation did not put it quite so bluntly, instead saying that at least 40 percent of the visas "shall be made available to natives of the foreign state the natives of which received the greatest number of visas issued under section 314 of the Immigration Reform and Control Act. . . .") After a three-year transition, the number of diversity visas would rise to fifty-five thousand.

The legislation also made visas more easily available for

Hong Kong, Lebanon, and selected other countries. It granted an eighteen-month "temporary protected status" for Salvadorans. And it eliminated certain exclusions of foreigners based on professed beliefs, past membership in the Communist party, and homosexuality.

That Congress could embrace such a precedent-shattering law so soon after its brush with illegal-alien hysteria said much about how quickly legislators' perception of the public mood could change. It perhaps said more, however, about the evolution of influence, and the way that Washington works. For as many had pointed out, the public was not exactly clamoring for such a bill. Nor, outside the community of experts, was America even much aware that such legislation was taking shape.

In the beginning, even those promoting the bill had no idea where it would lead. The most passionate were interested in getting a few more Europeans through the door. Others wanted to recruit workers or secure asylum for fugitives of war. Once lawmakers started down the road of letting certain groups in, other groups naturally followed; for Congress always finds adding easier than subtracting. The numbers (and variety) of constituencies who demanded consideration had changed radically from the era of the 1920s, when legislators, intent on boosting Western European immigration, could cavalierly ignore the rest of the world. Hispanic organizations, Asian-American groups, and a host of others irrelevant to debate at the turn of the century had suddenly become too important—and too savvy—to ignore.

Impelled by the most parochial of politics, Congress had ended up with a most expansive result—one ensuring that an already steady stream of strange people knocking on America's door would swell into a torrent, heightening not only the potential for ethnic enrichment but also for ethnic turmoil.

EPILOGUE

※

The Centrality of Race,
the Challenge of Diversity

B y limiting naturalization to whites, the first Congress of the United States made generations of judges into arbiters of racial purity. Time and again, would-be Americans of various hues—Mexicans, Japanese, Armenians, East Indians—were forced to be certified as "white" or as exceptions to the rule. As recently as the 1940s, trials of whiteness were still being held.

In 1942, a federal district court in Michigan denied citizenship to Yemen native Ahmed Hassan (in large part because of the petitioner's "undisputedly dark brown" skin), declaring, "The court is of the opinion that when one seeking citizenship is in fact clearly not white of skin a strong burden of proof devolves upon him to establish that he is a white person within the meaning of the act." Two years later, a federal district court in Massachusetts ruled on the same question when Mohamed Mohriez, also an Arab, applied for naturalization. In light of Ahmed Hassan's case, the Massachusetts court felt compelled to defend its opposite conclusion: "Both the learned and the unlearned would compare the Arabs with the Jews towards

whose naturalization every American Congress since the first
has been avowedly sympathetic. . . . Indeed, to earlier centuries as to the twentieth century, the Arab people stand as one
of the chief channels by which the traditions of white Europe,
especially the ancient Greek traditions, have been carried into
the present."

The 1952 McCarran-Walter Act, by eliminating all racial
restrictions to naturalization, brought such judicial race reck-
oning to an end. Shortly thereafter, the civil-rights movement
made unacceptable the very concept of blanket prohibitions
based exclusively on race. Nothing, however, could speedily
undo two centuries of tradition and legal and legislative history that rationalized (by blaming racism on its victims) the
Founding Fathers' decision in making race—not character, tal-
ent, or previous station—the key standard for judging prospective Americans. Excluding Asians from citizenship was not
discrimination, went the rationale, if they were inherently unassimilable—just as enslaving blacks was not a denial of freedom, if slavery were all they were fit for.

Such justifications, woven into custom, law, and values, made
race central to American identity and made exploitation of race-
based fears and animosities an easy route to political popular-
ity (and an ideal strategy for those with ethical or intellectual
failings in need of impenetrable camouflage). Racial distinctions were even manufactured where such differences had not
previously existed. For only if Eastern and Southern Europeans were viewed as inferior races could Madison Grant (and
his contemporaries) have any plausible basis for warning that
their coming would drive America into a "racial abyss."

The predicted calamity, of course, did not materialize. Italians, Russians, Romanians, and Poles were easily absorbed, as
much of today's Hispanic influx will be—despite widespread
talk of a "permanent underclass" of Hispanics. Rigid racial
distinctions among people who do not look very different become impossible to maintain once they share a language and
a culture—especially if they intermarry (as do nearly half of
second- and third-generation Hispanic-Americans in certain
areas). The progeny of a white immigrant from Cuba, Costa

Rica, or Argentina will ultimately be indistinguishable from the child of an immigrant from Greece, Italy, or Ireland.

For nonwhite Hispanics, for blacks, for Asians, for all those whose look is distinctive from the stereotypical American, history is less reassuring. This is not to say that easily identifiable "minorities" will share a common fate or face a future that is necessarily bleak; it is to say that America generally has had more of a problem with color than with simple ethnicity—though she continues to struggle with the implications of both. Prohibitions against Asian immigration, for instance, were erected earlier, built higher, and lasted longer than those thrown up against the purported lesser races of Europe. The history of black America is largely a history of watching various immigrant groups enter and surmount discrimination that black Americans could not overcome. While "national origins" was an invention of the twentieth century, American racism predated the American Revolution and has continually evolved since that time. Its roots, its rationalizations, and its ramifications go a good deal deeper than most Americans realize. Though, in the long run, acculturation and intermarriage will eliminate much of the basis for ethnic strife, it will not eradicate it.

The *San Francisco Chronicle* observed in 1905, "The individual Slav and Croat and Pole may be a dreary failure, but his children will be as clay in the hands of the potter and one generation will wipe away the squalor and freedom will banish even the inherited memories of repression." Such, the *Chronicle* argued, did not apply to Asians: "The Asiatic can never be other than as Asiatic, however much he may imitate the dress of the white man, learn his language and spend his wages for him." The internment camps of World War II indicated that U.S. leadership four decades later still assumed that Italians and Germans became Americans more quickly than did Japanese. Many see the emergence of a prosperous class of Asian Americans as evidence that such attitudes have finally died.

Without question, the new stereotype of Asians as a "model minority" (offensive though it may be) is an improvement on the old—which simply was no longer credible in light of the educational and entrepreneurial successes of so many Asian Americans, or of the economic explosion of Japan Incorporated. Yet even in heaping abuse on Asians during the "yellow peril" days of the nineteenth and twentieth centuries, white Americans had considered them fundamentally and mysteriously inscrutable—culturally and linguistically beyond understanding. Excluding them made them even more mysterious and prevented the nation from having an "Asian problem" on anything approaching the scale of its "black problem." Consequently, America invested less in her stereotypes of Asians than in her stereotypes of blacks, and was less inclined to cling to their unlikely truths; for she never felt that she knew Asians in the intimate way she believed she knew blacks and (to a lesser extent) Chicanos and Puerto Ricans.

The debates over the 1990 immigration act demonstrated anew, however, that no racial minority group has totally outgrown America's prejudice. The obsession with increasing "old seed" immigration, the insistence that some prospective immigrants are particularly deserving because of their forefathers' contributions, could only stem from a belief that certain ethnicities are more desirable than others, that where one comes from is, in the end, an important determinant of what one is worth—or at least of whether one should be entitled to American citizenship. Overcoming such an assumption means overcoming a large part of America's past. And a raft of recent surveys and studies indicates just how difficult that may be.

A Gallup Poll released in 1990 found that 54 percent of respondents believed too many immigrants came from Latin America. Nearly as many—49 percent—thought too many came from Asia, whereas only 31 percent felt similarly about Europe. A poll by the University of Chicago's National Opinion Research Center issued in 1991 revealed that nearly three fourths of non-Hispanic respondents thought Hispanics were more likely than whites to prefer welfare to employment. Hispanics were also considered more likely to be lazy, violence-prone, unintelligent, and unpatriotic. Blacks were viewed in an equally negative light, and Asians were seen as not much better. Former San Antonio mayor Henry Cisneros no doubt had such attitudes in mind when he predicted that increasingly, as cities are relegated to aged whites and young minorities, "People will not only say, 'Why should I be voting school bonds when my children have already gone through?' but 'Why should I be voting school bonds for people who don't look like me?' "

Signs of racial estrangement and isolation are ubiquitous. A major study completed in 1990 by the Carnegie Foundation for the Advancement of Teaching found college campuses in a virtual state of segregation: "At almost every campus we visited, Hispanic, Jewish, Polish, Italian, Muslim, Arab, Vietnamese, and Haitian student associations have organized themselves in their own separate groups." A *New York Times*/WCBS-TV News poll of New York City in 1990 found 10 percent of blacks convinced that the AIDS virus was "deliberately created in a laboratory in order to infect black people." Another 19 percent thought such a conspiracy might exist. The poll also revealed that one fourth of black respondents felt the government "deliberately makes sure that drugs are easily available in poor black neighborhoods in order to harm black people."

Distressingly often, disaffection and rage in minority neighborhoods have bubbled up in violence. In 1990, following the acquittal of several policemen responsible for the death of a Puerto Rican suspected drug dealer, outraged residents of Miami's small Puerto Rican community overturned several cars and set buildings ablaze. "It's sad that this is the only way we have gotten recognition," complained Betzaida Ferrer, state director of the National Puerto Rican Forum. Several months later, rioting broke out in a largely Hispanic area in Washington, D.C., after police shot a Salvadoran man. Mario Vasquez, a construction worker from Honduras, tried to explain the residents' frustration: "The police believe we're all dumb, illegal and drunk. They don't treat us as well as they treat blacks."

Such alienation is so pervasive as to be the norm in many communities. A study of Southeast Asian youths in San Diego found that though they were generally better students than native-born Americans, nearly all reported personal encounters with racism on U.S. soil. "No one who is not white can ever truly become an 'American,' " concluded one Khmer girl. Enrique Benjamin, a black Costa Rican who settled in Brooklyn, said he initially could not understand the attitudes of those around him. "I would see people looking at me kind of funny. I'd look around to see if it was me they were looking at. It took me awhile to realize that they looked at me that way because I was black. In my country, that never would have happened." As a consequence, he told a reporter, he had become uncomfortable. "With these looks, I don't feel free here." Nor did Haitian asylee Wilky Fortunat feel truly welcome. Rescued at sea by U.S. authorities after becoming ill during his clandestine flight from Haiti, Fortunat was placed in detention, where he faced racial epithets and physical abuse. Americans, he concluded, "don't care about black Haitians."

Even those Americans quick to complain of discrimination against native-born blacks often view foreign-born minorities with deep suspicion. Concerned that the once-black neighborhoods of south-central Los Angeles were becoming more and more Latino, the Reverend Charles Floyd accused Republicans of importing the Latinos to weaken black voting strength. "This is definitely by design," he said. "You have to ask yourself, how is it that people can come across the border with a green card and in six months or so buy a house?" In New York, state NAACP president Hazel Dukes complained of waiters who could not speak English. "Why let foreigners, newcomers, have these jobs while blacks, who have been here for hundreds of years, can't support themselves or their families?" asked Dukes. A group of Ecuadorian waiters were so enraged by her comments that they demonstrated in midtown Manhattan carrying signs declaring, HAZEL DUKES ES RACISTA.

A similar conflict surfaced at the nation's premier civil-rights coalition in 1990 when two major Hispanic organizations (the National Council of La Raza and the Mexican American Legal Defense and Education Fund) created turmoil by threatening to withdraw from the Leadership Conference for Civil Rights over what they saw as insensitivity to Hispanic concerns. The breach was repaired in an emotional rapprochement on the eve of the organization's fortieth-anniversary celebration. A week later, when feelings had calmed, MALDEF president Antonia Hernández recalled the commemorative and celebratory video shown at the anniversary dinner focusing on the heroes and high points of America's civil-rights struggle. "As I sat there, I took . . . pride . . . but it was . . . vicarious, because I wasn't part of that. I was excluded."

More such confrontations are inevitable as nonblack minority groups increasingly try to transform or supplant social-service, advocacy, and political organizations previously concerned primarily about blacks. The battle for inclusion in the civil-rights establishment is, at most, however, a minor skirmish in the larger struggle for acceptance into American society. That struggle touches schools, businesses, neighborhoods, and countless other institutions, including those devoted to the arts—as the theater world realized in 1990 when Actors Equity Association denied permission to Jonathan Pryce (a white English actor) to play a Eurasian role in a Broadway-bound play entitled *Miss Saigon*. During the acrimonious debate that proceeded Equity's reversal of its decision, the union argued "the casting of an Asian actor, in this role, would be an important and significant opportunity to break the usual pattern of casting Asians in minor roles."

The *Los Angeles Times* called Equity's position "monstrous." *The Washington Post* termed it "ludicrous." The *Chicago Tribune, Boston Globe, New York Times,* and countless others lambasted the union in similar terms. Minority artists and activists joined the fray, complaining that minority actors in general and Asians in particular were disproportionately relegated to minor roles. While whites—often with eye makeup or skin darkeners—were widely permitted to play minorities, they said, minorities were rarely chosen to play whites and often not even permitted to play themselves. "The only roles traditionally available to Asian-American acting professionals have been minor roles, often stereotyped and more often negative in the image they project," said Paul Igasaki, Washington representative of the Japanese American Citizens League. Producer and

director Shirley Sun complained of the "hypocrisy of those who
refuse to address the plight of Asian and Asian-American actors and instead turn it into an issue of 'artistic freedom.' All
that Asian and Asian-American actors are seeking is the opportunity to compete fairly and openly for a leading part."
"From the early westerns, when armies of white males painted
themselves as American Indians and collected paychecks while
real Indians went jobless, movies have served up an endless
pageant of whites playing nonwhite roles, hardly ever the reverse," wrote one black actress. An Asian actress, she added,
had once told her, "At least you work every once in a while.
Do you realize my only hope is to go out in a touring company
of 'The Flower Drum Song' or 'Teahouse of the August Moon'?"

Like members of a dysfunctional family, the two camps—
white critics and performers and minority activists and artists—were not so much having a dialogue as a shouting match,
and about entirely different things. One group was expressing
outrage over violation of an abstract principle, the other giving voice to an intensely personal pain; one focused on artistic
freedom, the other on lack of opportunity; one claimed white
racism was the basic problem, the other saw it as a minor factor in the general scheme of things. Such exchanges typify
those that too often go on between minorities and whites; and
they demonstrate a communications breakdown inevitable
among those who occupy largely different worlds.

After analyzing an array of studies regarding race relations
in America—and in particular those data concerning whites
and blacks—the National Research Council concluded, "At the
core of black-white relations is a dynamic tension between many
whites' expectations of American institutions and their expectations of themselves." Though whites generally supported the
concept of equal opportunity, said the NRC, they tended to
avoid blacks "in those institutions in which equal treatment is
most needed."

Despite the historic 1954 Supreme Court decision abolishing "separate but equal" educational facilities, many Americans, white and minority alike, cling to the idea that separate
neighborhoods, separate social lives, and separate aspirations

are inevitable, that the best that can be hoped for is peaceful—and occasionally cordial—coexistence. More often than not, behind such thinking lies an assumption that minorities (with few exceptions) are destined to lead lives of wretched mediocrity.

A review of *New York Times* stories in 1990, for instance, finds that Hispanics are nearly twelve times as likely (and blacks nearly twice as likely) to be described as poor than as middle class. Whites, conversely, are more than three times more likely to be described as "middle class" than as poor. In truth, while roughly 26 percent of Hispanics *are* below poverty level, as are 30 percent of blacks and 9 percent of whites, the majority of all three groups are not. Suppositions, however, create a truth of their own; so that to many, "minority," "poor," "free-loader," "criminal," and "unqualified" become largely interchangeable words. Without anyone intending to cause harm, minorities are routinely relegated to the margins of the mainstream.

Despite a widespread belief that affirmative action has led to a boom in minority opportunity and rampant "reverse discrimination," a 1991 Urban Institute study found that when young black and white men seeking entry-level jobs in Chicago and Washington were matched for age, qualifications, experience, education, demeanor, and physique, whites were three times as likely as blacks to receive preferential treatment from prospective employers—roughly the same advantage given Anglos over Hispanics in a comparable investigation (see Chapter 12) conducted for the U.S. General Accounting Office. Urban Institute researcher Margery Turner predicted that the research would shake up the thinking of those "who believe that the discrimination problem has been licked."

Such an outcome seems unlikely. Those who don't believe discrimination exists generally attribute its workings to an unbiased marketplace penalizing minorities' dearth of ability or initiative. And in a world where inequality is taken to be inevitable, many minorities resign themselves to a life of endless rejection and failure, and, in so doing, ensure that it will be. The result is not only complacent acceptance of discrimination but often competition among minorities for recognition as the most victimized group at the bottom of the social and economic hierarchy. The alternative, in many eyes, is not to aspire to something better but to plunge into an undefined state of nothingness.

Though an end to such attitudes (and the actions that cause and flow from them) can be encouraged by law, the law can hardly mandate changes in what are, essentially, matters of the heart—even if they are also matters of national concern. For barring major changes in U.S. immigration policy and birthrates, a steadily increasing proportion of new Americans will continue to be "minority." We can respond either by breaking down the walls separating so many from each other and from society's mainstream or risk the prospect of the nation's largest-growing segments floundering in alienation.

Noting the nation's growing ethnic diversity, author Ben J. Wattenberg has concluded that the United States is in the process of becoming the world's first "universal nation." Certainly America is in the process of assembling an array of ethnicities and races unlike anything previously assembled. And if we are wise, we will choose to make that a virtue. We will realize that the differences various groups bring to the table represent a potential gold mine of fresh ideas, if only we can learn to be open to them. We will realize as well that the problems of blacks, or Latinos, or whites, or Asian-Americans, inevitably, in an inextricably interrelated society, affect us all.

Exclusion and self-delusion are, unfortunately, arts in which we have had a great deal of practice. Those of us who are minorities consistently lie, to others and to ourselves, about the immutability of the burdens imposed upon us and about our readiness to let go of the rationalizations of the past. Whites routinely lie as well—about the degree of mobility society offers and about the depth of America's goodwill toward those who do not easily fit in. We have mastered words and phrases that shut down communication instead of facilitating it, that masquerade as dialogue but say nothing—while providing unlimited excuses for avoiding true contact.

For a nation experiencing a larger influx of nonwhites than

at any time since the height of the slave trade, that is profoundly troubling. For while it is true America's history is one of absorbing successive waves of immigrants, it is also a history of intermittent outbreaks of anti-immigrant hysteria, and of unremitting friction with racial minorities, whether native or foreign-born.

Given that, one can expect America's latest wave of immigration to be a magnet for conflict and hostility for years to come—despite a widely held belief that America has put the worst of her ethnic turmoil behind her. Optimistic forecasts notwithstanding, racial animosity has proven to be both an enduring American phenomenon and an invaluable political tool. Rather than a fire that flares up and burns itself out, it has more resembled a virus that at times lies dormant but can suddenly erupt with vengeance—particularly during periods of stress.

Flare-ups as gruesome as the draft riots in New York or the anti-Chinese rampage in San Francisco are not likely to be repeated. Hostilities are no longer quite so naked. But anyone who doubts that they exist need only put a group of whites and "minorities" together and induce a frank discussion of discrimination, affirmative action, or the state of race in America. If the participants are at all typical, pain, frustration, and anger will soon flood the room. Few would likely come away convinced that America's racial problems are solved or that conflict will not erupt again. Such a prognosis is not necessarily a reason for despair. It should, however, be a cause for concern and an incentive for confronting America's racial sickness with candor, determination, and intelligence. In so doing, we may reduce the intensity of future eruptions and may conceivably, in time, even eliminate the virus itself—provided we do not lapse into complacency or self-delusion and end up mistaking the calm for the cure.

NOTES

Introduction: In Search of
the Perfect American

9   *If a lawyer . . . certified for less: Annals of Congress,* July 1797, p. 423.

10   *"a moment of enthusiasm":* Ibid. p. 427.

10   *"We did not . . . sell it to others.":* Ibid. p. 430.

10   *"the sale . . . based on wealth.": Congressional Record,* daily edition, Oct. 27, 1990, H12361–62.

11   *"No one supposed . . . their own pleasure.": Dred Scott* versus *John F. A. Sandford,* U.S. Supreme Court, decided Dec. 1856.

11   *Great Britain ranked . . . Haiti and Iran:* U.S. Department of Justice, Immigration and Naturalization Service, *Statistical Yearbook of the Immigration and Naturalization Service: 1988* (Washington, D.C.: Government Printing Office, 1989).

12   *"still a beacon . . . toward home.":* "Transcript of Reagan's

Farewell Address to American People," *New York Times,* Jan. 12, 1989.

13   *Hispanics, Asians, blacks . . . is growing:* U.S. Bureau of the Census, "Projections of the Hispanic Population: 1983 to 2085," *Current Population Reports, Population Estimates and Projections, Series P-25, No. 955* (Washington, D.C.: Bureau of the Census, 1986); Judith Waldrop and Thomas Exter, "What the 1990 Census Will Show," *American Demographics,* Jan. 1990, p. 25.

13   *"Someday soon . . .":* William A. Henry III, "Beyond the Melting Pot," *Time,* April 9, 1990.

Chapter 1: Roots of Intolerance

17   *Nonetheless . . . Americans were Protestant:* Benjamin Hart, "The Wall That Protestantism Built: The Religious Reasons for the Separation of Church and State" (Washington, D.C.: Heritage Foundation) *Policy Review,* Fall 1988.

17   *During . . . in their communities:* See Thomas J. Curran, *Xenophobia and Immigration, 1820–1939* (Boston: Twayne Publishers, 1975), pp. 12–15.

18   *And when the Quakers:* See Marcus Lee Hansen, *The Atlantic Migration* (Cambridge, Mass.: Harvard University Press, 1951), pp. 34–35.

18   *So despite . . . political rights:* Ray Allen Billington, *The Protestant Crusade* (New York: Macmillan, 1938), pp. 6–9.

18   *"jail birds . . . die in England.":* Edith Abbott, ed., *Historical Aspects of the Immigration Problem: Select Documents* (Chicago: University of Chicago Press, 1926), p. 542.

18   *Maryland enacted:* Joseph G. Rayback, *A History of American Labor* (New York: Free Press, 1966), p. 8.

18   *In the mid-eighteenth . . . inferior quality:* See George M. Stephenson, *A History of American Immigration: 1840–1924* (Boston: Ginn and Company, 1926), p. 45.

19   *"of substance . . . refuse of their people.":* Extract from *Minutes of the Provincial Council of Pennsylvania*, May 15, 1755, rpt. in *Historical Aspects of the Immigration Problem: Select Documents*, ed. Edith Abbott (Chicago: University of Chicago Press, 1926), p. 415.

19   *"ignorant a set . . . of their own nation.":* Benjamin Franklin, letter to Peter Collison, May 1753, Ibid.

19   *"May not our government . . .":* Thomas Jefferson, *Notes on the State of Virginia* (1782), rpt. in Paul Leicester Ford, ed., *The Works of Thomas Jefferson*, Vol. III (New York: G. P. Putnam's Sons, 1904), pp. 484–88.

20   *"will probably never end . . .":* Ibid. Vol. IV, p. 49.

21   *In others . . . granted denization:* "Naturalization and Citizenship," *Harvard Encyclopedia of American Ethnic Groups* (Cambridge, Mass.: Harvard University Press, 1980), p. 735.

21   *denization valid outside any specific colony:* See Curran, p. 11.

21   *The law granted citizenship:* Ibid. p. 14.

22   *"It is not composed . . . not an easy place":* J. Hector St. John de Crèvecoeur, *Letters from an American Farmer* (1782; rpt. in New York: Fox, Duffield & Company, 1904), p. 49.

22   *"were as so. . . . in the world.":* Ibid. pp. 52–53.

22   *An open letter . . . one's own language:* "An Open Letter from Welsh Immigrants in Pennsylvania, 1800," Edith Abbott, ed., *Historical Aspects of the Immigration Problem: Select Documents*, p. 28.

22   *"If you knew . . . come hither.":* Samuel Crabtree, letter of April 10, 1818, Ibid. p. 28.

23   *In the same session . . . government officials:* See David S. Bogen, "The Free Speech Metamorphosis of Mr. Justice Holmes," *Hofstra Law Review*, Fall 1982.

24   *With the Sedition Acts . . . :* See Kenneth L. Karst, "Paths to Belonging: The Constitution and Cultural Identity," *North Carolina Law Review*, Jan. 1986.

24   *As president . . . naturalization waiting period:* See Frank H. Easterbrook, "Presidential Review," *Case Western Reserve Law Review*, 1990; Jeffery A. Smith, "Prior Restraint: Original Intentions and Modern Interpretations," *William & Mary Law Review*, Spring 1987.

24   *One launched in Antwerp . . . those brought in:* See Arthur E. Kellogg, "Two Centuries of Immigration Laws," *I & N Reporter,* Winter 1975–76, p. 30.

25   *The society started:* Hansen, p. 108.

25   *Massachusetts charged ship captains:* See *George Smith* versus *William Turner,* U.S. Supreme Court, decided Jan. 1849.

25   *"We think it . . . physical pestilence.":* The Mayor, Aldermen, and Commonalty of the City of New York versus *George Miln,* U.S. Supreme Court, decided Jan. 1837.

26   *In the 1820s . . . three fourths of America's immigrants:* U.S. Department of Justice, Immigration and Naturalization Service, *Statistical Yearbook of the Immigration and Naturalization Service: 1989* (Washington, D.C.: Government Printing Office, 1990), p. 2.

26   *Worried that destitute Irishmen:* William Forbes Adams, *Ireland and Irish Emigration to the New World* (1932; rpt. in Baltimore: Genealogical Publishing Co., 1980), pp. 277–83.

27   *Previously, the majority . . . urban areas:* Ibid. p. 70.

27   *"the present class of . . . murderers.":* from *Niles' Weekly Register,* 1834, rpt. in ed. Edith Abbott, *Historical Aspects of the Immigration Problem: Select Documents,* p. 570.

27   *"Gospel doctrines . . .":* Billington, p. 53.

27   *The phenomenal immigrant-driven:* See Ibid. p. 37; John Higham, *Send These to Me: Jews and Other Immigrants in Urban America* (New York: Atheneum, 1975), p. 21.

27   *Rumors abounded:* Curran, p. 26.

27   *In 1834 . . . basement of the nunnery:* Billington, pp. 71–89.

28   *The gathering was disrupted . . . city elections:* Curran, pp. 29–30.

28   *The party's candidates:* Billington, pp. 200–202.

28   *In addition to fighting. . . . numerous civilians:* Curran, pp. 38–43; Billington, pp. 220–34.

29   *Largely propelled . . . previous history:* William Forbes Adams, pp. 238–39.

29   *Irish nationals comprised:* from *Report of the Select Committee to Whom Was Referred the Memorial of the City of New York Relative to the Landing of Alien Passengers,* 1845 New York State Assem-

bly, rpt. in ed. Edith Abbott, *Historical Aspects of the Immigration Problem: Select Documents,* p. 581.

29   *"protection of American institutions . . . at any price.":* Congressional Globe, Appendix, Dec. 18, 1845, pp. 46–48.

30   *"a bill to accommodate . . . pitiable ignorance.":* Congressional Globe, Appendix, Feb. 1, 1847, pp. 385–87.

30   *And a Supreme Court ruling: George Smith* versus *William Turner,* U.S. Supreme Court, decided Jan. 1849.

Chapter 2: Years of Confusion, Days of Rage

31   *from which . . . through fiscal 1850:* U.S. Department of Justice, Immigration and Naturalization Service, *Statistical Yearbook of the Immigration and Naturalization Service: 1989* (Washington, D.C.: Government Printing Office, 1990), p. 2.

31   *"one of the most worthy . . .":* Mary Roberts' Coolidge, *Chinese Immigration* (1909; rpt. in New York: Arno Press, 1968), pp. 22–25.

31   *When a report:* Ibid. p. 17; See Charles J. McClain, Jr., "The Chinese Struggle for Civil Rights in Nineteenth Century America: The First Phase, 1850–1870," *California Law Review,* July 1984.

32   *The assembly responded . . . Chinese travelers:* Ibid.

32   *"morally a far . . .":* "Chinese Citizenship," *Daily Alta California,* May 21, 1853.

32   *"semi-human Asiatics . . . price of labor":* Peregrine Pilgrim, "The Chinese in California," *Daily Alta California,* July 29, 1853.

32   *Around the same . . . against whites:* McClain.

32   *Shortly thereafter . . . passage from China:* Ibid.

33   *Because six years . . . thought to be legal: George Smith* versus *William Turner,* U.S. Supreme Court, decided Jan. 1849; McClain.

33   *Close to 3 million:* U.S. Department of Justice, *Statistical Yearbook of the Immigration and Naturalization Service: 1989* (Wash-

ington, D.C.: Government Printing Office, 1990), p. 2.

33   *At the time:* See Stephen E. Maizlish, "The Meaning of Nativism and the Crisis of the Union: The Know-Nothing Movement in the Antebellum North," in ed. Stephen E. Maizlish, *Essays on American Antebellum Politics, 1840–1869* (Arlington, Texas: University of Texas at Arlington, 1982), pp. 166–68.

33   *They also wanted:* See Thomas J. Curran, *Xenophobia and Immigration, 1820–1939* (Boston: Twayne Publishers, 1975), p. 59.

33   *When asked:* Ibid. pp. 44–46.

34   *"all Pagan nations . . .":* Ray Allen Billington, *The Protestant Crusade* (New York: Macmillan, 1938), p. 291.

34   *A tour of America:* Billington, pp. 301–303; Alexander DeConde, *Half Bitter, Half Sweet* (New York: Charles Scribner's Sons, 1971), pp. 51–52; Carl Wittke, *Refugees of Revolution* (Westport, Conn.: Greenwood Press, 1952), pp. 135–37.

34   *"Had we no Irish . . .":* "Foreign Hornets," *New York Herald,* Feb. 1, 1854.

34   *"the chief source of crime . . .":* Samuel S. Busey, *Immigration: Its Evils and Consequences* (1856; rpt. in New York: Arno Press, 1969), pp. 108–20.

34   *"In the great cities . . .":* *Congressional Globe,* 33rd Congress, Jan. 25, 1855, pp. 389–91.

34   *"You may search . . .":* *Congressional Globe,* July 12, 1854, p. 1701.

35   *Similarly, when the Homestead Act:* See *Congressional Globe,* July 12, 1854, p. 1709.

35   *"by the next apportionment . . . in this body.":* *Congressional Globe,* June 20, 1856, p. 1413.

36   *"Debar the half-million . . . or any other nation.":* Parke Godwin, "Secret Societies—The Know-Nothings," *Putnam's Monthly,* V (Jan. 1855), pp. 95–97.

36   *In an attempt:* Billington, pp. 426–28.

37   *"In regard to Germans . . .":* Roy Bosler, ed., *The Collected Works of Abraham Lincoln,* Vol. IV (New Brunswick, N.J.: Rutgers University Press, 1953), p. 203.

38   *In December of 1862:* John Higham, *Strangers in the Land* (New

Brunswick, N.J.: Rutgers University Press, 1955), p. 13.

38   *"While the demand . . .":* Roy Bosler, ed., *The Collected Works of Abraham Lincoln,* Vol. VII, p. 40.

38   *"not only rescuing . . .":* "National Colonial Emigration Society," *Times* (London), June 4, 1863.

38   *"with flaming placards . . .":* "The Civil War in America," *Times* (London), June 4, 1863.

39   *"and if it should . . .":* John Sherman, *Congressional Globe,* 38th Congress, first session, March 21, 1864, p. 865.

39   *"one of the principal . . .":* Roy Bosler, ed., *The Collected Works of Abraham Lincoln,* Vol. VIII, p. 141.

39   *"material for the army":* "A Singular Letter from Mayor Gunther," *New York Times,* Sept. 15, 1864.

39   *They often were resented:* See Emerson David Fite, *Social and Industrial Conditions in the North During the Civil War* (New York: Macmillan, 1910), p. 190.

39   *At the same time:* See William Julius Wilson, *The Declining Significance of Race* (Chicago: University of Chicago Press, 1978), p. 48.

39   *Though Congress had exempted:* See James Ford Rhodes, *History of the United States,* Vol. IV (Port Washington, N.Y.: Kennikut Press, 1899), p. 113.

40   *That June:* Emerson David Fite, p. 189.

40   *The following Monday . . . gold-headed cane:* Iver Bernstein, *The New York City Draft Riots* (New York: Oxford University Press, 1990), pp. 28–30; "A Day of Infamy and Disgrace," *New York Times,* July 14, 1863.

40   *For several days . . . from a tree:* "A Day of Infamy and Disgrace," *New York Times,* July 14, 1863; "Continuation of the Riot—the Mob Increased in Numbers," *New York Times,* July 15, 1863; "Another Day of Rioting," *New York Times,* July 16, 1863; "The Riot Subsiding," *New York Times,* July 17, 1863.

Chapter 3: An Aroused West, an Excluded East

42   *"The pressing want . . .":* *Congressional Globe*, Jan. 31, 1866, p. 550.

43   *With the Union Pacific:* See Henry Kirke White, *History of the Union Pacific Railway* (1895; rpt. in Clifton, N.J.: Augustus M. Kelley Publishers, 1973); Alexander Saxton, *The Indispensable Enemy: Labor and the Anti-Chinese Movement in California* (Berkeley: University of California Press, 1971), pp. 60–65.

43   *Charles Crocker . . . direct from China:* See John Holt Williams, *A Great & Shining Road* (New York: Times Books, 1988), pp. 94–98.

43   *The Chinese . . . of the Sierra Nevada:* Saxton, pp. 60–65; Williams, p. 114.

44   *"Let the white . . .":* *Congressional Globe*, June 16, 1866, pp. 3213–17.

44   *"plunder league . . . for Governor.":* "The Issue Before the People," *San Francisco Examiner*, July 1, 1867.

44   *"protest against corruption . . .":* "Serenades to the Governor, Sheriff and County Clerk Elect," *Daily Alta California*, Sept. 6, 1867.

44   *"degrade the right . . . to earn a livelihood.":* Mary Roberts Coolidge, *Chinese Immigration* (1909; rpt. in New York: Arno Press, 1968), p. 65.

45   *"never intended . . .":* E. P. Hutchinson, *Legislative History of American Immigration Policy, 1798–1965* (Philadelphia: University of Pennsylvania Press, 1981), p. 56.

45   *George Williams, of Oregon:* *Congressional Globe*, Dec. 22, 1869, pp. 300–301.

45   *"Because we did . . .":* *Congressional Globe*, July 4, 1870, pp. 5150–53.

45   *When Sumner insisted:* *Congressional Globe*, July 4, 1870. p. 5154.

45   *In 1867:* Saxton, pp. 72–73.

45   *In 1871:* Shin-Shan Henry Tsai, *The Chinese Experience in America* (Bloomington: Indiana University Press, 1986), p. 67.

46   *"If their further immigration . . .":* In re Ah Fong, Circuit Court, D. California, decided Sept. 21, 1874.

46   *"The laws which govern. . . . and complaint.":* Henderson et al. versus *Mayor of The City of New York,* U.S. Supreme Court, decided Oct. 1875.

47   *"the great proportion . . . purposes of prostitution.":* Arthur E. Kellogg et al., "Two Centuries of Immigration Law," *I & N Reporter,* Winter 1975–76; Hutchinson, pp. 65–68.

47   *A woman subsequently: United States* versus *Johnson,* Circuit Court, S.D. New York, decided May 19, 1881.

47   *Neither passed:* Kellogg et al.; Coolidge, pp. 85–87.

47   *Around the same time . . . Americans could live:* Coolidge, pp. 85–87.

47   *Anti-Chinese planks:* Saxton, p. 105, f. 42.

48   *In Chico . . . were found guilty:* "The Chico Outrages: Arrest of Murderers and Incendiaries," *San Francisco Examiner,* March 27, 1877; "The Chico Outrages: The Prisoners Arrive at Oroville—Chinamen Raising Money to Aid in the Prosecution," *San Francisco Examiner,* March 29, 1877; "The Chico Murder," *San Francisco Examiner,* March 31, 1877.

48   *"There is now . . .":* "Hiring Chinamen," *San Francisco Examiner,* April 26, 1877.

49   *The evening of . . . Chinese were killed:* "The Scenes of Last Night," *San Francisco Examiner,* July 24, 1877; "The Hoodlum Outbreak," *San Francisco Examiner,* July 25, 1877; "The Hoodlum's Work," *San Francisco Examiner,* July 26, 1877; Saxton, pp. 114–15.

49   *"Before you and the world . . .":* Sandmeyer, p. 65.

50   *While ratifying the new:* See Saxton, p. 128; Coolidge, pp. 119–24.

50   *"Men of all parties . . .":* Congressional Record, Nov. 1, 1893, S3047.

50   *Congress responded in 1879:* See Tsai, p. 59.

50   *"Neither in popular language . . . right of naturalization.":* In re

Ah Yup, Circuit Court, D. California, decided April 29, 1878.

51 *"absolutely prohibit . . . the territory.":* See Tsai, p. 61; Coolidge, pp. 160–61; Hiroshi Motomura, "Immigration Law After a Century of Plenary Power: Phantom Constitutional Norms and Statutory Interpretation," *Yale Law Journal,* Dec. 1990.

51 *"servile people . . . upon this continent.":* Congressional Record, Feb. 28, 1882, S1480–86.

51 *"hereafter no state court . . . .":* Hutchinson, p. 82.

52 *That same year:* Kellogg et al.

52 *In September 1885:* Saxton, pp. 202–205.

53 *"act in self-defense . . . to both nations.":* Congressional Record, Nov. 2, 1893, S3088–89.

53 *"one of the great . . .":* Congressional Record, April 4, 1902, S3654.

53 *"The Chinese question":* Congressional Record, April 4, 1902, S3681.

54 *"It would be a perversion . . .":* Chew Heong versus *United States,* U.S. Supreme Court, decided Dec. 8, 1884.

55 *A California circuit court: In re Ah Ping,* Circuit Court, D. California, decided March 30, 1885.

55 *"To preserve its independence . . .":* Chae Chan Ping versus *United States,* U.S. Supreme Court, decided May 13, 1889.

55 *"paupers, criminals and persons . . . peace and security.":* Ibid.

55 *In one case involving Ah Fawn: United States* versus *Ah Fawn,* District Court, S.D. California, decided Sept. 18, 1893.

56 *"The right of a nation . . .":* Fong Yue Ting versus *United States; Wong Quan* versus *United States; Lee Joe* versus *United States,* U.S. Supreme Court, decided May 15, 1893.

56 *"The power of naturalization . . .":* United States versus *Wong Kim Ark,* U.S. Supreme Court, decided March 28, 1898.

Chapter 4: Radicals, Race, and New Restrictions

59 *In the ensuing . . . subsequently executed:* The Supreme Court refused to overturn the convictions. See *Spies* versus *Illinois,*

U.S. Supreme Court, decided Nov. 2, 1887; also see Paul Avrich, *The Haymarket Tragedy* (Princeton, N.J.: Princeton University Press, 1984).

59   *"[W]hat started the craze . . .":* "The Assassin Makes a Full Confession," *New York Times,* Sept. 8, 1901.

59   *A new immigration act:* Act of March 3, 1903 (32 Stat. 1213).

60   *Though only 26,000 . . . over 160,000.:* U.S. Department of Justice, Immigration and Naturalization Service, *Statistical Yearbook of the Immigration and Naturalization Service: 1989* (Washington, D.C.: Government Printing Office, 1990), pp. 2–3.

60   *and in 1885 prodded:* Act of Feb. 26, 1885 (23 Stat. 332).

60   *Ethnicity, however:* John Higham, *Strangers in the Land* (New Brunswick, N.J.: Rutgers University Press, 1955), pp. 92–93; Alexander DeConde, *Half Bitter, Half Sweet* (New York: Charles Scribner's Sons, 1971), pp. 121–26.

61   *The House Judiciary Committee:* E. P. Hutchinson, *Legislative History of American Immigration Policy, 1798–1965* (Philadelphia: University of Pennsylvania Press, 1981), pp. 97–101.

61   *"persons suffering . . . moral turpitude.":* Arthur E. Kellogg et al., "Two Centuries of Immigration Law," *I & N Reporter,* Winter 1975–76; Act of March 3, 1891 (31 Stat. 143).

61   *"the wholesale infusion . . .":* Hutchinson, p. 117.

62   *"ethnic explanation . . . saddle upon our ethnic types.":* William Z. Ripley, *The Races of Europe* (New York: D. Appleton, 1899), pp. 522–23.

62   *"noble and royal . . . downfall of nations.":* David Starr Jordan (president of Leland Stanford Jr. University), *The Blood of the Nation* (Boston: American Unitarian Association, 1902), pp. 25, 28.

63   *"Much more care . . .":* Francis Galton, *Hereditary Genius* (1869, 1892; rpt. in London: Macmillan, 1925), xxvi.

63   *"our race is above . . .":* Ibid. p. 330.

63   *Total immigration . . . from Turkey and India:* U.S. Department of Justice, *Statistical Yearbook of the Immigration and Naturalization Service: 1989* (Washington, D.C.: Government Printing Office), p. 3.

63   *For restrictionists:* See Daniel J. Kevles, *In the Name of Eugenics* (New York: Alfred A. Knopf, 1985), p. 72.

64   *"tricky, deceitful . . .":* George M. Stephenson, *A History of American Immigration: 1840–1924* (Boston: Ginn and Company, 1926), p. 268.

64   *"Japanese Invasion . . .":* "Japanese Invasion; The Problem of the Hour," *San Francisco Chronicle*, Feb. 23, 1905.

64   *"inundating torrent . . . fight us in future years.":* Ibid.: "Crime and Poverty Go Hand in Hand with Asiatic Labor," *San Francisco Chronicle*, Feb. 24, 1905; "Japanese a Menace to American Women," *San Francisco Chronicle*, March 1, 1905; "Grave Danger in the Orient: Says Japanese Are a Menace," *San Francisco Chronicle*, Feb. 25, 1905.

64   *In the climate:* "State Senate Adopts Resolution Against Unrestricted Immigration of Japanese," *San Francisco Chronicle*, March 2, 1905.

64   *As its contribution . . . children in San Francisco:* Carey McWilliams, *Prejudice: Japanese-Americans: Symbol of Intolerance* (Boston: Little, Brown, 1944), p. 31; Benjamin Ringer, *We the People, and Others* (London: Tavistock Publications, 1983), pp. 689–99.

65   *The Japanese government . . . bribes from bordellos:* "Ruef and Schmitz Indicted for Extortion: Grand Jury Finds the Mayor and His Boss Guilty of Blackmailing French Restaurants," *San Francisco Examiner*, Nov. 16, 1906; see also Lately Thomas, *A Debonair Scoundrel* (New York: Holt, Rinehart and Winston, 1962); Fremont Older, *My Own Story* (New York: Macmillan, 1926).

65   *In the course:* McWilliams, p. 26; Alexander Saxton, *The Indispensable Enemy: Labor and the Anti-Chinese Movement in California* (Berkeley: University of California Press, 1971), p. 253.

65   *A cooperative Congress:* Act of Feb. 20, 1907 (34 Stat. 898).

65   *Later experts would dispute:* See discussion in Maldwyn Allen Jones, *American Immigration* (Chicago: University of Chicago Press, 1960), pp. 177–206.

66   *"persons who . . . any time previously.":* Act of March 3, 1903 (32 Stat. 1213).

66   *In 1907:* Act of Feb. 20, 1907 (34 Stat. 898).

67   *The act also:* Act of Feb. 5, 1917 (39 Stat. 874).

67   *The latter condition:* see Hutchinson, p. 164.

Chapter 5: A War Ends, an Era of
Isolation Begins

68   *"found advocating or teaching . . .":* Act of Feb. 5, 1917 (39
      Stat. 889).

68   *"all organized government":* Act of Oct. 16, 1918 (40 Stat. 1012).

68   *In June 1920:* Act of June 5, 1920 (41 Stat. 1008).

69   *"I do not consider . . .":* "249 Reds Sail, Exiled to Soviet Rus-
      sia; Berkman Threatens to Come Back: Second Shipload May
      Leave This Week," *New York Times,* Dec. 22, 1919; See Louis
      F. Post, *The Deportations Delirium of Nineteen-Twenty* (Chicago:
      Charles H. Kerr & Co., 1923), pp. 1–27.

70   *One of the . . . or similar reasons:* Post, pp. 84–100; See *Colyer
      et al.* versus *Skeffington, Commissioner of Immigration. Katzeff et
      al.* versus *Same* (three cases). *In re Harbatuk et al. In re Mack et
      al.,* District Court, D. Massachusetts, decided June 23, 1920.

70   *Of the nearly:* Post, p. 192.

70   *"to create an . . . acquire useful knowledge.":* *Meyer* versus *Ne-
      braska,* U.S. Supreme Court, decided June 4, 1923; *Bartels*
      versus *State of Iowa; Bohning* versus *State of Ohio; Pohl* versus
      *State of Ohio; Nebraska District of Evangelical Lutheran Synod of
      Missouri, Ohio, and Other States, et al.* versus *Mckelvie et al., etc.,*
      U.S. Supreme Court, decided June 4, 1923.

70   *Concerned about:* U.S. Department of Labor, Bureau of Im-
      migration, *Annual Report of the Commissioner General of Immi-
      gration to the Secretary of Labor* (Washington, D.C.: Government
      Printing Office, 1918), pp. 15–16.

71   *"the popular belief . . .":* Carl C. Brigham, *A Study of American
      Intelligence* (Princeton, N.J.: Princeton University Press, 1923),
      p. 190.

71   *It also showed . . . some white genes:* Ibid. pp. 190, 192.

71   *"American intelligence is declining . . .":* Ibid. p. 210.

71   *The solution:* Ibid. vi–vii, p. 210.

71   *"the gradual dying . . .":* in Madison Grant, *The Passing of the Great Race* (1918; rpt. in New York: Arno Press, 1970), ix.

71   *Grant, expanding on William Ripley's:* Ibid. xx–xxi.

72   *The 1920 Republican:* Party platform statements excerpted in *Congressional Record,* April 8, 1924, S5806.

72   *Commissioner of Immigration:* "Immigration Menace Is Called America's Gravest Problem Now," *Minneapolis Journal,* Dec. 5, 1920.

72   *The* Literary Digest: *Literary Digest,* Dec. 18, 1920, p. 7.

72   *"If urging their exclusion . . .": Japanese Immigration: Hearings Before the Committee on Immigration and Naturalization,* 66th Congress, second session (Washington, D.C.: Government Printing Office, 1921), p. 4.

72   *"The fecundity . . .":* Ibid. p. 105.

72   *The* Los Angeles Times: *Los Angeles Times,* Jan. 11, 1920; *Sacramento Bee,* Feb. 26, 1920.

73   *In 1918: Annual Report of the Commissioner General of Immigration,* p. 21.

73   *"Most of the . . .":* "Immigration Menace Is Called America's Gravest Problem Now," *Minneapolis Journal,* Dec. 5, 1920.

73   *The House accepted:* E. P. Hutchinson, *Legislative History of American Immigration Policy, 1798–1965* (Philadelphia: University of Pennsylvania Press, 1981), p. 175.

73   *"It has not melted . . .": Congressional Record,* May 3, 1921, S958.

73   *"face to face . . .":* Ibid. S961.

74   *"Choose you this day . . .":* Ibid. S961–63.

74   *The business of reconciling:* Act of May 19, 1921 (42 Stat. 5).

74   *He calculated:* Lothrop Stoddard, *The Revolt Against Civilization* (New York: Charles Scribner's Sons, 1922), p. 113.

75   *"We are facing . . .": Scientific Monthly,* pp. 561–70. Vol. XV, No. 6. (Dec. 1922), p. 41.

75   *"If immigrants are not: Hearings Before the Committee on Immigration, U.S. Senate, 77th Congress, Jan. 24, 1923* (Washington, D.C.: Government Printing Office, 1923), p. 17.

75   *Ozawa contended: Takao Ozawa* versus *United States,* U.S. Supreme Court, decided Nov. 13, 1922.

76   *The U.S. Justice Department:* Ibid.

76   *Bhagat Singh Thind: United States* versus *Bhagat Singh Thind,* U.S. Supreme Court, decided Feb. 19, 1923.

77   *"It is obvious . . . owning agricultural lands.":* Terrace et al. versus *Thompson, Attorney General of the State of Washington,* U.S. Supreme Court, decided Nov. 12, 1923.

78   *The practice had become:* See Benjamin Ringer, *We the People, and Others* (London: Tavistock Publications, 1983), pp. 711–22.

78   *"hundreds of thousands . . . beneficial to this country.":* Congressional Record, April 8, 1924, S5804–5.

78   *"The Supreme Court . . .":* Ringer, p. 793.

79   *"be deeply resented . . .":* Congressional Record, April 8, 1924, S5811.

79   *"an open declaration . . .":* Ringer, p. 816.

79   *The Immigration Act:* Act of May 28, 1924 (43 Stat. 240).

80   *For two years:* See *Harvard Encyclopedia of American Ethnic Groups* (Cambridge, Mass.: Harvard University Press, 1980), p. 493.

Chapter 6: A Second War, Some Second Thoughts

82   *Total immigration:* U.S. Department of Justice, Immigration and Naturalization Service, *Statistical Yearbook of the Immigration and Naturalization Service: 1989* (Washington, D.C.: Government Printing Office, 1990), p. 3.

83   *They "must not . . . a hundred votes.":* "Roosevelt to Aid Refugees Here: 12,000 to Stay After Visas Expire," *New York Times,* Nov. 19, 1938; see Roland Sanders, *Shores of Refuge* (New York: Henry Holt and Company, 1988), pp. 451–58.

83   *"to prevent possible . . .":* "Refugee Ship Idles Off Florida Coast," *New York Times,* June 5, 1939; Sanders, pp. 466–67.

83   *The legislation's sponsors:* See Deborah E. Lipstadt, "In 1939, Sympathy but No Help for the Jews," *Newsday,* April 9, 1989; Toney Anaya, "Because There Are Still Many Who Wait for Death," *Hofstra Law Review,* Fall 1986.

84   *In June 1940:* Act of June 28, 1940 (54 Stat. 670).

84   *"stop all cars . . .":* "Japanese Aliens' Roundup Starts," *Los Angeles Times,* Dec. 8, 1941.

84   *"Those who know . . . sometimes shuffle.":* "How to Tell Your Friends from the Japs," *Time,* Dec. 22, 1941.

85   *"immediate evacuation . . .":* Benjamin B. Ringer, *We the People, and Others* (London: Tavistock Publications, 1983), pp. 866–67.

85   *"organized and ready . . . action will be taken.":* See Glenn P. Harris, "Sovereign Immunity," *George Washington Law Review,* May 1987.

85   *"first triumph . . . for the purpose.":* "Weekend Raids Jam West Coast Jails," *Los Angeles Times,* Feb. 23, 1942.

85   *Congress quickly passed:* Act of March 21, 1942 (56 Stat. 173).

86   *That group:* See Fred W. Riggs, *Pressures on Congress* (New York: King's Crown Press, 1950).

86   *They scored . . . to help win the war:* Ibid. pp. 65–91.

87   *To avoid alarming:* Ibid., p. 138.

87   *"thank the Chinese . . .":* "Hurting China, Helping Japan," *New York Times,* June 13, 1943.

87   *"I regard this legislation . . .":* Riggs, p. 211.

88   *"To date we have . . .":* *Congressional Record,* Oct. 20, 1943, H8581.

88   *The Court saw no merit: Hirabayashi* versus *United States,* U.S. Supreme Court, decided June 21, 1943; *Yasui* versus *United States,* U.S. Supreme Court, decided June 21, 1943.

89   *"Korematsu was not excluded . . .": Korematsu* versus *United States,* U.S. Supreme Court, decided Dec. 18, 1944.

89   *"This exclusion of . . .":* Ibid.

89   *"Loyalty is a matter . . .": Ex parte Mitsuye Endo,* U.S. Supreme
      Court, decided Dec. 18, 1944.

90   *Struggling to explain: Korematsu* versus *United States.*

91   *"We can speak most . . .":* "A Plea for Hitler's Victims," *New
      York Times,* Oct. 1, 1946.

91   *"The fact is . . .":* "The Text of President Truman's Call on
      Congress to Meet the Country's Grave Problems," *New York
      Times,* Jan. 7, 1947.

91   *"The only civilized route . . .":* "Text of Truman's Message on
      Admission of D.P.s to U.S.," *New York Times,* July 8, 1947.

92   *"This is a most begrudging . . .":* "Truman's Statement on Ref-
      ugee Bill," *New York Times,* June 26, 1948.

92   *"the vanguard . . .":* "U.S. City Welcome Ship With 813 DP's,
      1st Under New Act," *New York Times,* Oct. 31, 1948; see United
      States Displaced Persons Commission, *Memo to America: The
      DP Story* (Washington, D.C.: Government Printing Office,
      1952), pp. 64–65.

93   *Between 1943 and 1946:* See Gertrude D. Krichefsky, "Impor-
      tation of Alien Laborers," *I & N Reporter,* July 1956.

93   *"particularly during harvest . . .":* Albert Del Guercio, "Some
      Mexican Border Problems," *Monthly Review* (Department of
      Justice, INS), April 1946.

Chapter 7: Keeping Them Out

95   *"It would appear . . .":* Milton R. Konvitz, *Civil Rights in Im-
      migration* (Ithaca, N.Y.: Cornell University Press, 1953), pp.
      13–14.

95   *Such embarrassment led:* Act of Aug. 1, 1950 (64 Stat. 384).

95   *With the Internal Security:* Act of Sept. 23, 1950 (64 Stat. 987).

96   *"thought control.":* *Congressional Record* (daily edition), June 25,
      1952, H8084.

96   *"obviously unconstitutional . . . bill contemplate.":* Judy Wurtzel,
      "First Amendment Limitations on the Exclusion of Aliens,"

New York University Law Review, April 1987.

96   *"a virtual block . . .":* United States Displaced Persons Commission, *Memo to America: The DP Story* (Washington, D.C.: Government Printing Office, 1952), p. 71.

96   *That legislation:* Act of June 27, 1952 (66 Stat. 163).

97   *"The countries of Eastern . . .": Public Papers of the Presidents: Harry S Truman, 1952–53* (Washington, D.C.: Government Printing Office, 1966), p. 443.

97   *"demeaning process":* Mike Masaoka, interviewed Feb. 22, 1990.

97   *"frustrated and handicapped . . .":* U.S. President's Commission on Immigration and Naturalization, *Whom We Shall Welcome* (Washington, D.C.: Government Printing Office, 1953), p. 52.

98   *The Refugee Relief:* Act of Aug. 7, 1953 (67 Stat. 400); see Deborah Anker and Michael Posner, "The Forty Year Crisis: A Legislative History of the Refugee Act of 1980," *San Diego Law Review,* Vol. 16, No. 1 (Dec. 1981).

98   *"the wetback traffic . . .": Migratory Labor in American Agriculture,* report of the President's Commission on Migratory Labor (Washington, D.C.: Government Printing Office, 1951), p. 69.

98   *"perhaps the greatest . . .":* William F. Kelly, "The Wetback Issue," *The I & N Reporter,* Jan. 1954.

99   *During a fact-finding:* Ibid.

99   *"that he . . .":* Joseph Swing, from interview done in 1971 for "Eisenhower Administration Project" of the Oral History Research Office, Columbia University.

99   *In the meantime:* Anthony Leviero, "Eisenhower Backs 'Wetbacks' Drive," *New York Times,* Aug. 18, 1953.

99   *Brownell and acting:* Ibid; also see *Congressional Record,* March 1, 1954, H2424–26.

99   *A group of women's:* Gladwin Hill, "Wetback Traffic Again Sets Record—105,529 Persons Intercepted in August—Farmers Balk at New Federal Drive," *New York Times,* Sept. 15, 1953.

99   *"Imperial County has . . . public health problems.":* "Excerpts from the CBS Radio Network Presentation of 'The Wetbacks,' April 4, 1954, in *Congressional Record,* June 14, 1954, H8132.

100   *"No one could guess . . .":* Richard P. Eckels, "Hungry Work-

ers, Ripe Crops, and the Nonexistent Mexican Border," *The Reporter,* April 13, 1954.

100   *"cheap labor subsidy . . .":* Letter from Cristobal Aldret, state chairman, American GI Forum of Texas, *Congressional Record,* March 1, 1954, H2425.

100   *Mexico's foreign minister:* AP, "Mexico Cites Difficulties," *New York Times,* Aug. 18, 1953.

100   *Brownell spoke at length: Congressional Record,* June 14, 1954, S8131.

100   *"I want the Senate . . .": Congressional Record,* June 14, 1954, S8127.

101   *Swing promptly hired:* J. W. Swing, "A Workable Labor Program," *I & N Reporter,* Nov. 1955.

101   *Thirty days after:* Ibid.; Joseph Swing, "Eisenhower Administration Project"; "United States Mopup of Wetback Labor Slated," *Washington Post and Times Herald,* June 10, 1954.

101   *In late 1955:* J. W. Swing, "A Workable Labor Program."

101   *One scholar:* Juan Ramon García, *Operation Wetback: The Mass Deportation of Mexican Undocumented Workers in 1954* (Westport, Conn.: Greenwood Press, 1980), pp. 227–28.

102   *Politicians, satisfied:* Bills S.3660 and S.3661; see *Congressional Record,* June 14, 1954, S15175.

102   *Following Operation Wetback:* Gertrude D. Krichefsky, "Importation of Alien Laborers," *I & N Reporter,* Jan. 1954.

Chapter 8: A Reluctant Reform

103   *He did so through:* Russell Baker, "Eisenhower Acts," *New York Times,* Nov. 9, 1956; Deborah E. Anker and Michael H. Posner, "The Forty Year Crisis: A Legislative History of the Refugee Act of 1980," *San Diego Law Review,* Vol. 16, No. 1 (Dec. 1981), p. 15.

104   *"Send me your . . .":* John Kennedy, *A Nation of Immigrants*

(New York: Anti-Defamation League of B'Nai B'Rith, 1958), pp. 33–34.

104   *The following year:* E. P. Hutchinson, *Legislative History of American Immigration Policy, 1798–1965* (Philadelphia: University of Pennsylvania Press, 1981), p. 339.

104   *Days before Kennedy's:* "Statement and Notes in Cuba Break," *New York Times,* Jan. 4, 1961.

104   *Countless more were:* Max Frankel, "Hong Kong Crisis on Refugees Puts U.S. in a Dilemma," *New York Times,* May 23, 1962.

104   *"to end the spectacle . . .":* Ibid.

104   *The administration again:* "Transcript of the President's News Conference on Foreign and Domestic Matters," *New York Times,* May 24, 1962.

105   *Kennedy called for:* Hutchinson, p. 359.

105   Under the current system: Immigration, Hearing before Subcommittee #1 of the Committee of the Judiciary, House of Representatives, 88th Congress, part II (Washington, D.C.: Government Printing Office, 1964), p. 879.

105   *The day Kennedy:* "Negroes Break Off Los Angeles Talks," *New York Times,* July 24, 1963; R. Hart Phillips, "Negroes Resume Drive in Florida," *New York Times,* July 24, 1963; Peter Kihss, "143 More Seized in Protest Here," *New York Times,* July 24, 1963.

105   *In Cambridge, Maryland:* Ben A. Franklin, "Pact Is Reached for Racial Peace in Cambridge, Md.," *New York Times,* July 24, 1963.

105   *Hill insiders predicted:* See Tom Wicker, "President Urges Repeal of Quotas for Immigration," *New York Times,* July 24, 1963.

106   *"Let us carry . . .":* Lyndon B. Johnson, "The State of the Union—Address of the President of the United States," *Congressional Record,* Jan. 8, 1964, H113.

106   *Afterward, Johnson sent:* Garner J. Cline, former staff director House Immigration Subcommittee, interviewed July 6, 1990.

106   *The public backed:* Louis Harris, "By Vote of 2 to 1, Public Feels Congress Is Dragging Its Feet," *Washington Post,* Jan. 6, 1964.

107   *"incompatible with our . . .":* Lyndon B. Johnson, *Message from the President of the United States Relative to Changes in New Immigration Laws with Accompanying Papers,* Jan. 13, 1965, 89th Congress.

107   *"Everywhere else in . . .":* Hearings Before Subcommittee No. 1 of Committee on the Judiciary, U.S. House of Representatives, 88th Congress (Washington, D.C.: Government Printing Office, 1964), p. 412.

107   *The public . . . poll respondent:* Louis Harris, "U.S. Public Is Strongly Opposed to Easing of Immigration Laws," *Washington Post,* May 31, 1965.

108   *"a very sizable . . .":* Mrs. Robert V. H. Duncan, president general, National Society, Daughters of the American Revolution, statement, Hearings Before Subcommittee No. 1 of the Committee on the Judiciary, U.S. House of Representatives (Washington, D.C.: Government Printing Office, 1964), pp. 735, 740.

108   *"colored folks . . .":* Ibid., p. 30.

108   *Others worried about:* See Emanuel Celler, testimony, Hearings Before Subcommittee No. 1 of the Committee on the Judiciary, U.S. House of Representatives, p. 4; Mrs. William Henry Sullivan, Daughters of the American Revolution, statement, Hearings Before Subcommittee on Immigration and Naturalization, Committee on the Judiciary, U.S. Senate (Washington, D.C.: Government Printing Office, 1965), p. 711.

108   *"Take the English speaking . . .":* Hearings Before Subcommittee on Immigration and Naturalization, Committee on the Judiciary, U.S. Senate (Washington, D.C.: Government Printing Office) p. 63.

108   *Under the new legislation:* Nicholas deb Katzenbach, testimony, Hearings Before Subcommittee No. 1 of the Committee on the Judiciary, U.S. House of Representatives (Washington, D.C: Government Printing Office, 1965), p. 21.

109   *"The bill will not . . .":* Ibid. pp. 2–3.

109   *"but we do not expect . . .":* Hearings Before Subcommittee No. 1 of the Committee on the Judiciary, U.S. House of Representatives (Washington, D.C.: Government Printing Office), p. 418.

109   *"with the greatest . . .":* "Letter to the President of the Senate
        and to the Speaker of the House on Revision of the Immi-
        gration Laws," July 23, 1963, *Public Papers of the Presidents,*
        John F. Kennedy: 1963 (Washington, D.C.: Government Print-
        ing Office, 1964), p. 595.

109   *"more or less like . . .":* Pete Rodino, interviewed March
        22, 1990.

110   *If Asians were treated:* See Marion T. Bennett, "The Immigra-
        tion and Nationality (McCarren-Walter) Act of 1952, as
        Amended to 1965," in ed. Edward P. Hutchinson, *The Annals*
        of the American Academy of Political and Social Science (Philadel-
        phia: American Academy of Political and Social Science, 1966),
        p. 131.

110   *In return for abolishing:* Edward M. Kennedy, "The Immigra-
        tion Act of 1965," in *The Annals of the American Academy of*
        Political and Social Science, p. 147.

110   *Congressman Henry Gonzalez:* Henry Gonzalez, *Congressional*
        Record, Sept. 30, 1965, H25714.

110   *"Before we knew . . .":* Raúl Yzaguirre, interviewed Feb.
        23, 1990.

110   *"internationally oriented":* Abba P. Schwartz, *The Open Society,*
        p. 125.

111   *"There was a sense . . .":* Dale S. deHann, former counsel to
        Senate subcommittee on refugees, interviewed March 22, 1990.

112   *"The bill that we sign . . .":* Lyndon B. Johnson, "Remarks at
        the Signing of the Immigration Bill, Liberty Island, New York,
        Oct. 3, 1965," *Public Papers of the Presidents, Lyndon B. Johnson,*
        1965 (Washington, D.C.: Government Printing Office, 1966),
        p. 1038.

113   The New York Times: "Responding to Castro," *New York Times,*
        Oct. 5, 1965.

113   *Congress rejected:* Joyce Vialet, *U.S. Immigration Law and Policy:*
        1952–1986 (Washington, D.C.: Government Printing Office,
        1988), pp. 58–59.

113   *"Canada could entirely . ‹ .":* *Congressional Record,* Sept. 30, 1965,
        H25714.

114   *By then, total:* U.S. Department of Justice, 1975 *Annual Report:*

Immigration and Naturalization Service (Washington, D.C.: Government Printing Office, 1975), p. 44.

114 *Fierro told Eilberg:* Manny Fierro, former lobbyist for *El Congresso*, National Congress of Hispanic American Citizens, interviewed (phone) July 24, 1990; Garner J. Cline.

114 *"It may be . . .":* Congressional Record, Sept. 29, 1976, H33633.

115 *Meanwhile, bills whizzed:* Spencer Rich and Richard L. Lyons, "Senate Kills Clean Air Bill," *Washington Post*, Oct. 2, 1976.

115 *Byrd temporarily withdrew: Congressional Record*, Oct. 1, 1990, S34537.

Chapter 9: A Legacy of Vietnam

116 *"The Vietnam cease-fire . . .":* Flora Lewis, "Vietnam Peace Pacts Signed; America's Longest War Halts," *New York Times*, Jan. 28, 1973.

116 *"to rediscover those . . .":* Richard M. Nixon, "Transcript of President Nixon's Address to the Nation Announcing His Resignation," *New York Times*, Aug. 9, 1974.

116 *"the internal wounds . . .":* Gerald Ford, "Transcript of Address by New President," *New York Times*, Aug. 10, 1974.

117 *A sympathetic and solicitous:* Richard L. Madden, "Congress Unanimously Passes a Pledge of Cooperation with the New President," *New York Times*, Aug. 10, 1974.

117 *As Da Nang succumbed:* Le Kim Dinh, "For Those Who Flee, Life Is 'Hell on Earth,'" *New York Times*, March 31, 1975.

117 *"I still think . . .":* Gerald Ford, "Transcript of President's News Conference on Foreign and Domestic Matters," *New York Times*, April 4, 1975.

117 *A Pentagon contingency:* David E. Rosenbaum, "U.S. Considers Corridor to Evacuate Vietnamese," *New York Times*, April 17, 1975.

117 *Senate Foreign Relations: Congressional Record*, 94th Congress, April 21, 1975, S11017.

117   *Senator Thomas Eagleton: Congressional Record,* 94th Congress, April 21, 1975, S11029.

117   *Many wondered whether:* See *Congressional Record,* 94th Congress, April 21, 1975, S11278.

118   *"When the Americans saw . . .":* Nguyen Van Thieu, "Excerpts from Address on Resignation," *New York Times,* April 22, 1975.

118   *"But it cannot be . . .":* Gerald Ford, "Excerpts from Ford Address at Tulane," *New York Times,* April 24, 1975.

118   *Many were picked up:* Ambassador L. Dean Brown, director, Interagency Task Force on Indochina, U.S. Department of State, *Indochina Refugees,* Hearings Before Subcommittee on Immigration, Citizenship and International Law, U.S. House of Representatives, 94th Congress (Washington, D.C.: Government Printing Office, 1975), p. 5.

118   *Governor Edmund Brown, Jr.:* "Refugees: Unexpected Guests," *The Economist,* May 3, 1975.

119   *A Gallup Poll:* "Ford Asks $507 Million Refugee Aid," *Facts on File,* May 10, 1975.

119   *"We must strive . . .":* Indochina Refugees, Hearings Before Subcommittee on Immigration, Citizenship and International Law, U.S. House of Representatives, 94th Congress (Washington, D.C.: Government Printing Office, 1975), pp. 1–2.

119   *"Given the small number . . .":* "All Those Refugees—Who They Are, Where They're Going," *U.S. News & World Report,* May 12, 1975.

119   *"Christmas Brings Happy . . .":* "Christmas Brings Happy Ending for Vietnam Refugees," *U.S. News & World Report,* Dec. 29, 1975.

119   *"I guess nobody . . .":* Ibid.

120   *Even years after arriving:* See Nathan Caplan et al., *Southeast Asian Refugee Self-Sufficiency Study: Final Report* (Washington, D.C.: U.S. Department of Health and Human Services, 1985), pp. 123–35.

120   *"I hope they all . . .":* "A Ray of Hope; An Arkansas Town That Took in 2,000 Refugees," *U.S. News & World Report,* Aug. 6, 1979.

120   *"From time to time . . .":* Ibid.

120 *Despite the government's: Report to Congress: Refugee Resettlement Program* (Washington, D.C.: U.S. Department of Health and Human Services, 1988), p. 117.

121 *Night and day:* See, "Flurry in Capital: U.S. Opens Its Doors to the 'Floating Refugees,'" *U.S. News & World Report,* Aug. 15, 1977.

121 *In all, twenty-three thousand: Report to Congress: Refugee Resettlement Program* (Washington, D.C.: U.S. Department of Health and Human Services, 1988), p. A-1.

121 *Early in 1976:* Joyce Vialet, *U.S. Immigration Law and Policy: 1952–1986* (Washington, D.C.: Government Printing Office, 1988), p. 72.

121 *Bell, however, argued:* Susan W. Stewart, "Bell Defends Refugee Admission," *Washington Post,* Aug. 5, 1977.

122 *Edward Kennedy, then:* Jerry Tinker, Senate Subcommittee on Immigration and Refugee Affairs, interviewed March 19, 1990.

122 *"Refugees are hostage . . .":* Joyce Vialet, *U.S. Immigration Law and Policy: 1952–1986* (Washington, D.C.: Government Printing Office, 1988), p. 73; Christopher Dickey, "Administration to Request Reform of Refugee Laws," *Washington Post,* Dec. 11, 1978.

122 *In late 1978:* Henry Kamm, "Thai Irritation on Refugees Grows," *New York Times,* Jan. 25, 1978; Lee Lescaze, "Swelling Tide of Refugees Inundates Asian Camps, Despite Resettlement Push," *Washington Post,* Dec. 5, 1978.

122 *One group of. . . . the ordeal began:* "U.S. Accepting More Refugees from Vietnam," *Washington Post,* Nov. 21, 1978; "The Boat People Get Someone to Take Pity at Last," *The Economist,* Dec. 2, 1978.

122 *Equally horrible incidents:* "Malaysia Lifts Ban on Boat People," *Facts on File,* Dec. 8, 1978.

123 *"For President Carter . . .":* George Bush, "Our Deal with Peking: All Cost, No Benefit: Even the Chinese Now Know We Cannot Be Relied on Too Much," *Washington Post,* Dec. 24, 1978.

123 *The next year: Report to Congress: Refugee Resettlement Program,* p. A-1.

123 *Unlike the first:* See Nathan Caplan et al., *Southeast Asian Refugee Self-Sufficiency Study: Final Report.*

123   *"parasites. . . . forced to do so."*: AP, "Around the Nation; Oklahoma Catholic Aide Calls Refugees 'Parasites,' " *New York Times,* June 23, 1982.

123   *Attacks on Vietnamese:* "Disease, Ethnic Conflicts Prevail in U.S.," *Facts on File,* Sept. 7, 1979.

123   *"As long as . . ."*: Warren Brown, "Fishermen's Feud Now a Town's War; Simmering Anger About Vietnamese Refugees Boils Over in Seadrift, Tex.," *Washington Post,* Aug, 10, 1979.

124   *"What we have here . . ."*: Warren Brown, "Vietnamese Refugees Caught in Black-White Friction in New Orleans: A Different War," *Washington Post,* July 18, 1978.

124   *The Department of Health:* Donnel Nunes, "HEW Criticizes Resettlement Aid for Indochinese: HEW Faults Aid Offered to Indochinese Refugees," *Washington Post,* Jan. 26, 1980.

124   *A large part:* Joyce Vialet, p. 73; Christopher Dickey, "Administration to Request Reform of Refugee Laws," *Washington Post,* Dec. 11, 1978.

124   *"Sure, kid . . . there to Vietnam."*: Jerry Tinker.

125   *Shortly before succeeding:* Edward M. Kennedy, *The Refugee Act of 1979* (Washington, D.C.: U.S. Senate, 1979), p. 2.

125   *The Refugee Act:* Ibid., p. 5.

125   *This . . . does not . . ."*: Ibid.

125   "the United States has had strong . . .": Ibid., p. 6.

126   *During the first six:* Deborah E. Anker and Michael H. Posner, "The Forty Year Crisis: A Legislative History of the Refugee Act of 1980," *San Diego Law Review,* 19:9 (1981), pp. 69–70.

126   *"Virtually all . . ."*: Nathan Caplan et al.

126   *At the height:* "Rising Flood of Illegal Aliens: How to Deal With It," *U.S. News & World Report,* Feb. 3, 1975; "U.S. Job Market Pinched by Alien Trespassers," *U.S. News & World Report,* Jan. 26, 1976; "Illegal Immigrants Flood In," *The Economist,* Jan. 18, 1975.

127   *"With 10-million unemployed . . ."*: "The Illegal Jobholders," *Business Week,* Aug. 11, 1975.

127   *Two years later:* "What Illegal Aliens Cost the Economy," *Business Week,* June 13, 1977.

127   *"would just about . . ."*: Bob Reiss, "The Melting; Plot;

Grooming for the Green Card with Money-Order Brides,"
Potomac, magazine of the *Washington Post,* July 17, 1977.

127   *"The problem of the illegal . . .":* Marvin Stone, *U.S. News &
World Report,* May 30, 1977.

127   *The Texas legislature:* See *Plyler, Superintendent, Tyler Independent School District, et al.* versus *Doe, Guardian, et al.,* U.S. Supreme Court, decided June 15, 1982.

127   *In 1977, the Ku Klux Klan:* "Around the Nation," *Washington
Post,* Oct. 27, 1977.

127   *"firm, hard sealing":* Warren Brown, "House Committee Pro-
poses Sealing of Mexican Border," *Washington Post,* Dec. 21,
1978.

128   *"human tidal wave . . .":* Susan Jacoby, "Anti-Immigration
Campaign Begun," *Washington Post,* May 8, 1977.

128   *Before Chapman arrived:* See Charles B. Keely, "The Shadows
of Invisible People," *American Demographics,* March 1980.

128   *Pressed to make an:* Jacob S. Siegal et al., "Preliminary Review
of Existing Studies of the Number of Illegal Residents in the
United States (1980)," in *Selected Readings on U.S. Immigration
Policy and Law,* ed. Joyce Vialet (Washington, D.C.: Government Printing Office, 1980), pp. 6–10.

129   *Jimmy Carter not only:* Edward Walsh, "Permanent Resident
Status Proposed for Illegal Aliens: Change in Alien Status
Backed," *Washington Post,* Aug. 5, 1977; James W. Singer,
"Controlling Illegal Aliens—Carter's Compromise Solution,"
National Journal, Sept. 3, 1977.

Chapter 10: From Mariel to Miami

130   *"My revolutionary fervor . . .":* Braulio Saenz, interviewed
(phone) July 26, 1990.

131   *In 1961, with his wife:* Roberto Suarez, interviewed Sept. 29,
1987.

131   *Between 1960 and 1970: Hispanic Profile* (Miami: Metro-Dade

County Planning Department, 1985), p. 34.

131 *A school-board candidate:* "When It Takes Two Languages to Teach the Three R's . . ." *U.S. News & World Report,* July 7, 1975.

131 *"Many non-Latin Miamians . . .":* Larry Birger, "A New Mecca for Latin Shoppers," *Business Week,* Sept. 8, 1975.

131 *Their dramatic story:* Pat Sealey and Ron Sachs, "65 Fleeing Haiti Wash Ashore at Pompano," *Miami Herald,* Dec. 13, 1972.

132 *Six years later:* Mike Norton, "71 More Haitians Float In," *Miami Herald,* July 18, 1978.

132 *During the 1970s:* From 1972 to 1980, only 58 applications out of 5,795 were granted.

132 *Ira Kurzban:* Ira Kurzban, interviewed May 29, 1990.

133 *The legal work, however: National Council of Churches* versus *Egan* (S.D. Fla., 1979); *National Council of Churches* versus *Immigration and Naturalization Service* (S.D. Fla. 1979); *Haitian Refugee Center* versus *Civiletti* (S.D. Fla. 1979); *Louis* versus *Meissner* (S.D. Fla. 1981).

133 *In Delray Beach:* Jake C. Miller, *The Plight of Haitian Refugees* (New York: Praeger Publishers, 1984).

133 *In Miami scores of Haitians:* Shula Beyet, "Officials Seek New Homes for Haitians," *Miami Herald,* March 15, 1980; Jake C. Miller, *The Plight of Haitian Refugees* (New York: Praeger Publishers, 1984), pp. 149–50.

133 *On April 1:* Juan M. Clark, et al., *The 1980 Mariel Exodus: An Assessment and Prospect* (Washington: Council for Inter-American Security, 1981), p. 18, f. 8.

134 *News of the unguarded:* "1,500 Cubans Flee into Embassy," *Miami Herald,* April 6, 1980.

134 *Within twenty-four hours:* Guillermo Martinez, "8,000 Seeking Freedom Jam Embassy in Havana," *Miami Herald,* April 7, 1980.

134 *Florida's press:* Robert Rivas and Fredrick Tasker, "Only Imagination Limits Cuban Exodus," *Miami Herald,* April 23, 1980.

134 *The first Sunday:* Guillermo Martinez and Richard Morin, "Legal Cuban Immigration Halted," *Miami Herald,* May 5, 1980.

135   *One former science professor:* Braulio Saenz.

135   *Seeing no graceful way:* Dan Williams and Barbara O'Reilly, "U.S. Opens Arms to Cuba Exodus: New Wave of Refugees Rolling In," *Miami Herald,* May 6, 1980.

135   *When the Mariel exodus:* Brenda Pillors, interviewed May 4, 1990.

135   *"I was not sure . . .":* Rulx Jean-Bart, interviewed May 31, 1990.

136   *On May 14:* Tom Fiedler and Arnold Markowitz, "Offers a New Exodus on U.S. Ships, Planes," *Miami Herald,* May 15, 1980.

136   *The next day:* Robert Rivas and Janet Fix, "U.S. Patrols Intercept 5 Cuba-Bound Boats," *Miami Herald,* May 17, 1980.

136   *"We are third-class . . . up to that.":* Warren Brown, "Black Miami's Voices: Black Miami: Stories of Hatred and Love: Deep Undercurrents of Despair, Racial Hatred—and Love," *Washington Post,* May 23, 1980.

136   *"They bring everybody . . .":* Herbert Burkholz, "The Latinization of Miami," *New York Times Magazine,* Sept. 21, 1980.

136   *"From every angle . . .":* Warren Brown.

137   *After deliberating:* Gene Miller, "Laying the Blame: Jury Chief Ties Acquittal to 'Mishandled' Investigation," *Miami Herald,* May 19, 1980.

137   *An ex-policeman:* Edna Buchanan, "Ex-Officer Who Testified, Veverka, 'Numb' at Verdict," *Miami Herald,* May 18, 1980.

137   *"They're guilty . . .":* Gene Miller and Joe Oglesby, "U.S. Probe Promises '2nd Look,' *Miami Herald,* May 18, 1980.

137   *By the time night:* William R. Amlong, "Angry Blacks, Police Clash: 4 Die in Night of Violence," *Miami Herald,* May 18, 1980.

137   *Several policemen contributed:* Carl Hiaasen and Joan Fleischman, "Guard-Duty Cops Vandalized Cars in Shopping Plaza," *Miami Herald,* May 20, 1980.

137   *By Monday:* Carl Hiassen, "18 Die in City Under Siege; Fire, Looting Toll Is Heavy," *Miami Herald,* May 19, 1980; Margot Hornblower, "Miami Violence Abates, but Blacks Simmer: Miami Blacks Decry Lack of Jobs, Justice," *Washington Post,* May 20, 1980.

137   *Through it all:* Janet Fix and Fitz McAden, "Survival Is Brutal for Refugees as 14 of Their Number Drowned," *Miami Herald,* May 19, 1980.

137   *"Members of the black . . .":* Neal R. Peirce and Roger Fillion, "Should the United States Open Its Doors to the Foreigners Waiting to Come In?," *National Journal,* March 7, 1981.

138   *Two of the refugees:* Arnold Markowitz and Robert Rivas, "Criminal Charges Await 2 Cuban Refugees," *Miami Herald,* May 13, 1980.

138   *"Miami Beach is filled . . .":* Fred Grimm, "Freedom Flotilla Brought Fear to the Beach's Elderly," *Miami Herald,* Oct. 23, 1980.

138   *Without doubt:* Juan Clark et al., pp. 7–8.

138   *The new arrivals:* Stephan Thernstrom, ed., *Harvard Encyclopedia of American Ethnic Groups* (Cambridge, Mass.: Harvard University Press, 1980), p. 257.

138   *By the end of May:* Tom Fiedler and Guy Gugliotta, "How Resettlement Has Become a Mess," *Miami Herald,* June 1, 1990.

139   *The ceremony occurred:* "Duvalier Weds in Style; Haiti, the Hemisphere's Poorest Nation, to Pay $3 Million for Flowery Nuptials," *Washington Post,* May 27, 1980; Leslie Burdick, "Fairy Tale or Nightmare in Haiti?," *Christian Science Monitor,* July 23, 1980.

139   *Oliver Cromwell:* Oliver Cromwell, interviewed Nov. 5, 1990.

139   *He paroled the refugees:* "Text of State Dept. Statement on a Refugee Policy," *New York Times,* June 21, 1980.

140   *The new designation:* Walter Jacob, "Lack of Cash and Poor Coordination Plague U.S. Refugee Policies," *National Journal,* July 26, 1980; Charles R. Babcock, "Funding Gap Prompts Criticism of Carter's Refugee Policy," *Washington Post,* June 21, 1980.

140   *"not at a level . . .":* Charles R. Babcock, Ibid.

140   *"After two months . . .":* "Domestic News," June 21, 1980, Reuters Ltd.

140   *"The administration has . . .":* Charles R. Babcock.

140   *"We will do everything . . .":* Associated Press, "Miami Schools Deny Special Programs to Refugees," *New York Times,* July 19, 1980.

140   *"You could get food . . .":* Rulx Jean-Bart.

141   *"what they found was . . .": Haitian Refugee Center* versus *Benjamin Civiletti,* U.S. District Court, S.D. Florida, July 2, 1980.

141   *Later that year:* "Haitians Win the Right to Hold Jobs in Florida," *New York Times,* Oct. 22, 1980.

142   *"I urge you and your . . .":* Grace A. Rockafellar, "Close-Up of the Illegal Immigration Issue," *New York Times,* May 16, 1982.

142   *By September 26:* Juan Clark et al., pp. 7–8.

142   *In a poll:* Reported in Herbert Burkholz.

142   *"We have been Cubanized . . .":* Janis Johnson, "Anti-Latin Rage: A War of Words Waged in Miami: Miamians Waging a War of Languages," *Washington Post,* Aug. 30, 1980.

142   *"We'd like to keep . . .":* Robert M. Press, "English-Only Drive Mirrors Deeper Miami Unrest," *Christian Science Monitor,* Oct. 20, 1980.

142   *The referendum:* Ibid.

143   *"This statement implies . . .":* Jo Thomas, "Miami Area Divided Over Ballot Proposal to Drop Spanish as Second Official Language," *New York Times,* Nov. 2, 1980.

143   *"What is United . . . before English":* George Volsky, "Approval of Antibilingual Measures Causes Confusion and Worry in Miami," *New York Times,* Nov. 9, 1980.

143   *Such reservations notwithstanding:* Ibid.

143   *An estimated 71:* Ibid.

143   *Latinos—while over:* Janis Johnson, "Anti-Latin Rage: A War of Words Waged in Miami: Miamians Waging a War of Languages," *Washington Post,* Aug. 30, 1980.

143   *"No way . . .":* Herbert Burkholz.

143   *"the country's failure . . .":* "The Economic Consequences of a New Wave," *Business Week,* June 23, 1980.

Chapter 11: After the Deluge

145   *"Can we doubt . . .":* Ronald Reagan, "Text of Reagan's Speech Accepting the Republicans' Nomination," *New York Times,* July 18, 1980.

146   *Colorado governor Richard:* William L. Chaze, "Will U.S. Shut the Door on Immigrants?" *U.S. News & World Report*, April 12, 1982.

146   *"America is no . . .":* Ibid.

146   *Eighty percent wanted:* Roper Poll cited in William L. Chaze.

146   *"Backlash is already . . .":* "Immigration Under Law," *Christian Science Monitor*, May 16, 1980.

146   *"minority cultures . . . of our time":* Theodore H. White, *America in Search of Itself: The Making of the President, 1956–1980* (New York: Harper and Row, 1982), pp. 350, 362.

147   *Troubled by the:* Wayne King, "In El Paso, Hope Floats with Peso," *New York Times*, March 21, 1983; "Regional News," UPI, March 30, 1983.

147   *"You can be sitting . . .":* Richard Meyer and Mike Goodman, "Marauders from Inner City Prey on L.A.'s Suburbs," July 12, 1981.

147   *"the Latinos have taken . . .":* Ibid.

147   *In Sacramento:* Robert Lindsey, "Vietnamese Fishermen Stir Bitterness on Coast," *New York Times*, July 8, 1982.

147   *"It's the influx . . .":* Bob Schwartz, "Influx of Aliens Sparks Angry Response: Many Cite Problems but Steps Taken to Improve Conditions," *Los Angeles Times*, July 29, 1986.

147   *In the San Gabriel:* Mark Arax, "San Gabriel Valley: Asian Influx Alters Life in Suburbia," *Los Angeles Times*, April 5, 1987.

148   *"came out here . . .":* University of California, Irvine sociologist Marc Baldassare, quoted in Bob Schwartz, "Influx of Aliens Sparks Angry Response: Many Cite Problems but Steps Taken to Improve Conditions," *Los Angeles Times*, July 29, 1986.

148   *In Arlington, Virginia:* Nancy Scannell, "After the Influx, a County Copes: Change," *Washington Post*, Feb. 18, 1982.

148   *In Arizona:* "Regional News," UPI, Sept. 8, 1982.

148   *In Washington:* Francis X. Clines and Bernard Weinraub, "Briefing," *New York Times*, Nov. 19, 1981.

148   *"like trying to . . .":* Stewart Powell et al., "Illegal Aliens: Invasion Out of Control?," *U.S. News & World Report*, Jan. 29, 1979.

148   *"We have neither . . .":* Statement at Joint Hearing Before
        Subcommittee on Immigration, Refugees, and International
        Law of House Committee on the Judiciary and Subcommittee
        on Immigration and Refugee Policy of the Senate Committee
        on the Judiciary, 97th Congress, first session (1981).

148   *"serious national problem . . .":* Ronald Reagan, "High Seas
        Interdiction of Illegal Aliens," Proclamation 4865, *Public Pa-
        pers of the Presidents,* September 29, 1981; Ronald Reagan,
        "Interdiction of Illegal Aliens," Executive Order 12324, *Pub-
        lic Papers of the Presidents,* Sept. 29, 1981.

149   *"We have to remember . . .":* Ronald Reagan, "Excerpts from
        an Interview with Walter Cronkite of CBS News," *Public Pa-
        pers of the Presidents,* March 3, 1981.

149   *"If it is a truism . . .":* Select Commission on Immigration and
        Refugee Policy, *U.S. Immigration Policy and the National Interest*
        (Washington, D.C.: Government Printing Office, 1981), p. 2.

149   *"One does not have . . .":* Ibid. p. 12.

150   *"Nothing about immigration . . .":* Ibid. pp. 4–5.

150   *"No longer exploitable . . .":* Ibid. p. 13.

150   *"will contribute to . . .":* Ibid. p. 13.

150   *"Many undocumented/illegal . . .":* Ibid, p. 12.

151   *"closing the back . . .":* Ibid. p. 3.

151   *In striving to maintain:* See Robert Pear, "No Changes Sought
        on Excluding Aliens," *New York Times,* Feb. 15, 1981; see also
        Lawrence H. Fuchs, "Directions for U.S. Immigration Policy:
        Immigration Policy and the Rule of Law," *University of Pitts-
        burgh Law Review,* Winter 1983.

151   *"For . . . Americans who . . .":* Statement by Vilma Martinez,
        MALDEF, *Final Report on the Select Commission on Immigration
        and Refugee Policy,* Joint Hearings Before Subcommittee on
        Immigration of Senate Committee on Judiciary and Subcom-
        mittee on Immigration, Refugees, and International Law of
        House Committee on the Judiciary (Washington, D.C.: Gov-
        ernment Printing Office, 1981), p. 149.

152   *"Illegal aliens come . . .":* Richard L. Strout, "Law Would Pro-
        hibit Hiring of Illegal Aliens," *Christian Science Monitor,* March
        18, 1982.

152   *Despite Reagan administration:* See Stuart Taylor, Jr., "Smith Sees Immigration Plan as a Means to Avert Boatlifts," *New York Times,* Oct. 23, 1981.

152   *"have to go back home.":* Robert Pear, "Bipartisan Legislation Introduced to Restructure Immigration Laws," *New York Times,* March 18, 1982.

153   *Criminal justice, he realized:* Romano Mazzoli, interviewed June 28, 1990.

153   *Nonetheless, Rodino:* Peter Rodino, interviewed March 22, 1990.

153   *Because undocumented workers:* Alan K. Simpson, interviewed May 14, 1990.

154   *"I'm fully aware . . . Mexico or Canada.":* Neal R. Peirce and Roger Fillion, "Should the United States Open Its Doors to the Foreigners Waiting to Come In?," *National Journal,* March 7, 1981.

154   *When the Simpson-Mazzoli:* "Not Nativist, Not Racist, Not Mean," *New York Times,* March 18, 1982.

154   *"Such admiration was":* Mary Thornton, "Hill Chairmen Propose New Immigration Bill," *Washington Post,* March 18, 1982; Robert Pear, "Bipartisan Legislation Introduced to Restructure Immigration Laws," *New York Times,* March 18, 1982.

154   *"A law that requires . . .":* Richard L. Strout, "Law Would Prohibit Hiring of Illegal Aliens," *Christian Science Monitor,* March 18, 1982.

155   *Simpson's insistence:* Mary Thornton, "Hill Chairmen Propose New Immigration Bill."

155   *The bill had died:* Peter Rodino, interviewed March 22, 1990; Joyce Vialet, *U.S. Immigration Law and Policy: 1952–1986* (Washington, D.C.: Government Printing Office, 1988), pp. 86–89; "A Plan to Slow the Flood of Illegal Aliens," *Business Week,* Aug. 11, 1975.

155   *"put us . . . on . . .":* Raúl Yzaguirre, interviewed Feb. 23, 1990.

156   *"We knew . . .":* Charles Kamasaki, interviewed, May 9, 1990.

156   *"carry out really . . .":* Ibid.

156   *"The Simpson-Mazzoli H-2":* Joaquin G. Avila, "Simpson-Maz-

zoli Immigration Bill: Back to the Bracero Fiasco?," *New York Times,* Oct. 2, 1982.

156   *"I would dance . . .":* Antonia Hernández, interviewed, May 16, 1990.

156   *"confirming and giving . . .":* Ibid.

157   *LULAC executive director:* Arnoldo Torres, interviewed (phone) July 24, 1990.

157   *"then who are we . . .":* J. Michael Myers, interviewed June 7, 1990.

157   *"It became obvious . . .":* Wade Henderson, interviewed Sept. 6, 1990.

157   *"equal protection . . .":* "Don't Shut Court Doors on Aliens," *New York Times,* Aug. 23, 1982.

157   *"What's all the shouting . . .":* "Showing ID at the Golden Doors," *New York Times,* Sept. 24, 1982.

157   *"Save Simpson-Mazzoli . . .":* "Save Simpson-Mazzoli," *Washington Post,* Sept. 21, 1982.

158   *"as delicately balanced . . .":* "Why Break the Immigration Clock?," *New York Times,* Dec. 3, 1982.

158   *Mazzoli complained:* Margot Hornblower, "Immigration Law Revision May Be Derailed in House," *Washington Post,* Dec. 5, 1982.

159   *"There was always . . .":* J. Michael Myers.

159   *Uncomfortable with the idea:* Wade Henderson.

159   *"You don't ask . . .":* Charles Kamasaki.

160   *"at the worst . . .":* *Congressional Record,* Dec. 16, 1982, H31674.

160   *Mazzoli lauded Rodino: Congressional Record,* Dec. 16, 1982, H31796.

160   *"Central Americans fleeing . . .":* *Congressional Record,* Dec. 16, 1982, H31805.

160   *Do Latino congressmen: Congressional Record,* Dec. 16, 1982, H31804.

161   *"The sensitivities involved . . .":* *Congressional Record,* Dec. 18, 1982, H32169.

161   *Hyde's tribute went:* Romano Mazzoli.

Chapter 12: No Room for Compromise

162 *"All we needed . . .":* Robert Pear, "Discussion Ended on Aliens Measure," *New York Times,* Dec. 19, 1982.

162 *"I think . . .":* Romano Mazzoli, interviewed June 28, 1990.

162 *When Congress reconvened:* Robert Pear, "What the House Said in Not Voting an Immigration Bill," *New York Times,* Dec. 27, 1982; Kathy Sawyer, "Senate Stymied in Efforts to Pass Spending Measure; House Passes Farm Aid Bill," *Washington Post,* Dec. 19, 1982.

162 *"An impressive win . . .":* "When Senators Guard the Border,"
  ▪ *Christian Science Monitor,* May 20, 1983.

162 *"before the rush . . .":* "Momentum for Immigration Reform," *Washington Post,* May 20, 1983.

163 *At the fiesta:* Ronald Reagan, "Remarks at Cinco de Mayo Ceremonies," Pres. Doc. 661, *Public Papers of the Presidents,* May 5, 1983.

163 *"of the values . . .":* Ronald Reagan, "National Hispanic Heritage Week, 1983: Remarks at a White House Ceremony," Pres. Doc. 1231, *Public Papers of the Presidents,* Sept. 12, 1983.

163 *"where eighty percent . . .":* Francis X. Clines, "If This Is Washington, It Must Be 'Hispanic Week,' " *New York Times,* Sept. 16, 1983.

163 *"Mr. Reagan's idea":* Ibid.

164 *"shares the Hispanic . . . modern history":* Sarah Peterson and John W. Mashek, "Hispanics Set Their Sights on Ballot Box," *U.S. News & World Report,* Aug. 22, 1983.

164 *Though the most:* U.S. Bureau of the Census, *Statistical Abstract of the United States: 1989* (Washington, D.C.: Government Printing Office, 1989), p. 16; Robert Reinhold, "Hispanic Leaders Open Voter Drive," *New York Times,* Aug. 9, 1983; Dick Kirschten, "The Hispanic Vote—Parties Can't Gamble

That the Sleeping Giant Won't Awaken," *National Journal,* Nov. 19, 1983.

164   *At a Congressional Hispanic Caucus:* Dick Kirschten, "The Hispanic Vote—Parties Can't Gamble That the Sleeping Giant Won't Awaken," *National Journal,* Nov. 19, 1983.

164   *At one point:* Alan K. Simpson, interviewed May 14, 1990.

165   *"How can you guys . . .":* Ibid.

165   *Blazing with such:* Ibid.

165   *Attorney General:* Robert Pear, "O'Neill Says Bill on Illegal Aliens Is Dead for 1983," *New York Times,* Oct. 5, 1983.

165   *The survey reported:* Dick Kirschten, "The Hispanic Vote—Parties Can't Gamble That the Sleeping Giant Won't Awaken"; UPI, "California Regional News," Aug. 2, 1983.

166   *"We can now destroy . . .":* From an undated "Dear Member" solicitation from the Federation for American Immigration Reform.

166   *Only thirty-four:* Frank Sotomayor, "The Times Poll: Most Latinos Back Amnesty for Aliens," *Southern California's Latino Community,* series reprint from *Los Angeles Times,* 1983 (Los Angeles: Times Mirror, 1984), p. 26.

166   *"Though leaders . . .":* "The Speaker, on the Border," *New York Times,* Sept. 25, 1983.

166   *"Who the hell . . .":* Charles Kamasaki, interviewed May 9, 1990.

167   *LULAC's Torres:* Arnoldo Torres, interviewed (phone) July 24, 1990.

167   *"Are reports true . . .":* "Let the House Vote on the Immigration Bill," *Christian Science Monitor,* July 25, 1983.

167   *"Perhaps a partisan . . .":* "The Speaker, on the Border," *New York Times,* Sept. 25, 1983.

167   *He had heard:* T. R. Reid, "Suspects Double-Cross: O'Neill Exercises Power, Bars Immigration Bill," *Washington Post,* Oct. 5, 1983; Robert Pear, "O'Neill Says Bill on Illegal Aliens Is Dead for 1983," *New York Times,* Oct. 5, 1983.

167   *"Do I think . . .":* T. R. Reid, Ibid.

167   *"There's nobody . . .":* T. R. Reid, "Political System Runs Aground on Vexing Immigration Issue," *Washington Post,* Oct. 7, 1983.

167   *"put his neck . . .":* Robert Pear, "Immigration and Politics," *New York Times,* Oct. 6, 1983; Mary Thornton, "Hispanics Hail O'Neill for Halting Immigration Bill," *Washington Post,* Oct. 6, 1983.

167   *Newspapers, however:* See "Immigration Reform, O'Neill Style," *New York Times,* Oct. 9, 1983; "Free the Immigration Bill," *Washington Post,* Oct. 6, 1983.

168   *And Simpson vowed:* Julia Malone, "Hispanic Political Pressure Stops Immigration Reform in Congress," *Christian Science Monitor,* Oct. 6, 1983.

168   *"The President sent . . .":* "Immigration Reform Legislation: Statement by the Principal Deputy Press Secretary," *Public Papers of the Presidents,* Oct. 4, 1983, Pres. Doc. 1390.

168   *"I want to sign . . .":* Ronald Reagan, "The President's News Conference of October 19, 1983," *Public Papers of the Presidents,* Pres. Doc. 1465.

168   *Around the same:* "Does Immigration Reform Live?," *Washington Post,* Nov. 4, 1983; Julia Malone, "Speaker O'Neill Opens House Door to Immigration," *Christian Science Monitor,* Dec. 5, 1983.

168   *"You don't even . . .":* Alan K. Simpson.

168   *"I didn't . . .":* Ibid.

168   *O'Neill was:* Martin Tolchin, "O'Neill Now Favors Revision of Immigration Laws," *New York Times,* Nov. 30, 1983.

169   *Gary Hart said:* Dan Balz, "Hart Espouses Aid for Mexico in Bid for Hispanic Votes," *Washington Post,* April 30, 1984.

169   *"We cannot have . . .":* "Responses of Democratic Presidential Candidates Mondale, Hart and Jackson to Questionnaire of American Civil Liberties Union," BNA *Daily Labor Report,* April 2, 1984.

169   *"until the House . . .":* Memo from Arnoldo Torres to George Dalley, March 14, 1984.

169   *During the conversation:* Robert Pear, "O'Neill to Delay Debate on Aliens," *New York Times,* May 3, 1984.

169   *"single most important . . .":* "Statement of AFL-CIO President Kirkland on Immigration Reform Before Senate Judiciary Subcommittee on Immigration," BNA *Daily Labor Report,* March 7, 1983.

169 *"There have been no . . .":* "Organized Labor Hit for 'Nit-Picking' on Immigration Bill," BNA *Daily Report for Executives,* March 10, 1983.

170 *"For the party . . .":* Robert Pear, "Bill on Aliens a Divisive Issue for Democrats," *New York Times,* April 22, 1984.

170 *"more confident than . . .":* George Dalley, interviewed Aug. 23, 1990.

170 *"It became clear . . .":* Ibid.

170 *"We want Fritz!":* Howell Raines, "Labor Parley Endorses Mondale for Presidency," *New York Times,* Oct. 6, 1983; Kathy Sawyer, "Exuberant AFL-CIO Delegates Wrap Up Endorsement of Mondale," *Washington Post,* Oct. 6, 1983.

171 *"Bottom line . . .":* George Dalley.

171 *"It is a great . . .":* *Congressional Record,* June 20, 1984, p. 17233.

171 *"We really have . . .":* *Congressional Record,* June 20, 1984, pp. 17239, 17241.

172 *"I looked at that . . .":* Romano Mazzoli.

172 *The final vote:* Robert Pear, "House, by 216–211, Approves Aliens Bill After Retaining Amnesty Plan in Final Test," *New York Times,* June 21, 1984.

172 *"Nothing in my . . .":* Romano Mazzoli.

172 *"For a while . . .":* Ibid.

172 *"As Hispanics become . . .":* Mario Obledo, Dear Delegate letter, July 11, 1984.

173 *"conscience and conviction":* Paul Taylor and Juan Williams, "Hispanic Delegates Urged to Withhold First Ballot," *Washington Post,* June 23, 1984.

173 *Less than a month:* Press release issued July 16, 1984, in Los Angeles following Hispanic Conference on Immigration Reform.

173 *"Already we have . . .":* Ibid.

173 *"It is imperative . . .":* Memorandum from Mario Obledo to Hispanic Elected Officials, July 16, 1984.

173 *"We recognize the boldness . . .":* Mario Obledo, Dear Delegate letter, July 11, 1984.

174 *"It was the most . . .":* Arnoldo Torres.

174 *"harmful . . . for the convention":* UPI, "The Democrats in San Francisco; Mondale Promises Caucus He'll Fight Immigration Bill," *New York Times,* July 18, 1984.

174 *At a Hispanic caucus . . . kill the bill:* Ibid.; Cynthia Gorney, "Hispanic Delegates Split Over Call for Boycott on First Ballot Tonight," *Washington Post,* July 18, 1984.

175 *"We're going to fight . . .":* Paul Taylor, "Some Hispanics Abstain from First Ballot," *Washington Post,* July 19, 1984.

175 *"I said then . . .":* Ibid.

175 *"long record . . .":* Ken Flynn, "Regional News," UPI, June 22, 1984.

175 *At the meeting:* Arnoldo Torres.

176 *Early on, negotiations:* Maxwell Glen, "Immigration Bill Knocked Out in Final Round, but Sponsors Promise Rematch," *National Journal,* Nov. 3, 1984.

176 *Negotiations finally collapsed:* Robert Pear, "Immigration Bill Conferees Reach a Major Compromise," *New York Times,* Sept. 22, 1984.

176 *"I just decided . . .":* Alan K. Simpson.

177 *"You could see that . . .":* Ibid.

177 *"In my judgment":* Romano Mazzoli.

177 *"A couple of people . . .":* Harris N. Miller, interviewed, May 7, 1990.

177 *"The last vote . . .":* Charles Kamasaki.

177 *"Ultimately it was . . .":* Wade Henderson, interviewed Sept. 6, 1990.

177 *"and he wasn't pushing . . .":* Garner J. Cline, interviewed July 6, 1990.

177 *"I stated I would . . .":* Peter Rodino, interviewed March 22, 1990.

178 *"one real item . . .":* Alan K. Simpson.

178 *"I could have . . .":* Romano Mazzoli.

178 *"He took body blows . . .":* Ibid.

178 *Even though the Democrats:* Democrat Frank McCloskey was seated in the Eighth District over Republican Richard McIntyre. See Steven V. Roberts, "House Refuses to Order Spe-

cial Indiana Election," *New York Times,* May 1, 1985.

179 *When Simpson finally:* Richard Day, minority counsel, Senate Immigration Subcommittee on Immigration and Refugee Affairs, interviewed April 30, 1990.

179 *"good elements . . .":* J. Michael Myers, interviewed June 7, 1990.

179 *"You can only sustain . . .":* Rick Swartz, interviewed Feb. 19, 1990.

179 *"What the Hispanics . . .":* Jerry Tinker, March 19, 1990.

179 *In explaining: Congressional Record,* May 23, 1985, p. 13586.

179 *"go down in flames":* Antonia Hernández, interviewed May 16, 1990.

180 *The antisanctions lobby:* Robert Pear, "Panel Approves Immigration Bill but Accepts 2 Key Amendments," *New York Times,* July 31, 1985.

180 *Kennedy ridiculed: Congressional Record,* daily edition, Sept. 18, 1985. S11686; Robert Pear, "Senate Votes Bill Designed to Curb Illegal Migrants," *New York Times,* Sept. 20, 1985.

181 *"This immigration . . .":* Peter Rodino.

181 *"There is a reason . . .":* Tom Gorman, "750 Protest Immigration Policies of United States," *Los Angeles Times,* July 5, 1986.

182 *While 49 percent:* Robert Pear, "New Restrictions on Immigration Gain Public Support, Poll Shows," *New York Times,* July 1, 1986.

182 *Fifty-two percent of whites:* Those identifying themselves as Hispanic, regardless of race, were not included in the totals for blacks and whites.

183 *"The opportunity to make . . .":* ". . . And a Failure on Immigration," *Washington Post,* Sept. 30, 1986.

183 *"This is like Rasputin . . .":* Robert Pear, "House Approves Immigration Bill Considered Dead Two Weeks Ago," *New York Times,* Oct. 10, 1986.

183 *"We can take in . . .": Congressional Record,* daily edition, Oct. 9, 1986, H9785.

183 *"I still claim . . .":* Romano Mazzoli.

183 *Negotiators did accept: Immigration Reform and Control Act of 1986:*

Conference Report (Washington, D.C.: U.S. House of Representatives, 1986).

184   *"You may still . . .":* Charles Kamasaki.

184   *"Let there be no . . .":* *Congressional Record,* daily edition, Oct. 15, 1986, H10583.

184   *"Most members . . .":* Ibid.

184   *"Millions of people . . .":* Ibid. H10527.

185   *"Because it is called . . .":* *Congressional Record,* daily edition, Oct. 16, 1986, S16611.

185   *As finally enacted: Immigration Reform and Control Act of 1986: Conference Report* (Washington, D.C.: U.S. House of Representatives, 1986).

185   *At a White House:* Ronald Reagan, "Immigration Reform and Control Act of 1986: Remarks on Signing S. 1200 into Law," *Public Papers of the Presidents,* Pres. Doc. 1533, Nov. 6, 1986.

186   *"probably the best . . .":* Robert Pear, "Congress, Winding Up Work, Votes Sweeping Aliens Bill; Reagan Expected to Sign It," *New York Times,* Oct. 18, 1986.

186   *"to mess with . . .":* Richard J. Meislin, "To Mexicans, Law on Aliens Is Cruel Joke," *New York Times,* June 24, 1984.

186   *They came in cars:* See Richard W. Stevenson, "U.S. Work Barrier to Illegal Aliens Doesn't Stop Them," *New York Times,* Oct. 9, 1989; Paul Weingarten, "Refugee Kids Flocking to Texas—All Alone, *Chicago Tribune,* March 12, 1989; William Glaberson, "6 Seized in Smuggling Asians into New York," *New York Times,* May 5, 1989; Peter Applebome, "79 Suspect Aliens Arrested on a Jet," *New York Times,* Feb. 28, 1989; Peter Applebome, "Smugglers of U.S. Aliens Held More Sophisticated, *New York Times,* March 2, 1989.

187   *"There has been . . .":* Wayne Cornelius, quoted in Roberto Suro, "1986 Amnesty Law Is Seen as Failing to Slow Alien Tide," *New York Times,* June 18, 1989.

187   *Studies conducted by:* Pauline Yoshihashi, "Employer Sanctions Show Little Success Halting Illegal Immigration, Study Says," *Wall Street Journal,* April 20, 1990; Richard W. Stevenson, "Study Finds Mild Gain in Drive on Illegal Aliens," *New York Times,* April 21, 1990.

187   *"Almost immediately . . .":* "Second Report on the Implementation of IRCA," *INS Reporter,* Summer 1989, p. 3.

187   *In fact, fewer:* U.S. Immigration and Naturalization Service, *Statistical Yearbook of the Immigration and Naturalization Service: 1989* (Washington, D.C.: Government Printing Office, 1990), p. 111.

187   *Although legislators:* Statistical Division, Office of Plans and Analysis, U.S. Immigration and Naturalization Service, "Provisional Legalization Application Statistics," Aug. 27, 1990.

187   *"Thousands of people . . .":* Larry Rohter, "Mexicans Crowd a Last Opening to U.S.," *New York Times,* June 20, 1988.

188   *On the other:* "Second Report on the Implementation of IRCA," *INS Reporter,* Summer 1989, pp. 6–7.

188   *"a success by . . .":* Robert L. Bach and Doris Meissner, *Employment and Immigration Reform: Employer Sanctions Four Years Later* (Washington, D.C.: Carnegie Endowment for International Peace, 1990), p. 5.

188   *"widespread discrimination":* U.S. General Accounting Office, "Immigration Reform: Employer Sanctions and the Question of Discrimination" (Washington, D.C.: General Accounting Office, 1990), p. 3.

188   *Nineteen percent:* Ibid. p. 38.

188   *"For example, although . . .":* Ibid. p. 49.

189   *"We want to make sure . . .":* Richard Day.

189   *"Our fear . . .":* Raúl Yzaguirre, interviewed Feb. 23, 1990.

189   *"I didn't see . . .":* "Judiciary Committee's Democrats Revolt, Oust Mazzoli from Immigration Panel Chair," BNA *Daily Labor Report,* Feb. 10, 1989.

190   *"passed a couple . . . better for it":* Romano Mazzoli.

Chapter 13: A Movement for the Eighties

190   *"We're never going . . .":* James Fallows, "Immigration: How It's Affecting Us," *Atlantic Monthly,* Nov. 1983.

191 *In an opinion:* Plyler, Superintendent, Tyler Independent School District, et al. versus *Doe, Guardian, et al.,* U.S. Supreme Court, decided June 15, 1982.

191 *Shortly thereafter:* See Linda Witt, "Following Conscience, Not Law, an Underground Railroad Smuggles Threatened Salvadorans to Safety in America," *People,* Aug. 9, 1982.

191 *By 1985:* Miriam Davidson, "Sanctuary Movement Under Fire," *Christian Science Monitor,* Oct. 22, 1985.

192 *Around that same:* Victor Merina, "Cities vs. the Ins: Sanctuary: Reviving an Old Concept," *Los Angeles Times,* Nov. 17, 1985; Robert Lindsey, "Aid to Aliens Said to Spur Illegal Immigration," *New York Times,* Dec. 23, 1985; James Coates, "In New Sanctuary Debate, Fine Line Divides Criminal, Refugee," *Chicago Tribune,* Dec. 29, 1985; "New Mexico Is Declared Sanctuary for Refugees," *New York Times,* March 30, 1986.

192 *The accused:* Wayne King, "Trial Opens for 11 Who Aided Central Americans," *New York Times,* Nov. 16, 1985; Leviticus 19:33.

192 *In May 1986:* Jay Mathews, "Jury Convicts 8 Sanctuary Defendants," *Washington Post,* May 2, 1986.

192 *Four years later:* Katherine Bishop, "U.S. Adopts New Policy for Hearings on Political Asylum for Some Aliens," *New York Times,* Dec. 20, 1990; See *American Baptist Churches in the U.S.A., et al.* versus *Edwin Meese III, in his official capacity as Attorney General of the United States, and Alan Nelson, in his official capacity as Commissioner of the Immigration and Naturalization Service,* U.S. District Court for the Northern District of California, decided March 24, 1989.

192 *From 1981 through 1986:* U.S. Immigration and Naturalization Service, *Statistical Yearbook of the Immigration and Naturalization Service: 1986* (Washington, D.C.: Government Printing Office, 1987), pp. 55, 108.

192 *Many of those:* Jane Applegate, "Idealism of '60s Reborn in Pleas for Immigrants," *Los Angeles Times,* June 1, 1986.

193 *In 1987:* Philip Hager and Laurie Becklund, "Ezell's Ouster Urged Over Statements Called Racist," *Los Angeles Times,* Sept. 24, 1987.

193   *The most notorious. . . . a baseball bat:* Details taken from court
       and other legal records; *People of the State of Michigan* versus
       Ronald Ebens and Michael Nitz, Wayne County Circuit Court;
       United States of America versus *Ronald Ebens,* U.S. Court of Ap-
       peals, Sixth Circuit; from 1987 statements given by Jimmy
       Choi, Gary Koivu, Morris Cotton, and other witnesses to at-
       torneys Brescoll and Associates representing Lily Chin; from
       transcript of tape recording of interviews with Robert Si-
       rosky, Gary Koivu, Jimmy Choi made by attorney Liza Chan
       on April 13, 1983.

193   *Ebens pleaded guilty: State of Michigan* versus *Ronald Ebens and
       Michael Nitz.*

193   *As a result:* "Jury to Investigate Murder of a Chinese-Ameri-
       can," *New York Times,* Aug. 5, 1983; John Holusha, "2 Fined
       in Detroit Slaying Are Indicted by Federal Jury," *New York
       Times,* Nov. 3, 1983.

193   *Nitz was acquitted:* "Ex-Auto Worker Guilty in Slaying," *New
       York Times,* June 29, 1984; "Around the Nation," *Washington
       Post,* Sept. 19, 1984.

193   *"real Americans.":* The Rev. Wesley Woo of the Presbyterian
       Church U.S.A., in Marvine Howe, "Group Raises Concern
       Over Anti-Asian Violence," *New York Times,* Oct. 1986.

194   *"peaceably hand over . . . with their pants down":* John Tanton,
       WITAN IV memorandum, Oct. 10, 1986.

194   *"an anti-Catholic . . .":* Zita Arocha, "Dispute Fuels Campaign
       Against 'Official English': Foes Say Memo Shows Racism's Be-
       hind Plan," *Washington Post,* Nov. 6, 1988.

194   *"To ignore them . . .":* Melinda Yee, interviewed Feb. 9, 1990.

194   *"It's sort of . . .":* Frank Sharry, interviewed April 4, 1990.

Chapter 14: A Better Class of Immigrant

196   *"the issues addressed . . .":* Immigration Reform and Control Act of
       1986, Conference Report (Washington, D.C.: U.S. House of
       Representatives, 1986), p. 98.

196   *It housed:* Legal Immigration Legislation, Hearings Before Subcommittee on Immigration, Refugees, and International Law, of Committee on the Judiciary, U.S. House of Representatives (Washington, D.C.: Government Printing Office, 1988), p. 11.

196   *At the peak:* U.S. Immigration and Naturalization Service, *Statistical Yearbook of the Immigration and Naturalization Service: 1989* (Washington, D.C.: Government Printing Office, 1990), p. 2.

196   *In 1986:* Ibid., p. 4.

196   *"large numbers are . . .":* Congressional Record, daily edition, Sept. 30, 1986, H8760.

196   *By couching:* The "adversely affected" countries identified by the U.S. State Department were Albania, Algeria, Argentina, Austria, Belgium, Bermuda, Britain and Northern Ireland, Canada, Czechoslovakia, Denmark, East Germany, West Germany, Finland, France, Gibraltar, Guadeloupe, Hungary, Iceland, Indonesia, Ireland, Italy, Japan, Liechtenstein, Luxembourg, Monaco, Netherlands, New Caledonia, Norway, Poland, San Marino, Sweden, Switzerland, Tunisia, and the Soviet republics of Estonia, Latvia, and Lithuania.

197   *The scheme touched:* Esther B. Fein, "Dreams of Citizenship Ride on Deluge of Mail," *New York Times*, Jan. 22, 1987; Linda Wheeler, "Applicants Rush for Extra Allotment of Visas," *Washington Post*, Jan. 22, 1987.

197   *In Ireland:* UPI, "Irish Flood Mails with U.S. Visa Applications," *Los Angeles Times*, Jan. 20, 1987; "Thousands Flock to Window That Would Let Them into U.S.," *Chicago Tribune*, Jan. 22, 1987.

197   *Exports and industrial:* See "How the Government Spent the People into a Slump," *The Economist*, Jan. 24, 1987; "Ulster's Other Troubles," *The Economist*, Nov. 29, 1986.

197   *Irish nationals:* AP, "10,000 Win Residency in U.S.," *New York Times*, Feb. 23, 1987.

197   *"At the end . . .":* Ken Franckling, "Biggest Emigration Wave Since Potato Famine: Wearin' of the Green Card Gets Irish Eyes Smiling," *Los Angeles Times*, Jan. 31, 1988.

197   *"the cream . . .":* Francis X. Clines, "Ireland's Woes Again Forcing out the Young," *New York Times*, April 27, 1987.

198   *"needs their skills":* "Immigration Injustice," *Boston Globe,* Sept. 26, 1988.

198   *"special relationship . . .":* Susan Diesenhouse, "Green-Carpet Treatment for Boston's New Immigrants," *New York Times,* Nov. 6, 1987; "Boston Plans Help for Illegal Aliens," *New York Times,* Oct. 11, 1987.

198   *When Congressman Joseph:* Mary Jo Hill, "Immigration Bid: Bay Staters Push Proposals to Open US Doors Wider for Irish Entrants," *Christian Science Monitor,* Oct. 21, 1987; Morton Kondracke, "Moral Borders: Politics, Mercy, and Immigration," *New Republic,* Nov. 23, 1987.

198   *"Many of those . . .":* *Congressional Record,* daily edition, Oct. 27, 1987, S15238.

198   *"discrimination . . . against Irish . . .":* *Congressional Record,* daily edition, Oct. 16, 1986, S16419; *Legal Immigration Reforms,* Hearings Before Subcommittee on Immigration and Refugee Affairs of the Committee on the Judiciary, U.S. Senate (Washington, D.C.: Government Printing Office, 1989), p. 2.

198   *"If our current . . .":* *Legal Immigration Legislation,* p. 29.

198   *"The countries which . . .":* *Congressional Record,* daily edition, Aug. 6, 1987, S11487.

199   *"for older sources . . .":* Ibid.

199   *"The goal . . .":* *Congressional Record,* daily edition, Aug. 6, 1987, H7213.

199   *"had set this . . .":* Richard Day, interviewed April 30, 1990.

199   *Widely heralded research:* William B. Johnston and Arnold S. Packer, *Workforce 2000: Work and Workers for the 21st Century* (Indianapolis: The Hudson Institute, 1987).

200   *The actual statistic:* See Frank Swoboda, "Students of Labor Force Projections Have Been Working Without a 'Net'; Omissions in 1987 Summary Left Role of White Males Understated," *Washington Post,* Nov. 6, 1990.

200   *"permanently to the . . .":* Roger D. Semerad, "2000: Labor Shortage Looms: The U.S. Will Need a More Productive and More Competitive Workforce in the Year 2000. How Do We Get There from Here?," *Industry Week,* Feb. 9, 1987.

200   *About one fourth:* John M. Goering, *Legal Immigration to the United*

States: A Demographic Analysis of Fifth Preferences Visa Admission (Washington, D.C.: Government Printing Office, 1987).

200   *That category:* U.S. Immigration and Naturalization Service, *Statistical Yearbook of the Immigration and Naturalization Service: 1987* (Washington, D.C.: Government Printing Office, 1988), p. 12.

200   *In early 1988: Congressional Record,* daily edition, Feb. 4, 1988, S671; *Congressional Record,* daily edition, Feb. 4, 1988, E170.

200   *The bill: Congressional Record,* daily edition, Oct. 18, 1988, S16484.

201   *"fears of being . . .":* Paul Igasaki, "Immigration: A Japanese American Issue," *Pacific Citizen,* Jan. 26, 1990.

201   *"could produce . . .":* Susan F. Rasky, "Senate Backs Bill on Aliens That Emphasizes Job Skills," *New York Times,* March 16, 1988.

201   *"the tremendous progress . . .": Legal Immigration Reforms,* Hearings Before Subcommittee on Immigration and Refugee Affairs of the Committee on the Judiciary, U.S. Senate (Washington, D.C.: Government Printing Office, 1989), p. 5.

201   *"undercurrent . . . that Kennedy-Simpson . . .":* Dale Frederick "Rick" Swartz, interviewed Feb. 19, 1990.

202   *"I am asked . . .": Reform of Legal Immigration,* Hearings Before Subcommittee on Immigration, Refugees, and International Law, of the Committee on the Judiciary, House of Representatives (Washington, D.C.: Government Printing Office, 1989), p. 200.

202   *"The same people . . .":* Charles Kamasaki, interviewed Feb. 5, 1990.

202   *"It's only fair . . .":* Melinda Yee, interviewed Feb. 9, 1990.

202   *"The irony . . .":* William Tamayo, interviewed April 11, 1990.

202   *"Citizenship is something . . .":* Milton Morris, interviewed Feb. 9, 1990.

202   *After projecting: Immigration Reform: Major Changes Likely Under S. 385* (Washington, D.C.: General Accounting Office, 1989), p. 3.

203   *"Some would argue . . .":* Ibid., p. 51.

203   *"Determinations and analysis . . .":* Janet Norwood, statement

before Subcommittee on Immigration, Refugees, and International Law, U.S. House of Representatives, March 1, 1990.

203 *"quite simplistic":* Richard Belous, vice president, National Planning Association, testimony before Subcommittee on Immigration, Refugees, and International Law, U.S. House of Representatives, March 1, 1990.

203 *"in the name . . .":* Doris Meissner, Carnegie Endowment for International Peace, statement before Subcommittee on Immigration, Refugees, and International Law, U.S. House of Representatives, March 1, 1990.

203 *"virtually excluded . . .":* Immigration Reform: Major Changes Likely Under S. 385, pp. 55–56.

203 *"distorted the whole . . .":* Congressional Record, daily edition, July 13, 1989, S7863.

204 *"I do not care . . .":* Ibid. S7862.

204 *"My guess is . . .":* Ibid. S7863.

204 *Morrison's bill: Family Unity and Employment Opportunity Immigration Act of 1990,* Report together with dissenting views, Judiciary Committee, U.S. House of Representatives (Washington, D.C.: U.S. House of Representatives, 1990).

205 *"Every poll taken . . .":* Dissent of Lamar Smith, Carlos Moorheard, et al., in Family Unity and Employment Opportunity Immigration Act of 1990, p. 137.

205 *"We can either . . .":* Lamar Smith, opening statement, markup of HR 4300, Judiciary Committee, U.S. House of Representatives, July 31, 1990.

205 *"can no longer afford . . .":* Congressional Record, daily edition, Oct. 3, 1990, H8713.

205 *"The authors . . .":* Ibid. H8717.

205 *"If this legislation . . .":* Congressional Record, daily edition, Sept. 24, 1990, S13628.

206 *"best honest effort . . .":* Congressional Record, daily edition, Oct. 12, 1990, S15036.

206 *"his long curly . . .":* Congressional Record, daily edition, Oct. 26, 1990, H12984–85.

206 *"This immigration bill helps . . .":* Congressional Record, daily edition, Oct. 27, 1990, H12320–321.

206   *Conversely, congressman:* Ibid. H12358.

207   *The act divided visas: Immigration Act of 1990,* Conference Report to accompany S358, U.S. House of Representatives, Oct. 26, 1990.

Epilogue: The Centrality of Race, the Challenge of Diversity

209   *"The court is . . .":* In re Ahmed Hassan, No. 162148, District Court, E.D. Michigan, S.D., decided Dec. 15, 1942.

209   *"Both the learned . . .":* Ex parte Mohriez, No. 1500, District Court, D. Massachusetts, decided April 13, 1944.

210   *"racial abyss":* Madison Grant, *The Passing of the Great Race* (1918; rpt. in New York: Arno Press, 1970), p. 263.

210   *Rigid racial distinctions:* See Gary A. Cretser and Joseph H. Leon, eds., *Intermarriage in the United States* (New York: Haworth Press, 1982).

211   *"The individual Slav . . .":* "Japanese Invasion: The Problem of the Hour," *San Francisco Chronicle,* Feb. 23, 1905.

212   *A Gallup Poll:* "America's Changing Face," *Newsweek,* Sept. 10, 1990.

212   *A poll by the University:* AP, "Poll Finds Whites Use Stereotypes," *New York Times,* Jan. 10, 1991; Lynne Duke, "Whites' Racial Stereotypes Persist: Most Retain Negative Beliefs About Minorities, Survey Finds," *Washington Post,* Jan. 9, 1991.

213   *"People will not . . .":* Henry Cisneros, opening address at "Demographic Change and Public Policy: Challenge for the 21st Century," conference organized by the Population Resource Center, March 29, 1990.

213   *"At almost every . . .":* The Carnegie Foundation for the Advancement of Teaching, *Campus Life: In Search of Community* (Princeton, N.J.: Princeton University Press, 1990), p. 29.

213   *A New York Times/WCBS-TV:* Jason Deparle, "Talk of Gov-

ernment Being Out to Get Blacks Falls on More Attentive Ears," *New York Times,* Oct. 29, 1990.

213 *"It's sad . . .":* Steven A. Holmes, "Miami Melting Pot Proves Explosive," *New York Times,* Dec. 9, 1990.

216 *"The police believe . . .":* Mary Jordan, "Residents Differ on Where to Focus Their Anger," *Washington Post,* May 7, 1991.

213 *"No one who . . .": The Adaptation of Southeast Asian Refugee Youth: A Comparative Study* (Washington, D.C.: U.S. Department of Health and Human Services, 1988), pp. 96–97.

214 *"I would see people . . .":* Robert Friedman, "Huddled Masses by the Millions: Immigration Surge Accents New York Life," *Newsday,* June 24, 1990.

214 *"don't care . . .":* Wilky Fortunat, interviewed July 10, 1990.

214 *"This is definitely . . .":* Hector Tobar, "Column One: Changing the Face of South L.A.: As Housing Prices Rise and Gang Violence Persists, Blacks Are Moving Out. Latino Immigrants Are Taking Their Place," *Los Angeles Times,* March 30, 1990.

214 *"Why let foreigners . . . es racista":* David Gonzalez, "Criticism Aimed at Statements on Immigrants," *New York Times,* Oct. 5, 1990; Alison Carper, "Dukes Apologizes for 'Foreigners' Comments; NAACP President's Remarks Called 'Insensitive,' " *Newsday,* Oct. 5, 1990; T. J. Collins and Molly Gordy, "Immigrants Vow Lawsuit against NAACP's Dukes," *Newsday,* Oct. 13, 1990.

214 *A similar conflict:* Roberto Rodríguez, "Latinos Confront Civil Rights Establishment," *Hispanic Link Weekly Report,* May 14, 1990.

215 *"As I sat there . . .":* Antonia Hernández, interviewed May 16, 1990.

215 *"the casting of . . .":* Mervyn Rothstein, "Union Won't Allow White Actor to Play a Eurasian on Broadway," *New York Times,* Aug. 8, 1990.

215 *The* Los Angeles Times: " 'Miss Saigon' Watch: Equity Regained," *Los Angeles Times,* Aug. 17, 1990.

215 *The* Washington Post: "This Is Equity?," *Washington Post,* Aug. 15, 1990.

215 *"The only roles . . .":* Paul Igasaki, "That Was Equity," *Washington Post,* Aug. 18, 1990.

215   *Producer and director:* Shirley Sun, "Why the Furor Over 'Miss Saigon' Won't Fade; For Asians Denied Asian Roles, 'Artistic Freedom' Is No Comfort," *New York Times,* Aug. 26, 1990.

216   *"From the early westerns . . ."* Ellen Holly, "Why the Furor Over 'Miss Saigon' Won't Fade: 'The Ideal World We All Long for' Is Not the World We Live In," *New York Times* Aug. 26, 1990.

216   *"At the core . . .":* Gerald David Jaynes and Robin M. Williams, Jr., eds., *A Common Destiny: Blacks and American Society* (Washington, D.C.: National Academy Press, 1989), p. 5.

217   *A review:* The computer was programmed to look for "black," "Hispanic," or "white" within two words of "middle class" or "poor." In instances where the adjective clearly described something other than race, the case was eliminated. Since each case was not examined in depth, some such couplings were likely missed, but not enough to affect the basic observation.

217   *In truth:* U.S. Bureau of the Census, *Statistical Abstract of the United States, 1989* (Washington, D.C.: Government Printing Office, 1990), p. 455.

217   *Despite a widespread:* Lynne Duke, "Entry Level Hiring Bias Found Here," *Washington Post,* May 15, 1991; U.S. General Accounting Office, "Immigration Reform: Employer Sanctions and the Question of Discrimination" (Washington, D.C.: General Accounting Office, 1990), passim.

217   *"who believe that . . .":* Ibid.

218   *Noting the nation's:* Ben J. Wattenberg, *The First Universal Nation* (New York: The Free Press, 1990).

Partial Bibliography

Books, Monographs, and Reports

Abbott, Edith, ed. *Historical Aspects of the Immigration Problem: Select Documents*. Chicago: University of Chicago Press, 1926.

Adams, William Forbes. *Ireland and Irish Emigration to the New World*. 1932; rpt. Baltimore: Genealogical Publishing Co., 1980.

The Adaptation of Southeast Asian Refugee Youth: A Comparative Study. Washington, D.C.: U.S. Department of Health and Human Services, 1988.

Avrich, Paul. *The Haymarket Tragedy*. Princeton, N.J.: Princeton University Press, 1984.

Bach, Robert L., and Doris Meissner. *Employment and Immigration Reform: Employer Sanctions Four Years Later*. Washington, D.C.: Carnegie Endowment for International Peace, 1990.

Bernstein, Iver. *The New York City Draft Riots*. New York: Oxford University Press, 1990.

Billington, Ray Allen. *The Protestant Crusade*. New York: The Macmillan Company, 1938.

Bosler, Roy, ed. *The Collected Works of Abraham Lincoln,* Volume Four. New Brunswick, N.J.: Rutgers University Press, 1953.

———. *The Collected Works of Abraham Lincoln,* Volume Seven. New Brunswick, N.J.: Rutgers University Press, 1953.

———. *The Collected Works of Abraham Lincoln,* Volume Eight. New Brunswick, N.J.: Rutgers University Press, 1953.

Brigham, Carl C. *A Study of American Intelligence.* Princeton, N.J.: Princeton University Press, 1923.

Busey, Samuel S. *Immigration: Its Evils and Consequences.* 1856; rpt. New York: Arno Press, 1969.

Caplan, Nathan, et al. *Southeast Asian Refugee Self-Sufficiency Study: Final Report.* Washington: U.S. Department of Health and Human Services, 1985.

Carnegie Foundation for the Advancement of Teaching. *Campus Life: In Search of Community.* Princeton, N.J.: Princeton University Press, 1990.

Clark, Juan M., et al. *The 1980 Mariel Exodus: An Assessment and Prospect.* Washington, D.C.: Council for Inter-American Security, 1981.

Coolidge, Mary Roberts. *Chinese Immigration.* 1909; rpt. New York: Arno Press, 1968.

Cretser, Gary A., and Joseph H. Leon, eds. *Intermarriage in the United States.* New York: Haworth Press, 1982.

Crèvecoeur, J. Hector St. John de. *Letters from an American Farmer.* 1782; rpt. New York: Fox, Duffield & Company, 1904.

Curran, Thomas J. *Xenophobia and Immigration, 1820–1939.* Boston: Twayne Publishers, 1975.

DeConde, Alexander. *Half Bitter, Half Sweet.* New York: Charles Scribner's Sons, 1971.

Final Report on the Select Commission on Immigration and Refugee Policy: Joint Hearings Before the Subcommittee on Immigration of the Senate Committee on the Judiciary and Subcommittee on Immigration, Refugees, and International Law of the House Committee on the Judiciary. Washington, D.C.: United States Government Printing Office, 1981.

Fite, Emerson David. *Social and Industrial Conditions in the North During the Civil War.* New York: The Macmillan Company, 1910.

Galton, Francis. *Hereditary Genius.* 1869, 1892; rpt. London: Macmillan and Company, 1925.

García, Juan Ramon. *Operation Wetback: The Mass Deportation of Mexican Undocumented Workers in 1954.* Westport, Conn.: Greenwood Press, 1980.

Goering, John M. *Legal Immigration to the United States: A Demographic Analysis of Fifth Preferences Visa Admission.* Washington, D.C.: United States Government Printing Office, 1987.

Grant, Madison. *The Passing of the Great Race.* 1918; rpt. New York: Arno Press, 1970.

Konvitz, Milton R. *Civil Rights in Immigration.* Ithaca, N.Y.: Cornell University Press, 1953.

Hansen, Marcus Lee. *The Atlantic Migration.* Cambridge, Mass.: Harvard University Press, 1951.

Hearings Before the Committee on Immigration, U.S. Senate, 77th Congress. Washington, D.C.: United States Government Printing Office, 1923.

Hearings: Subcommittee No. 1 of the Committee on the Judiciary, U.S. House of Representatives. Washington, D.C.: United States Government Printing Office, 1964.

Hearings: Subcommittee on Immigration and Naturalization, Committee on the Judiciary, U.S. Senate. Washington, D.C.: United States Government Printing Office, 1965.

Higham, John. *Send These to Me: Jews and Other Immigrants in Urban America.* New York: Atheneum, 1975.

———. *Strangers in the Land.* New Brunswick, N.J.: Rutgers University Press, 1955.

Hispanic Profile. Miami: Metro-Dade County Planning Department, 1985.

Hutchinson, Edward P., ed. *The Annals of the American Academy of Political and Social Science.* Philadelphia: American Academy of Political and Social Science, 1966.

———. *Legislative History of American Immigration Policy, 1798–1965.* Philadelphia: University of Pennsylvania Press, 1981.

Immigration: Hearings Before Subcommittee #1 of the Committee of the Judiciary, House of Representatives, 88th Congress, part II. Washington, D.C.: United States Government Printing Office, 1964.

Immigration Reform and Control Act of 1986: Conference Report. Washington, D.C.: United States House of Representatives, 1986.

Indochina Refugees: Hearings Before the Subcommittee on Immigration, Citizenship and International Law, U.S. House of Representatives, 94th Congress. Washington, D.C.: United States Government Printing Office, 1975.

Japanese Immigration: Hearings Before the Committee on Immigration and Naturalization. Washington, D.C.: United States Government Printing Office, 1921.

Jaynes, Gerald David, and Robin M. Williams, Jr., eds. *A Common Destiny: Blacks and American Society.* Washington, D.C.: National Academy Press, 1989.

Jefferson, Thomas. *Notes on the State of Virginia* (1782); rpt. in *The Works of Thomas Jefferson,* Volume III. New York: G. P. Putnam's Sons, 1904.

————. *The Works of Thomas Jefferson,* Volume IV. New York: G. P. Putnam's Sons, 1904.

Johnston, William B., and Arnold S. Packer. *Workforce 2000: Work and Workers for the 21st Century.* Indianapolis: The Hudson Institute, 1987.

Jones, Maldwyn Allen. *American Immigration.* Chicago: University of Chicago Press, 1960.

Jordan, David Starr. *The Blood of the Nation.* Boston: American Unitarian Association, 1902.

Kennedy, Edward M. *The Refugee Act of 1979.* Washington, D.C.: United States Senate, 1979.

Kennedy, John. *A Nation of Immigrants.* New York: Anti-Defamation League of B'Nai B'Rith, 1958.

Kevles, Daniel J. *In the Name of Eugenics.* New York: Alfred A. Knopf, 1985.

Legal Immigration Legislation: Hearings Before the Subcommittee on Immigration, Refugees, and International Law of the Committee on the Judiciary, U.S. House of Representatives. Washington, D.C.: United States Government Printing Office, 1988.

Legal Immigration Reforms: Hearings Before the Subcommittee on Immigration and Refugee Affairs of the Committee on the Judiciary, U.S. Senate. Washington, D.C.: United States Government Printing Office, 1989.

McWilliams, Carey. *Prejudice: Japanese-Americans: Symbol of Intolerance.* Boston: Little, Brown and Company, 1944.

Maizlish, Stephen E., ed. *Essays on American Antebellum Politics, 1840–1869.* Arlington, Texas: University of Texas at Arlington, 1982.

Miller, Jake C. *The Plight of Haitian Refugees.* New York: Praeger Publishers, 1984.

Older, Fremont. *My Own Story.* New York: The Macmillan Company, 1926.

Post, Louis F. *The Deportations Delirium of Nineteen-Twenty.* Chicago: Charles H. Kerr & Company, 1923.

President's Commission on Migratory Labor. *Migratory Labor in American Agriculture.* Washington, D.C.: United States Government Printing Office, 1951.

Public Papers of the Presidents: Lyndon B. Johnson, 1965. Washington, D.C.: United States Government Printing Office, 1966.

Public Papers of the Presidents: John F. Kennedy, 1963. Washington, D.C.: United States Government Printing Office, 1964.

Public Papers of the Presidents: Harry S Truman, 1952–53. Washington: D.C.: United States Government Printing Office, 1966.

Rayback, Joseph G. *A History of American Labor.* New York: Free Press, 1966.

Reform of Legal Immigration: Hearings Before the Subcommittee on Immigration, Refugees, and International Law of the Committee on the Judiciary, House of Representatives. Washington, D.C.: United States Government Printing Office, 1989.

Refugee Resettlement Program. Washington, D.C.: United States Department of Health and Human Services, 1988.

Report to Congress: Refugee Resettlement Program. Washington, D.C.: United States Department of Health and Human Services, 1988.

Rhodes, James Ford. *History of the United States,* Volume Four. Port Washington, N.Y.: Kennikut Press, 1899.

Riggs, Fred W. *Pressures on Congress.* New York: King's Crown Press, 1950.

Ringer, Benjamin. *We the People, and Others.* London: Tavistock Publications, 1983.

Ripley, William Z. *The Races of Europe.* New York: D. Appleton and Company, 1899.

Sanders, Roland. *Shores of Refuge.* New York: Henry Holt and Company, 1988.

Sandmeyer, E. C. *The Anti-Chinese Movement in California.* Urbana, Ill.: University of Illinois Press, 1973.

Saxton, Alexander. *The Indispensable Enemy: Labor and the Anti-Chinese Movement in California.* Berkeley: University of California Press, 1971.

Schwartz, Abba P. *The Open Society.* 1968; rpt. New York: Simon and Schuster, 1969.

Select Commission on Immigration and Refugee Policy. *U.S. Immigration Policy and the National Interest.* Washington, D.C.: United States Government Printing Office, 1981.

Southern California's Latino Community. Los Angeles: Times Mirror, 1984.

Stephenson, George M. *A History of American Immigration: 1840–1924.* Boston: Ginn and Company, 1926.

Stoddard, Lothrop. *The Revolt Against Civilization.* New York: Charles Scribner's Sons, 1922.

Thernstrom, Stephan, Ann Orlov, and Oscar Handlin, eds. *Harvard Encyclopedia of American Ethnic Groups.* Cambridge, Mass.: Harvard University Press, 1980.

Thomas, Lately. *A Debonair Scoundrel.* New York: Holt, Rinehart and Winston, 1962.

Tsai, Shin-Shan Henry. *The Chinese Experience in America.* Bloomington: Indiana University Press, 1986.

U.S. Bureau of the Census. "Projections of the Hispanic Population: 1983 to 2085." *Current Population Reports, Population Estimates and Projections, Series P-25, No. 955, 1986.*

U.S. Bureau of the Census. *Statistical Abstract of the United States: 1989.* Washington, D.C.: United States Government Printing Office, 1989.

United States Department of Justice. *1975 Annual Report: Immigration and Naturalization Service.* Washington, D.C.: United States Government Printing Office, 1975.

———. *Statistical Yearbook of the Immigration and Naturalization Service: 1986.* Washington, D.C.: United States Government Printing Office, 1987.

————. *Statistical Yearbook of the Immigration and Naturalization Service: 1987.* Washington, D.C.: United States Government Printing Office, 1988.

————. *Statistical Yearbook of the Immigration and Naturalization Service: 1988.* Washington, D.C.: United States Government Printing Office, 1989.

————. *Statistical Yearbook of the Immigration and Naturalization Service: 1989.* Washington, D.C.: United States Government Printing Office, 1990.

United States Department of Labor, Bureau of Immigration. *Annual Report of the Commissioner General of Immigration to the Secretary of Labor.* Washington, D.C.: United States Government Printing Office, 1918.

United States Displaced Persons Commission. *Memo to America: The DP Story.* Washington, D.C.: United States Government Printing Office, 1952.

United States General Accounting Office. *Immigration Reform: Employer Sanctions and the Question of Discrimination.* Washington, D.C.: United States General Accounting Office, 1990.

————. *Immigration Reform: Major Changes Likely Under S. 385.* Washington, D.C.: General Accounting Office, 1989.

United States President's Commission on Immigration and Naturalization. *Whom We Shall Welcome.* Washington, D.C.: United States Government Printing Office, 1953.

Vialet, Joyce, ed. *Selected Readings on U.S. Immigration Policy and Law.* Washington, D.C.: United States Government Printing Office, 1980.

————. *United States Immigration Law and Policy: 1952–1986.* Washington, D.C.: United States Government Printing Office, 1988.

Wattenberg, Ben J. *The First Universal Nation.* New York: The Free Press, 1990.

White, Henry Kirke. *History of the Union Pacific Railway.* 1895; rpt. Clifton, N.J.: Augustus M. Kelley Publishers, 1973.

White, Theodore H. *America in Search of Itself: The Making of the President, 1956–1980.* New York: Harper and Row, 1982.

Williams, John Holt. *A Great & Shining Road.* New York: Times Books, 1988.

Wilson, William Julius. *The Declining Significance of Race.* Chicago: University of Chicago Press, 1978.

Wittke, Carl. *Refugees of Revolution.* Westport, Conn.: Greenwood Press, 1952.

Magazines

"All Those Refugees—Who They Are, Where They're Going." *U.S. News & World Report,* May 12, 1975.

"America's Changing Face." *Newsweek.* Sept. 10, 1990.

Birger, Larry. "A New Mecca for Latin Shoppers." *Business Week,* Sept. 8, 1975.

Burkholz, Herbert. "The Latinization of Miami." *New York Times Magazine,* Sept. 21, 1980.

Chaze, William L. "Will U.S. Shut the Door on Immigrants?" *U.S. News & World Report,* April 12, 1982.

"Christmas Brings Happy Ending for Vietnam Refugees." *U.S. News & World Report,* Dec. 29, 1975.

Eckels, Richard P. "Hungry Workers, Ripe Crops, and the Nonexistent Mexican Border." *The Reporter,* April 13, 1954.

"The Economic Consequences of a New Wave." *Business Week,* June 23, 1980.

Fallows, James. "Immigration: How It's Affecting Us." *Atlantic Monthly,* Nov. 1983.

"Flurry in Capital: U.S. Opens Its Doors to the 'Floating Refugees.' " *U.S. News & World Report,* Aug. 15, 1977.

Glen, Maxwell. "Immigration Bill Knocked Out in Final Round, but Sponsors Promise Rematch." *National Journal,* Nov. 3, 1984.

Godwin, Parke. "Secret Societies—The Know-Nothings." *Putnam's Monthly,* Jan. 1855.

Harris, Glenn P. "Sovereign Immunity." *George Washington Law Review,* May 1987.

Henry, William A. III. "Beyond the Melting Pot." *Time,* April 9, 1990.

"How to Tell Your Friends from the Japs." *Time*, Dec. 22, 1941.

"The Illegal Jobholders." *Business Week*, Aug. 11, 1975.

Jacob, Walter. "Lack of Cash and Poor Coordination Plague U.S. Refugee Policies." *National Journal*, July 26, 1980.

Keely, Charles B. "The Shadows of Invisible People." *American Demographics*, March 1980.

Kirschten, Dick. "The Hispanic Vote—Parties Can't Gamble That the Sleeping Giant Won't Awaken." *National Journal*, Nov. 19, 1983.

Kondracke, Morton. "Moral Borders: Politics, Mercy, and Immigration." *New Republic*, Nov. 23, 1987.

Peirce, Neal R., and Roger Fillion. "Should the United States Open Its Doors to the Foreigners Waiting to Come In?" *National Journal*, March 7, 1981.

Peterson, Sarah, and John W. Mashek. "Hispanics Set Their Sights on Ballot Box," *U.S. News & World Report*, Aug. 22, 1983.

"A Plan to Slow the Flood of Illegal Aliens." *Business Week*, Aug. 11, 1975.

Powell, Stewart, et al. "Illegal Aliens: Invasion Out of Control?" *U.S. News & World Report*, Jan. 29, 1979.

"A Ray of Hope: An Arkansas Town That Took in 2,000 Refugees." *U.S. News & World Report*, Aug. 6, 1979.

Reiss, Bob. "The Melting Plot: Grooming for the Green Card with Money-Order Brides." *Potomac*, July 17, 1977.

Semerad, Roger D. "2000: Labor Shortage Looms: The U.S. Will Need a More Productive and More Competitive Workforce in the Year 2000. How Do We Get There from Here?" *Industry Week*, Feb. 9, 1987.

Singer, James W. "Controlling Illegal Aliens—Carter's Compromise Solution." *National Journal*, Sept. 3, 1977.

Waldrop, Judith, and Thomas Exter. "What the 1990 Census Will Show." *American Demographics*, Jan. 1990.

"What Illegal Aliens Cost the Economy." *Business Week*, June 13, 1977.

"When It Takes Two Languages to Teach the Three R's. . . ." *U.S. News & World Report*, July 7, 1975.

Witt, Linda. "Following Conscience, Not Law, an Underground Railroad Smuggles Threatened Salvadorans to Safety in America." *People*, Aug. 9, 1982.

Journals

Anaya, Toney. "Because There Are Still Many Who Wait for Death." *Hofstra Law Review*, Fall 1986.

Anker, Deborah, and Michael Posner. "The Forty Year Crisis: A Legislative History of the Refugee Act of 1980." *San Diego Law Review*, Dec. 1981.

Bogen, David S. "The Free Speech Metamorphosis of Mr. Justice Holmes." *Hofstra Law Review*, Fall 1982.

Easterbrook, Frank H. "Presidential Review." *Case Western Reserve Law Review*, 1990.

Fuchs, Lawrence H. "Directions for U.S. Immigration Policy: Immigration Policy and the Rule of Law." *University of Pittsburgh Law Review*, Winter 1983.

Guercio, Albert Del. "Some Mexican Border Problems." *Monthly Review* (INS, Department of Justice), April 1946.

Hart, Benjamin. "The Wall That Protestantism Built: The Religious Reasons for the Separation of Church and State." *Policy Review*, Fall 1988.

Karst, Kenneth L. "Paths to Belonging: The Constitution and Cultural Identity." *North Carolina Law Review*, Jan. 1986.

Kellogg, Arthur E. "Two Centuries of Immigration Laws." *I & N Reporter*, Winter 1975–76.

Kelly, William F. "The Wetback Issue." *The I & N Reporter*. Jan. 1954.

Krichefsky, Gertrude D. "Importation of Alien Laborers." *I & N Reporter*, July 1956.

McClain, Charles J., Jr. "The Chinese Struggle for Civil Rights in Nineteenth-Century America: The First Phase, 1850–1870." *California Law Review*, July 1984.

Motomura, Hiroshi. "Immigration Law After a Century of Plenary Power: Phantom Constitutional Norms and Statutory Interpretation." *Yale Law Journal*, Dec. 1990.

"Second Report on the Implementation of IRCA." *INS Reporter*, Summer 1989.

Smith, Jeffery A. "Prior Restraint: Original Intentions and Modern Interpretations." *William & Mary Law Review*, Spring 1987.

Swing, J. W. "A Workable Labor Program." *I & N Reporter*, Nov. 1955.

Wurtzel, Judy. "First Amendment Limitations on the Exclusion of Aliens." *New York University Law Review*, April 1987.

Court Cases

In re Ah Fong. Circuit Court, D. California. 1874.

In re Ah Ping. Circuit Court, D. California. 1885.

In re Ah Yup. Circuit Court, D. California. 1878.

In re Ahmed Hassan, U.S. District Court, E.D. Michigan. 1942.

American Baptist Churches in the U.S.A., et al., versus *Edwin Meese III and Alan Nelson*. U.S. District Court, Northern District of California. 1989.

Bartels versus *State of Iowa.; Bohning* versus *State of Ohio; Pohl* versus *State of Ohio; Nebraska District of Evangelical Lutheran Synod of Missouri, Ohio, and Other States, et al.* versus *McKelvie et al., etc.* U.S. Supreme Court. 1923.

Chae Chan Ping versus *United States*. U.S. Supreme Court. 1889.

Chew Heong versus *United States*. U.S. Supreme Court. 1884.

Colyer et al. versus *Skeffington, Commissioner of Immigration; Katzeff et al.* versus *Same; In re Harbatuk et al; In re Mack et al.* District Court, D. Massachusetts. 1920.

Dred Scott versus *John F. A. Sandford*. U.S. Supreme Court. 1856.

Fong Yue Ting versus *United States; Wong Quan* versus *United States; Lee Joe* versus *United States*. U.S. Supreme Court. 1893.

George Smith versus *William Turner*. U.S. Supreme Court. 1849.

Haitian Refugee Center versus *Civiletti*. U.S. District Court, S.D. Florida. 1979.

Haitian Refugee Center versus *Civiletti.* U.S. Court of Appeals, Fifth Circuit. 1980.

Henderson et al. versus *Mayor of the City of New York.* U.S. Supreme Court. 1875.

Hirabayashi versus *United States.* U.S. Supreme Court. 1943.

Korematsu versus *United States.* U.S. Supreme Court. 1944.

Louis versus *Meissner.* U.S. District Court, S.D. Florida. 1981.

Meyer versus *Nebraska.* U.S. Supreme Court, 1923.

Ex parte Mitsuye Endo. U.S. Supreme Court. 1944.

Ex parte Mohriez, U.S. District Court, Massachusetts. 1944.

National Council of Churches versus *Egan.* U.S. District Court, S.D. Florida. 1979.

National Council of Churches versus *U.S. Department of Immigration and Naturalization Service.* S.D. Florida. 1979.

New York versus *George Miln.* U.S. Supreme Court. 1837.

Plyler, Superintendent, Tyler Independent School District, et al. versus *Doe, Guardian.* U.S. Supreme Court. 1982.

Spies versus *Illinois.* U.S. Supreme Court. 1887.

Takao Ozawa versus *United States.* U.S. Supreme Court. 1922.

Terrace et al. versus *Thompson, Attorney General of the State of Washington.* U.S., Supreme Court. 1923.

United States versus *Ah Fawn.* District Court, S.D. California. 1893.

United States versus *Bhagat Singh Thind.* U.S. Supreme Court. 1923.

United States versus *Johnson.* Circuit Court, S.D. New York. 1881.

United States versus *Wong Kim Ark.* U.S. Supreme Court. 1898.

Yasui versus *United States.* U.S. Supreme Court. 1943.

INDEX

denization vs., 21
of "free white persons," 11, 23, 45,
    50, 52, 75–77, 209–210
of Japanese, 65, 75–76, 77
1740 British legislation on, 21
1773 legislation on, 21
1790 legislation on, 10–11, 23, 75–
    77
1795 legislation on, 23
1798 legislation on, 45
tax on, 9–10
waiting period for, 23, 24, 28, 29,
    33, 35
Nazism, 82–83, 90, 96, 98, 167
Neuman, Bob, 163
Nevada, 31, 45, 50
New Hampshire, 33
New Jersey, 21, 28, 60, 146
New Mexico, 31, 164, 192
New Republic, 198
New York, N.Y., 38–41, 69, 92, 105,
    108, 112, 214
anti-Catholicism in, 27–28, 33–34
draft riots in, 40–41, 219
immigrant taxes imposed by, 30,
    33, 46
Irish-Catholics in, 29, 39–41
Know-Nothings in, 33–34
New York Herald, 34
New York Protestant Association, 28
New York Society for the Prevention
    of Pauperism, 25
New York Times, 87, 91, 113, 142, 154,
    156, 157, 166, 167, 182, 186,
    213, 215, 217
New York Tribune, 33
Nguyen Van Thieu, 118
Niblack, William, 43–44
Nitz, Michael, 193
Nixon, Richard M., 116, 132, 155
North Atlantic Treaty Organization
    (NATO), 97
Norwood, Janet, 203

Oaxaca, Fernando, 173
Obledo, Mario, 172–175
O'Neill, Thomas "Tip," 162, 165,
    167–169, 171, 173

Operation Wetback (1954), 101–102,
    190
Oregon, 45, 48, 50, 53
Organization of Chinese Americans,
    194, 202
Orphan Asylum for Colored Chil-
    dren (New York), 40
Ortega, Katherine, 163
Osborn, Henry, 71
Ozawa, Takao, 75–76

Palmer, A. Mitchell, 69
parole authority, 103–104, 108, 113,
    118, 120, 121–122, 123, 124,
    125, 139–140, 141
Passing of the Great Race, The (Grant),
    71
Paul II, Pope, 153
paupers, 18, 20, 22, 25, 26, 27, 29,
    34, 36, 52, 55, 61, 63, 205
Pearl Harbor, 84
Penn, William, 18, 19
Pennsylvania, 18–19, 21, 22, 33, 42,
    59, 119, 138
anti-Catholicism in, 27, 28–29
Perkins, George, 50
Perlman, Philip, 97
Peru, 133–134
Pheland, James, 72
Philippines, 11, 90, 118
Pietists, German, 19
Pillors, Brenda, 135
Piper, William, 47
Poles, 60, 61, 64, 66, 71
police, 59, 136, 137, 143, 144, 213
polygamists, 61
Polynesia, 67
"popular sovereignty," 35
Portugal, 60
Preemption Act (1841), 37
preference system, 96–97, 105, 109,
    111, 113, 114, 200–201, 202,
    204
property ownership, 77
prostitutes, 46, 47, 50, 61, 64
Protestant, 27
Protestants, 11, 17–19, 27, 33, 191–
    192
Pryce, Jonathan, 215